FRENCH *ÉCOCRITIQUE*

STEPHANIE POSTHUMUS

French *Écocritique*

Reading Contemporary French Theory and Fiction Ecologically

UNIVERSITY OF TORONTO PRESS
Toronto Buffalo London

Toronto Buffalo London
www.utppublishing.com

ISBN 978-1-4875-0145-7 (cloth)

(University of Toronto Romance Series)

Library and Archives Canada Cataloguing in Publication

Posthumus, Stephanie, 1973–, author
French écocritique : reading contemporary French theory and fiction ecologically / Stephanie Posthumus.

Includes bibliographical references and index.
ISBN 978-1-4875-0145-7 (cloth)

1. French literature – 20th century – History and criticism. 2. Ecology in literature. 3. Nature in literature. 4. Ecocriticism – France. I. Title.

PQ307.E26P67 2017 840.9'36 C2017-902616-X

This book has been published with the help of a grant from the Federation for the Humanities and Social Sciences, through the Awards to Scholarly Publications Program, using funds provided by the Social Sciences and Humanities Research Council of Canada.

University of Toronto Press acknowledges the financial assistance to its publishing program of the Canada Council for the Arts and the Ontario Arts Council, an agency of the Government of Ontario.

Canada Council for the Arts Conseil des Arts du Canada

Funded by the Government of Canada
Financé par le gouvernement du Canada

Contents

Remerciements

Ce livre n'aurait jamais vu le jour sans l'appui, l'aide et l'encouragement de beaucoup de personnes autour de moi à Montréal et à des distances plus éloignées au Canada et en Europe. Je voudrais remercier tout d'abord les collègues qui m'ont écoutée et appuyée à différents moments de mes recherches et de la rédaction de mon manuscrit. Au groupe de chercheurs EcoLITT à l'Université d'Angers en France, je suis très reconnaissante qu'ils m'aient invitée à faire des conférences et à partager mes idées, ce qui m'a redonné envie de me mettre au travail lorsque je manquais d'inspiration. Les associations universitaires ASLE et ALECC m'ont fourni un milieu intellectuel amical où présenter mes premières idées sur une écocritique française. (Je pense ici à mon premier colloque ASLE à Boston en 2003 lorsque j'ai parlé de la figure du marin chez Michel Serres.) Grâce à l'encouragement et à l'appui précieux de Louisa Mackenzie à l'Université du Washington-Seattle, j'ai entrepris les démarches pour envoyer ma proposition de livre aux presses universitaires de Toronto. Au cours du long processus de rédaction, l'éditeur en chef Richard Ratzlaff m'a toujours répondu avec patience et bonne humeur, prêt à me donner des suggestions pratiques et stylistiques pour améliorer mon écriture en anglais. Deux lecteurs anonymes ont évalué soigneusement l'organisation des idées, l'approche littéraire et le développement des arguments, ce qui m'a convaincue encore une fois de la valeur du processus d'évaluation par les paires. Or, toute l'aide intellectuelle du monde entier n'aurait pas suffi pour mener à bien ce projet. Je voudrais donc remercier du fond de mon cœur les membres de ma famille sur la côte ouest et en Ontario qui m'ont donné l'amour, le soutien, et l'espace et le temps nécessaires pour terminer mon livre. Finalement, je dédie ce livre à Stéfan, Naomie et Élodie, les grands amours de ma vie.

FRENCH *ÉCOCRITIQUE*

Introduction: Ecological Readings

The "Ferry" effect

My aim in this book is to build a French *écocritique* on the premise of cultural difference. I am intentionally using the term *écocritique* in a book written in English to perform the central and productive tension at the heart of my method, which is to hold together the cultural specificity of French textual ecologies and the ways in which they extend beyond their linguistic and cultural boundaries. My readings of contemporary French literature are brought together with recent ecocritical theories in both French and English in order to complicate what might otherwise become a reductive notion of "French nature" or the simplistic deployment of a notion of "French culture." The ways in which an essentialized Frenchness has been extrapolated to an equally problematic universalism can be seen in one of the earliest and most influential critiques of environmental thinking in France, Luc Ferry's *Le Nouvel Ordre écologique* (1992), translated as *The New Ecological Order* (1995).

In his book, Ferry characterizes environmental philosophy and animal ethics as fundamentally anti-humanist. Granting rights to plants and animals can lead to ideological excesses, according to Ferry, who cites the medieval example of infanticide sows brought into court and sentenced to death by hanging. In his attack on deep ecology, which lumps together thinkers as diverse as Aldo Leopold and Michel Serres, Ferry calls for a renewal of humanism by going back to the thinking of Jean-Jacques Rousseau and Immanuel Kant. He reasserts the notion of a universal human nature and posits humans as necessarily anti-natural. Unflinchingly, he defends the position of the Moderns as the only foundation on which to build a democratic humanism and address social and political injustices:

> The most fundamental ethical requirement among Moderns, that of altruism, is in its very principle antinatural, since it requires a form of disinterestedness. It presupposes "good will" and is inevitably expressed in the form of an imperative. But the reference to universality, which is incomprehensible outside of the framework of this new philosophical anthropology, also becomes necessary. For the separation from historical-natural codes, through which man manifests his difference from animals, is still a refusal to allow oneself to be limited to any particularity. It is because he is capable of taking his distances not only from the cycle of his biological life but also from this particular language, nation, and culture that man can enter into communication with others. His capacity for universality is a direct function of this distancing.[1]

Refusing particular, socially constructed differences, Ferry reminds his readers that to be a French philosopher is to hold to a universal humanism.

Despite what was largely a reductive reading of ecological thinking at the time,[2] Ferry's book has had a long-lasting effect on environmental philosophy in France. In an interview in 2008, Catherine Larrère speaks of the "censoring effect" that Ferry's book had in the nineties, making environmentalism a taboo subject in philosophical circles in France. Emerging philosophers feared that any association with ecological issues would marginalize their work or that that their approach would not be considered serious, dismissed as mere "applied ethics." It has only been more recently, with the translation into French of important anglophone texts in environmental philosophy and environmentalism more generally, that these sub-disciplines have come to be recognized as valid subjects of philosophical inquiry in France.[3]

To grant so much weight to a single book may seem exaggerated, but Ferry's *Le Nouvel Ordre écologique* embodies a French humanist way of thinking that continues to dominate much of contemporary French philosophy. This tradition has meant that the work of thinkers like Michel Serres and Bruno Latour has had a very different reception in France than in North America, their contributions being better-recognized in France in science studies and/or epistemology than in the discipline of philosophy.[4] So while Ferry argues for a universal humanism, his book is evidence of the fact that thinking about the environment takes place in specific cultural and intellectual contexts. Ferry constructs a binary opposition between French-as-universal-humanism and American-as-liberal-individualism without realizing the extent to which this very position is culturally contingent.[5] Even though Ferry's position is diametrically opposed to my own, his book offers a perfect opening for discussing the need for a culturally situated ecocritical approach.

Reading ecologically

Ecocriticism has been defined in many different ways in the anglophone world: 1) as the study of the relationship between literature and environment (Glotfelty); 2) as the study of texts and ideas in terms of their coherence and usefulness as responses to environmental crisis (Kerridge); and 3) as the study of the relationship of the human and the non-human throughout human cultural history (Garrard).[6] Identifying a common thread for bringing together different literary texts and readings has given ecocriticism a sense of coherence and cohesion. But it has also glossed over important cultural differences when the emphasis has been on finding a common discourse to respond to planetary environmental issues. Without denying the relevance and urgency of the global ecological crisis, I will develop an ecocritical approach that moves more slowly through cultural specificities while also recognizing the need for cross-cultural dialogue. My analysis draws on a set of concepts and themes that illustrates specificities of ecological thinking in France, but that also points to ways of moving beyond a strictly French context for reading ecologically.

Given that ecocriticism first defined itself by foregrounding nature in literary texts, my choice to examine a corpus of contemporary French literary texts that do not promote a return to nature or an environmentalist message may seem counterintuitive.[7] Why not consider instead texts by Henri Bosco, Maurice Genevoix, Jean Giono, Paul Guimard, or Pierre-Jakez Hélias, to name a few French writers of the twentieth century known for their portraits of nature and the wild? Or texts by contemporary poets and authors such as Pierre Bergounioux, Thierry Beinstingel, Jean-Loup Trassard, Pierre Michon, and Richard Millet? Why not construct a French *écocritique* by examining literary texts that foreground trees, mountains, lakes, rivers, fields, animals, etc. – in short, natural landscapes, understood as unmodified by humans?

There are a number of reasons why I am not drawing on the literary tradition of writing about natural landscapes in my work on a French *écocritique*. First, research has already been done in this area by literary scholars, such as Pierre Schoentjes's overview of French contemporary novels in which natural landscapes play an important role and Alain

Suberchicot's comparative study of environmental texts in French, American, and Chinese literatures.[8] Second, I would like to challenge the idea that literary texts that focus on and accurately portray nature are necessarily ecological or environmental. As Dana Phillips states, "the success of our efforts to discover whatever we can about the ecological character of the natural world does not hinge on the right representation of nature."[9] While non-fiction texts such as Rachel Carson's *Silent Spring* have done much to increase environmental awareness, nature writing has also in some cases created a sense of nature as "out there," separate from culture, urban spaces, and humans in general. Critical of the nature/culture binary, Bernard Kalaora asserts that we need to create new "représentations paysagères" that reflect "les paysages post-modernes, paysages d'interfaces ... paysages où règnent des phénomènes d'échanges, de contact ou plutôt de contamination des milieux."[10] Taking up this assertion, I argue that a French *écocritique* needs to examine a mix of representations of environments and landscapes in literary texts, from industrial and urban to mixed and rebuilt, from devastated and contaminated to flourishing and exuberant.

What, then, constitutes an ecological reading, whether this be of a literary or a theoretical text? If not limited to a specific kind of landscape or environment, what makes a reading ecological? Does this entail a certain methodology or subject matter? The original etymology of the term *oikos* is helpful, as it means habitat, home, or a place in which one lives. In 1866, Ernst Haeckel coined the word *ecology* to refer to the study of organisms in their natural habitat. As Anna Bramwell explains, "when Haeckel coined *Oekologie* he was referring to the web that links organisms and their surrounding environment."[11] In other words, ecology refers to the study of the physical world as web-like, made up of many interrelated organisms. How, then, can reading be ecological? First, reading is part of the physical world and not removed from it. While we often imagine ourselves as disembodied subjects when reading, physical processes are as much a part of the experience as are mental and physiological ones. Remaining attentive to these multiple responses to the text as material object (whether this be an actual book or a screen) can be one way of arriving at an ecological reading. Second, reading can be ecological when it pays careful attention to the specific contexts of writing, production, and circulation of a text. Without reducing a text's meaning to its socio-historical context, ecological readings acknowledge the link between creativity, imagination, and the effects of particular world views and experiences of the world. Third, the question of interrelatedness is foundational, so that reading becomes a way of making connections between texts, readers, interpretive communities, authors. The choice of connections gives rise to a contextual and situated politics, one that reflects the orientation and perspective of that particular reading.

In this book, both theory and fiction will be read ecologically. While the field of cultural studies has accustomed anglophone scholars to reading fiction and theory together, the same is not true of French literary studies. The transformation of literary analysis into various "studies" (feminist studies, animal studies, cultural studies, postcolonial studies, etc.) has been met with quite a bit of resistance in France. This is why I make the pairing of a theorist and an author very evident in each chapter, using the methods of close reading to analyse both theory and fiction. In this way, I illustrate the benefits of using literary analysis that is attentive to form, structure, and poetics more generally to read beyond the literary text. At the same time, I am illustrating that theoretical readings are not just about "name-dropping" (as some French literary scholars have surmised) – that they can be used to engage with concepts as relevant to fiction and aesthetics as they are to philosophy or politics. While cultural studies and critical theory scholars may find this division between theory and fiction rigid, I am working to move French literary studies more slowly in the direction of ecological readings.

As a bilingual scholar, I have taken an approach indebted to two different literary and intellectual traditions. On the one hand, my emphasis on close readings reflects the kind of literary analysis that is still common in French literary studies today. I examine specific passages in terms of form and meaning to highlight the specificities and originalities of writing as producing a world rather than simply representing a world. On the other hand, my insistence on examining the novel's themes in terms of larger philosophical and political issues follows from a long interest in interdisciplinary scholarship. Over the years, literary theory has embraced concepts from philosophy, history, anthropology, and geography, to name just a few, thus creating a circulation of ideas between thinkers (who are also writers) and authors (who are also thinkers creating fictional worlds). Drawing on both the tradition of close literary analysis and recent developments in literary theory, my ecological readings of texts are inscribed within a particular set of linguistic, cultural, and cross-cultural contexts (not to mention those of class, gender, and race).

Corpus and concepts

The novels chosen for my analysis range from careful portrayals of the end of the traditional *paysan* or farmer to futuristic representations of a world in which a clone rediscovers the natural world outside his isolated residence. Rather than attempt an exhaustive overview of literary texts that grapple with today's changing landscapes, I have chosen a sampling of French contemporary texts in order to develop four key ecocritical concepts: ecological subjectivity, ecological dwelling, ecological politics, and ecological ends. The literary texts play a role in the shaping and forming of each concept, but are not reduced to nor fully determined by the concept. Each analysis includes threads that lead outwards from the literary text to social and political contexts, so that literature is brought into dialogue with other discourses about humans and the non-human world.

According to Dominique Viart and Bruno Vercier, contemporary French literature can be characterized in terms of a *retour au reel*.[12] This (re)turn to the real is not, however, an attempt to resurrect French literary realism of the nineteenth century as exemplified by high stylists such as Gustave Flaubert. French contemporary literature instead examines the possibility of writing about the real world in light of the criticisms raised by theorists of the *Nouveau Roman* in the 1950s and 1960s, according to whom literature is a way of "producing" a world sufficient to itself and not a way of "representing" a world outside of the text. Each of the novels in my corpus underscores the problem of representation and engages with real-world issues without reducing the novel to *un miroir qu'on promène le long d'un chemin* to borrow Stendhal's phrase from *Le Rouge et le noir* (1830).[13] In this way, they reflect more generally French contemporary literature's reengagement with the question of the real, not as a static, objective truth located outside the text, but as a collection of experiences, perceptions, expressions, and representations.

To illustrate ways of reading French texts ecologically, I have chosen four contemporary authors: Marie Darrieussecq, Marie-Hélène Lafon, Jean-Christophe Rufin, and Michel Houellebecq (in the order in which they are analysed in this book). While these authors all situate their stories in worlds very much like that of the present day, no one common theme runs through their novels. Darrieussecq and Lafon explore the intimacy of personal relationships to regional landscapes of France's Basque country and Cantal department respectively. And yet they situate these regions in larger concentric circles, contrasting country and city, France and Europe. Their novels raise the question of how the literary critic can read for a sense of place in changing and transforming global landscapes. Houellebecq and Rufin complicate an ecocritical reading of their novels, because their characters are explicitly critical of environmentalism in all its forms. These novels tap into an apocalyptic fear often exploited by environmentalist rhetoric and illustrate its dangerous political implications. Yet they also portray the possibility of interacting with the physical world in ways that go beyond consumer capitalism – Houellebecq from the perspective of a dark posthumanism, and Rufin from the perspective of a renewed humanism.

In terms of ecocritical themes, I have chosen Darrieussecq and Lafon because of their focus on the body and landscapes, and Rufin and Houellebecq because of their vision of globalization, science, and technology. Because of their diversity, the texts challenge an ecocriticism that focuses solely on one kind of relationship with the non-human world or one kind of descriptive or realist writing. At the same time, the texts engage with the problem of literary representation in a world in which the distinction between the real and the virtual is becoming more and more blurred. Darrieussecq and Lafon push the boundaries of fiction by writing *autofiction* (novels in which the main character shares biographical characteristics with the author), while Rufin and Houellebecq test the waters of speculative fiction by imagining future dystopian worlds. Engaging with contemporary issues as diverse as changing rural landscapes, globalization, consumer capitalism, political oligarchies, biotechnologies, ecoterrorism, and cloning, these authors attest to the richness of contemporary French literature that, far from sinking into oblivion, continues to nourish the global literary and intellectual scene.[14]

The first chapter of the book will focus on the concept of *ecological subjectivity* as a way of rethinking the role of human characters and interactions in literary texts from an ecocritical perspective. First, I will examine Félix Guattari's project of ecosophical thought and his calls for an ethical and aesthetic paradigm across three ecologies – mental, social, and environmental. Guattari's ecosophy articulates subjectivity not as a state of being or a fixed identity, but as processes taking place on an immanent plane of swirling differences and events. While Guattari points to the importance of art and literature in bringing about new subjectivities, Darrieussecq's novels *Un bref séjour chez les vivants* (2001) and *Le Pays* (2005) instantiate these processes.[15] In both novels, Darrieussecq explores subjectivity as a turning kaleidoscope of memories, events, places, bodies, and stories. Illustrating the instability of the genre of *autofiction*, the narrative voices circulate at multiple levels, tracing possible passages from the local to the global. Although the novels include references to nuclear power plants, toxic waste, and air pollution, Darrieussecq is not advocating for ecological change. The references remind the reader that textual worlds are necessarily anchored in a material reality.

The second chapter will examine an issue that has been considered central to contemporary environmental thought: What does it mean to live ecologically? I will use the expression *ecological dwelling* to refer not to a particular type of home or habitat with a green roof, geothermal heating system, or other forms of sustainable architecture, but to the ways in which place gives form to practices or ways of living. In particular, the chapter will focus on the figure of the *paysan* and rurality as they appear in Serres's work on the natural contract and in three novels by Lafon, *Les Derniers Indiens* (2008), *L'Annonce* (2009) and *Les Pays* (2012).[16] For Serres, farming practices and rural landscapes can serve as examples for imagining ecological dwelling on a global scale. Serres is not advocating that we all become farmers, but that we move toward a natural contract built on the principles of symbiosis and co-dependency characteristic of previous local ways of dwelling. Lafon's novels bring the reader back to personal contexts and stories, revealing the difficulties of rural life when one's former identity is threatened. Lafon avoids a backward-looking view of a better, more harmonious relationship between humans and the non-human world, adopting a realist aesthetic to narrate life as it is composed, renewed, and regenerated. Both Lafon and Serres assert the need to rethink relationships to the land in light of the figure of the *paysan*, which has been central to the French imaginary.

The third chapter will move from the question of dwelling and place to the broader issue of articulating a politics capable of representing as many human and non-human beings as possible. Avoiding the humanism/anti-humanism binary that has plagued French philosophy since Ferry's 1992 book *Le Nouvel Ordre écologique*, I adopt the expression *ecological politics* to include both critiques of environmentalism and calls for a new ecological paradigm. Latour offers a framework for radically rethinking the modern Constitution, that is, the way in which the Western world has separated nature from culture, and matters of fact from matters of concern.[17] He rejects anglophone environmental philosophy's argument about nature's intrinsic value and posits the always and already embedded agency of non-humans in cultural systems. Rufin's novels *Globalia* (2004) and *Le Parfum d'Adam* (2007)[18] are also highly critical of Anglo-American environmentalism, but they reassert the importance of the human in ecological politics. Holding to the ideal of universal social justice and equality, the novels raise the question of human voices that remain unheard in democratic political systems and illustrate the increasing problem of North-South relations in the era of globalization. Ecological politics becomes a way of addressing the global within the context of French discourses and attitudes toward nature and environmentalism.

The fourth chapter will come full circle by examining the issue of *ecological ends*. What future worlds may one day put an end to our ecological imagining? What role do other "ends" such as the end of the human or the end of nature play in our ecological imagining? According to Jean-Marie Schaeffer, it is time to put an end to the thesis of human exceptionalism and recognize the embeddedness of humans in the physical world.[19] Critiquing the long history of Cartesian dualism in France, Schaeffer draws on studies in cognitive psychology, biology, and the neurosciences to develop a non-reductionist continuism. As a philosopher, Schaeffer believes it is essential for the humanities to move toward a more scientifically informed notion of the human. Houellebecq's novels *Les Particules élémentaires* (1998) and *La Possibilité d'une île* (2005) also take up the question of the human as part of nature, but do so in the context of the possible end of the human race and the creation of a new species.[20] Even if Houellebecq's fiction falls into the trap of biological reductionism of which Schaeffer is so critical, both Schaeffer and Houellebecq adopt a common notion of humans as having value as *homo literatus*, that is, as tellers and writers of stories. Ecological ends are, then, not absolute ends, but a way of rethinking and resituating the human in the larger question of life on the planet.

The four concepts can be seen as forming constellations that are connected in multiple ways. First, the concept of ecological subjectivity raises the problem of the self and the subject, moving away from humanism's anthropocentrism by mapping out relational becoming. Second, ecological dwelling connects subjectivity to place, looking to understand how perceptual experiences are embedded in specific geographies. Third, ecological politics shifts the analysis from the *domos* to the *polis*, from the local to problems of representation in a globalized world, examining how non-humans and humans are given voice in a planetary city state. Lastly, the problem of ecological ends is brought to bear on the three other concepts and on the practices of ecocriticism more broadly: How will ecological subjectivity emerge if humans have evolved into a different life form? What will ecological dwelling look like in such an environment? Who will speak for whom in terms of an ecological politics? To what end can ecological imaginings be used? What are the end(s) of ecological readings?

From this overview, it should be clear that no universal set of ecological ethics and politics is being applied to the theoretical and literary texts discussed here. Instead, a micro-politics of diverse encounters, understandings, and positionings is being outlined. This does not mean that there is no passage from the micro-politics of an ecocritical reading of text to the macro-politics of ecological thought in contemporary France. But this passage very much resembles the one described by Serres in *Le Passage du Nord-Ouest*: singular, transitory, time-space dependent, full of obstacles, and yet extremely enriching and worthwhile. It brings the reader to the real world, but a real that is "frangé de sommeil et de songes," "plongé dans la démence et la beauté," "concret, flottant, solide, fragile, précis et fondu, résistant ou sans prise."[21]

Setting the stage: French ecological thinking

Offering a historical overview of French eco-thinking is beyond the scope of this introduction. It would mean going at least as far back as Michel Montaigne's essays on colonialism (1580) or Voltaire's poem about the Lisbon earthquake (1756) or Jean-Jacques Rousseau's writings about the *bon sauvage* (1755). Given that my area of interest is contemporary French theory and fiction, a more relevant starting point is Claude Lévi-Strauss's eco-thought. A twentieth-century structural anthropologist who was deeply influenced by Rousseau's thinking and highly critical of society's destruction of nature,[22] Lévi-Strauss attempted to develop what he called a more "ordered humanism" by placing "le monde avant la vie, la vie avant l'homme, le respect des autres êtres avant l'amour-propre."[23] According to Verena Andermatt Conley, "the anthropology that Lévi-Strauss mobilized through politics, ethics, and aesthetics inaugurated a decisive critique of Western expansion and materialism."[24] In many respects, Lévi-Strauss was a key figure in drawing attention to the West's destruction of the natural world.

In terms of ecological politics in France, interest in bringing environmentalism into the political sphere has been increasing from the 1950s and 60s on. The first French "green" political party, *les Verts*, was created in the 1970s, and the Ministère de l'Environnement was one of the first of such governance structures in Europe. Examining the work of Jean-Paul Deléage, Bruno Latour, Alain Lipietz, Edgar Morin, Serge Moscovici, Emmanuel Mounier, and Michel Serres, Kerry Whiteside argues that French eco-thought represents a strong counter-example to anglophone environmental philosophy: "French green theorists tend to study how conceptions of nature and human identity intertwine. They elaborate green thought more often by *reciprocally problematizing* 'nature' and 'humanity' than by refining the distinction between them."[25] The emphasis is on bringing ecological issues into the political sphere rather than establishing a set of policies around conserving and preserving nature in national parks.

It is clear that Ferry's book did not shut down eco-thinking in France in the 1990s. Rather, it polarized the difference between political ecology on the one hand and environmental philosophy and ethics on the other. While the former continued to take on different forms with the rise and fall of the Green party, the latter was largely marginalized in France. As Larrère points out, debates about environmental philosophy and ethics were much more characteristic of the anglophone world in the 1990s: "Ce débat affecte plus particulièrement la communauté de langue anglaise, américaine principalement ... La France, jusqu'à présent, est restée à l'écart."[26] While political ecology remained important in subsequent years, environmental issues were relegated to the sphere of a centralized government and the developments of science and technology, and thus deemed to have little to do with personal decisions and ethical living in France.[27] It is from this particular climate that contemporary French ecological thinking emerged.

The effects of this climate can be seen in the work of two contemporary thinkers at whom I will look in more depth in the following chapters. Both Serres and Latour avoid the term "environment" even though they engage with the urgency of planetary ecological issues. In *Le Contrat naturel* (1990), Serres describes his particular way of bringing together science, nature, and law as a *philosophie de la nature*, and does not once mention well-known eco-thinkers such as Aldo Leopold or Arne Naess. As for Latour, he distances himself from environmental philosophy, entitling his seminal work *Politiques de la nature* (1999). Moreover, Latour remains highly critical of the ways in which Green parties reduce ecological issues to problems related to nature and environment. Specific to the French context and intellectual climate,

Latour's and Serres's thinking cannot be reduced to a form of *philosophie environnementale*, or a French equivalent to North American environmental philosophy.

A similar point can be made about the emergence and development of environmental history. As Fabien Locher and Grégory Quenet note, this discipline emerged in the United States in the early 1970s, whereas the expression *histoire environnementale* has only been used more recently in France.[28] This is not because French historians have not been interested in the relationship between nature and history or in the emergence of laws and policies to protect natural and cultural landscapes in France. But there has been no one single umbrella term under which these diverse studies have gathered. Instead, expressions such as *éco-histoire* and *histoire écologique* have been used in the *Annales,* a key historical journal in France. Locher and Quenet conclude their comparison of the two fields by calling for more dialogue between American and French historians, not to unify their thinking about nature and the environment but to understand further the diversity of approaches.

This leads me to an important point about the work of comparative studies. The emergence of environmental philosophy and environmental history in France has been characterized as slow when the term "environment" is held up as the measuring stick. But such a comparison unfairly glosses over the fact that ecological thinking has evolved from different concepts and theoretical frameworks in France. Instead of pointing to a lag or delay, comparative studies need to consider the rise of ecological thought in light of various cultural and historical factors in France. This does not mean reifying the notion of cultural difference, since what constitutes difference changes as cultures come into contact. As Locher and Quenet point out, the French expression *histoire environnementale* is now used to refer to the parallel but distinct anglophone field of environmental history. Working from the notion of cultural difference offers a productive perspective for revisiting and reviewing issues that may already have a long history in anglophone scholarly communities.

Language is an important place to start when considering French eco-differences. As I have already noted, the terms "environment" and "environmental" do not have the same resonances in French as they do in English. The English "environment" is a relatively recent term, and comes partly from Middle French *environnement,* meaning surroundings, and partly from the Anglo-Norman *avirounement,* meaning proximity or perimeters.[29] The word's meaning remained fairly stable in English until the second half of the nineteenth century, when the term began to be used in science to refer to the place where an organism lives or develops and then to the natural environment more specifically. This more recent meaning was taken up in the 1960s by grass-roots movements in North America arguing for an environmentalism based on the principle of interrelatedness and a politics of countercultural resistance. Today the term "environment" still has the original sense of a surrounding, but it is more often than not associated with environmentalism as a political position.

In French, the term *environnement* has not undergone the same transformation, and has largely retained the original meaning of "environs" from Middle French.[30] While it does refer to that which surrounds an organism (its *milieu*), the word continues to connote the place at the centre of the surroundings. It is on these grounds that Serres rejects the word: "Oubliez donc le mot *environnement*, usité en ces matières. Il suppose que nous autres hommes siégeons au centre d'un système de choses qui gravitent autour de nous, nombrils de l'univers, maîtres et possesseurs de la nature."[31] Citing René Descartes's famous line – "maîtres et possesseurs de la nature" – Serres equates the word *environnement* with a long history of anthropocentric thinking in France. It is not surprising that he does not use the words *environnemental* and *environnementalisme* either, even though these terms appear regularly in the French media.[32] Instead, Serres uses the term *écologie* to refer to the kind of thinking needed to arrive at an understanding of the intertwined, reciprocal relationship between humanity and the planet.

In a similar vein, Latour and Guattari adopt the term *écologie* to differentiate their approaches from an environmental politics of saving the planet. For Latour, ecology becomes a verb – *écologiser* – that stands in opposition to *moderniser* and refers to the political and epistemological project of accounting for non-humans as actors in social networks. As for Guattari, he builds his *écosophie* on a triad of mental, social, and environmental ecologies. Although he uses the adjective *environnemental,* he opposes environmentalism's narrow focus on nature and articulates a broad understanding of interactions among organisms in many different environments.

To foreground the importance of the concept *écologie,* the current section is entitled "French ecological thinking." Using the more common expression "environmental thought" in English would gloss over the ways in which thinking about nature and culture have emerged in France over the last fifty years. Even though I am writing this book in

English, I will at times use less-common terms and expressions in order to keep this language/culture gap in sight. French quotations are also included strategically as a way of reminding readers of the work of translation, of the fact that language can hinder or facilitate expression. My point is not to discourage readers from understanding cultural differences, but to invite them to go back to original texts so as to grasp the ways in which meaning is formed situationally from constellations of words and concepts.

Thinking through/with cultural differences

To posit the need for a specifically French *écocritique* poses the question of what the adjective "French" means. I will respond to this question not by listing a set of characteristics or traits, but by looking at some of the ways in which French cultural differences have been constructed and deconstructed. A first obvious example is the notion of *l'exception française*. What this expression actually refers to – the *République*, universal humanism, *fraternité, égalité, liberté* – is not clear, and yet the idea has had long staying power, even in today's globalized world. As Roger Célestin, Eliane DalMolin, Marc Dambre, and Richard J. Golsan note, "the expression is invoked almost incessantly to emphasize the uniqueness or peculiarities of, among many other things … a national political and social model that has supposedly run its course."[33] The idea of a cultural and political exceptionalism may not map onto the contemporary situation in France today, but it continues to give rise to lively debates.[34]

In the November 2007 European edition of *Time* magazine, Donald Morrison published a feature article entitled "French culture is dead."[35] To no one's surprise, the article's main premise was rejected both within and outside of France. But as critics have pointed out, the article reveals more about the relationship between the USA and France than about the actual state of French culture.[36] My point is not to enter into the fray of the debate, but to look more closely at how the idea of "French culture" is being used in the article. The cover of the *Time* magazine issue – showing the famous Mr Bip character of actor Marcel Marceau, wearing a beret, miming sadness and holding a wilted red flower – reduces French culture to a set of clichés. References in Morrison's article to French art, cinema, literature, and culinary traditions – in short, to the easily exportable products of French culture – confirm this initial impression. Even the article's hopeful conclusion that French culture will one day "reclaim its reputation as a cultural power" does nothing to offer the reader a more complex view of French cultural difference.

Stereotypical images of French culture, such as wearing a beret, riding a bicycle, carrying a baguette, eating cheese, and drinking wine, are not useful for developing a French *écocritique*. To avoid such reductionist understandings of culture and cultural differences, it is helpful to consider comparative studies that discuss the specificities of the culture of nature and environment in France. Adopting a historical perspective, Caroline Ford notes that in nineteenth-century metropolitan France, emphasis was placed on landscape preservation to protect areas of great cultural and historical value: "Landscape protection represented a longer cultural continuum, harking back to the drive to protect France's architectural, historic, and aesthetic heritage as *patrimoine*."[37] The French government was initially concerned with saving landscapes as sites of cultural patrimony and not as sites of ecological value. Ford goes on to explain that it was upon obtaining large tracts of so-called "untouched" land in Algeria that France began to adopt the more American model of national parks meant to "preserve" wilderness spaces.[38] Ford's comparative historical study nicely illustrates the ways in which cultures of nature and environment are embedded in geographical realities.

Comparative studies are useful for framing French cultural differences, but they can also give rise to a problematic, essentialized view of culture. Adopting a sociological perspective, Jean Viard argues that Catholicism in France has led to a love of cultivated, tended nature and laws that are for the most part "restauratrice, nationaliste, [et] rentabilisatrice," whereas Protestantism in the US has developed a love of wilderness and the creation of conservation laws to save the natural beauty of national parks.[39] He goes so far as to propose the hypothesis that "c'est dans les tréfonds religieux de l'organisation de nos cultures qu'il faut plonger pour pouvoir penser pourquoi les uns ont favorisé les monuments naturels, les autres les monuments humains."[40] Comparing attitudes toward nature and environment along the lines of religious difference disembeds culture from geographical realities. It also raises the question of who is speaking for whom in cultural comparative analysis.

Anthropology and ethnography have become increasingly aware of the power structures inherent in marking cultural differences. In "Writing Against Culture," Lila Abu-Lughod critiques the normalizing effect of anthropological descriptions of cultural practices that project stable identities onto others.[41] As she explains, "culture is the ultimate tool for making other" (470). To avoid essentializing cultural differences, Abu-Lughod calls for ethnographies of the particular that focus on daily life and practices. She reminds anthropologists of the need for partial readings and explanations that remain situated in a particular time and place. Even though her field of specialization is ethnography, Abu-Lughod makes a point that is just as relevant for literary studies when she speaks of bringing the "language of the text" closer as a way of reversing the "mode of making other."[42] Through close reading, literary analysis can reveal how texts use language to subvert cultural norms and conventions.

Critical of the "cultural turn" in the humanities, Pál Nyíri and Joana Breidenbach question the explanation of everything from genocide to consumer habits in terms of a generalized notion of "culture."[43] They offer an in-depth analysis of the social and political conditions that have given rise to this notion of culture at the global level, the state level, the institutional level and the individual level. At the end of their book, Nyíri and Breidenbach come back to the problem that Abu-Lughod had outlined in her article almost twenty years earlier: How do we talk about culture without reducing it to some bounded, homogenous, unchanging whole that explains individual behaviour? Nyíri and Breidenbach advocate for a critical awareness of the power dynamics of making claims about culture, and they advise scholars to ask questions such as: Who is making statements about culture differences and similarities? Why are they making them? Who is speaking for whom? Whose voices are not being heard?[44]

These are the questions I will continue to ask in order to avoid reducing the notion of "French" to a list of clichés and stereotypes. While general studies about French attitudes toward nature and the environment, such as less concern for wilderness and more concern for cultural landscapes, can act as starting points, they need to be complemented by the study of particular texts that often illustrate the exception rather than the rule. In addition, it is essential to respond to the question of who is speaking in the name of cultural difference. Part of the reason I have been able to outline a French *écocritique* is because I am not working strictly within French literary studies but instead from a comparative perspective in a Franco-Canadian context. This has made me aware of the socio-historical and political factors that affect how literary studies are taught and practiced in both Canada and France. At the same time, I have had the opportunity to participate in transnational and global dialogues, making me more aware of the influences and exchanges that are possible between languages and cultures.[45]

According to Gayatri Spivak, a "responsible comparativism" avoids foregone conclusions by being especially attuned to the ways in which literary texts use language to subvert ideas about nationalist identity.[46]

She speaks of the "performativity of cultures as instantiated in narrative," drawing attention to the ways in which the literary text exploits the gap between nation and culture, between language and nation. In my literary analysis, I will highlight the ways in which narratives "perform culture" even as they deconstruct the notion of "belonging" to a single place. In addition, I will cultivate a "care for language and idiom"[47] when analysing literary and theoretical texts. When French words or concepts have no equivalent in English, they will be carefully explained so as to provide the necessary sociocultural context. In this sense, culture matters as an imagined community different from the nation and the state, but also as an evolving *oikos* or habitat for language and literature. In keeping with its original etymology, the word "culture" means a form of cultivation of practices and traditions, and a cultivation of the earth itself. Rather than a fixed set of representations, characteristics, or habits, culture is a living biophysical process in which we participate and are constantly adapting.

Cultures and climates of literary studies

Ecocriticism as an academic field has been aware of the need for comparative cultural approaches for some time. One of the key defenders of this idea, Ursula Heise, has pointed out the dangers of a dominant Anglo-American focus within ecocriticism as well as the problem of English as a hegemonic language.[48] Arguing for an eco-cosmopolitan approach, she states that we need an "expanded understanding of how different cultures approach nature."[49] More recently, one of the founders of North American ecocriticism, Lawrence Buell, has argued for the creation of a handbook of critical keywords that will allow anglophone ecocritics to become better-versed in linguistic and cultural differences, such as the fact that Chinese has no word for "watershed" and Spanish no term for "wilderness."[50] Although Heise and Buell seem to be arguing for a similar awareness of cultural diversity, they are doing so for quite different reasons. Heise argues for more cultural difference within ecocriticism, whereas Buell hopes to find a common language in which ecocritics can speak together against environmental destruction. The problem with Buell's position is that it once again reinstates English as the common language and relegates ecocritical work done in other languages to a secondary role.[51]

The tension around cultural differences within ecocriticism arises in part from the perceived need for a global response to environmental issues on the one hand, and the desire to be sensitive to other world views on the other. But it is not necessary to set up a division between the global and the cultural in this way.[52] As Heise clearly states in her book *Sense of Place, Sense of Planet,* we need an ecological awareness about planetary issues, but this awareness is necessarily discussed, represented, and imagined in specific sociocultural and linguistic contexts. Developing this awareness may mean that ecocritics who do not speak the language cannot always bridge differences. To cite Spivak once again, "the diversity of mother-tongues must challenge" the "uniformity" of "even a good globalization."[53]

The case of "French theory" is a fascinating example of the ways in which systems of thought migrate across cultures without transcending cultural or linguistic differences. The expression "French theory" is of English origin and describes a movement that thrived in North American universities in the 1970s, when identity politics were driving new feminist, African-American, gay and lesbian approaches, and cultural studies more generally. In France, such movements were almost completely absent from literary studies at the time.[54] As François Cusset explains, theorists like Jacques Derrida, Gilles Deleuze, Félix Guattari, and Michel Foucault garnered much more attention on the other side of the Atlantic in the seventies, eighties, and nineties than in France.[55] Even if these thinkers have become more recognized in France since then, queer studies, postcolonial studies, ethnic studies, and gender studies are just now emerging there.[56] For scholars working in these areas, it has been difficult and at times impossible to receive recognition within the French institutional and intellectual context.[57]

Aside from an initial special issue of *Mots pluriels* (1999) that brought together Francophone scholars around the question of literature and ecology,[58] ecocriticism has had little traction in French and francophone literary studies. The first scholars to introduce ecocriticism to a French readership were those working on American literature. In their introduction to ecocriticism, Tom Pughe and Michel Granger note that ecocriticism arises from "des préoccupations logées au cœur de l'histoire culturelle américaine."[59] Interest in ecocriticism in France has, moreover, largely come from Americanists working on nature writers like Rick Bass, Annie Dillard, and Henry David Thoreau.[60] This reception of ecocriticism is not in and of itself different from that of other literature departments outside North America. Ecocriticism first spread around the world in large part thanks to American and English literary studies in places as diverse as India, Korea, Japan, and Taiwan. It is only now that culturally specific ecocriticisms have been emerging.[61] What is different in terms of the reception of ecocriticism in France is the ways in which it has had to contend with other literary approaches to space, place and landscape.

According to Aline Bergé, French contemporary literature has undergone a "véritable tournant paysager" over the last twenty-five years.[62] She cites the fiction of Pierre Bergounioux, François Bon, Henri Cueco, Jean Echenoz, Henri Michon, Richard Millet, and Jean Rolin as proof of this "landscape turn." It is true that landscape has become an important topic for literature and literary critics in France.[63] And yet landscape studies draw largely on theories of aesthetics to define landscape as a representation of place and not as a physical, material reality. For example, one of the leading theorists of literary landscape studies, Michel Collot, explains that landscape is "cette image du monde, inséparable d'une image de soi, qu'un écrivain compose et impose à partir de traits disperses mais récurrents dans son œuvre."[64] From this perspective, landscape loses much if not all of its material connection to the real world. In a more recent text, Collot and Bergé recognize the need for a politics of landscape when they write: "Le paysage se présente … comme un recours voire un modèle pour inventer une relation plus harmonieuse entre cosmos et anthropos … un terrain d'action où se bâtit peut-être une nouvelle modernité capable de concilier le progrès des sciences et des techniques avec le respect de l'homme et de l'environnement."[65] And yet this vague assertion that science and technology will bring about harmony between humans and the cosmos hardly constitutes an ecological politics (see Larrère's earlier comment about how environmental issues are relegated to science and technology in France, eschewing the need for a more personal, ethical engagement).[66]

Bertrand Westphal's *géocritique* offers a way of bringing the material world back into the reading of literary representations of space and place. In his pioneering book *La Géocritique: Réel, fiction, espace* (2007), Westphal attempts to rethink referentiality and retheorize the relationship between the real and the fictional. Without mentioning ecocriticism, Westphal examines one of the problems at the heart of the ecocritical approach: How does the textual world relate to the real world? Drawing on work in architecture, geography, sociology, and urban studies, Westphal develops a methodology for analysing places (largely urban) in literary texts. Even though he goes beyond landscape studies to give place a physical referent in the real world, he does not go so far as to develop a politically engaged reading of texts.[67] It is important to note once again the difficulties faced by French literary scholars who attempt to engage in ecological readings of texts.[68]

While environmental studies have greatly influenced the emergence of North American ecocriticism, geography has played the key role in new literary approaches to space, place, and landscape in France. In his book *Pour une géographie littéraire*, Collot points to the importance of literary readings that bring together geography and literature, such as Marc Brosseau's work, Franco Moretti's distant reading, and Westphal's geocriticism.[69] Collot then goes on to develop his own methodology for reading place in literary texts that is based on semiotic theory. A closer look at Collot's approach reveals that once again the materiality of the referent is disregarded so that there is no object preceding or even interceding in the literary representation. Although he does not mention "eco" approaches, Collot reveals through his silence that a literary geography does not start from an ecological politics. It is clear that for literary scholars like Westphal and Collot, interest in rethinking the relationship between the text and the world lies in the spatial and not the ecological or environmental imagination.

This is much less true of *géopoétique*, an approach that places "emphasis on developing a body and mind relationship to the earth."[70] Founded by Kenneth White, a bilingual writer, traveller and philosopher, Scottish by birth, but who has been living in France for many years, geopoetics has spread quickly into an archipelago of different research centres, institutes and groups, some of which have homes in academic settings and others not. Its main goal is to develop practices of reading and writing that involve more careful and attentive relationships to the physical world. As White explains: "A world, well conceived, emerges from a contact between Mind and Earth. When the contact is sensitive, intelligent, subtle, you have a world in the full sense of the world. When the contact is stupid and brutal, you have nothing like a world, nothing like a culture, only, and more and more so, an accumulation of refuse, including a lot of 'cultural products.'"[71] At the heart of geopoetics is a transdisciplinary approach that aims to understand better the relationships between humans and diverse environments. In many respects, geopoetics and ecocriticism follow parallel paths, but have developed in largely distinct linguistic and intellectual communities.

In recent years, there has been more interest in politically oriented readings of representations of nature and the environment in French literary studies.[72] In their introduction to "Littérature et écologie," a special 2008 issue of *Écologie & Politique*, Nathalie Blanc, Denis Chartier, and Tom Pughe propose the term *écopoétique* to describe an ecological approach to reading literature and analysing art more generally.[73] They explain that an *éco-logique* dislodges the author or artist as the origin of meaning and turns instead to the material conditions of the production and reception of a work of art. They prefer the term *écopoétique* to *écocritique* because it more accurately reflects the fact that a creative work cannot be reduced to its content or themes and that a consideration of its aesthetic nature must be taken into account.

In *Ce qui a lieu. Essai d'écopoétique* (2015), Pierre Schoentjes adopts a similar position, presenting *écopoétique* as a way of redirecting attention back to "le travail de l'écriture."[74] He recognizes that there is overlap between the terms – *écopoétique* and *écocritique* – but he asserts that "la spécificité française s'accommode mieux d'un terme qui met moins l'accent sur l'engagement et plus sur la composante proprement littéraire."[75] Interestingly, Schoentjes defines his corpus using an approach that is typical of early work in ecocriticism, that is, he chooses texts in which natural spaces are given an important role. The concept of nature is not, however, examined or critiqued from a political or epistemological perspective. Literature is kept separate from these other discourses despite the fact that the nature question has been the focus of much French ecological thinking.[76]

And so the door has remained open to an approach that seeks to bring contemporary French literature and ecological thinking together. Drawing on various theoretical frameworks available for thinking nature and the human critically, a French *écocritique* proposes to read contemporary literature and fiction ecologically.[77] It remains attentive, however, to the formal and structural elements of the literary texts in question. As will become clear in the following chapters, I am keenly aware of the impossibility of reading texts purely thematically (in part because of my long engagement with structuralism and narratology). I am not, moreover, advocating for a general methodology; each of the texts I analyse determines the kind of attention to form and structure that is needed. The singularity of the text will necessarily come up against my attempts to read across literature, philosophy, and science for similar ideas and concepts. And so in each of the four chapters, close reading is used to emphasize formal and thematic singularities, while a broader, interdisciplinary approach is used to situate the text in its sociocultural and ecological contexts.[78]

The "French" effect

In her introduction to the *Vocabulaire européen des philosophies. Dictionnaire des intraduisibles*, editor Barbara Cassin carefully outlines two problematic positions for a project that aims to explain the ways in which philosophical concepts have been articulated differently in different European languages.[79] On the one hand, she denounces "a logical universalism" that looks to bridge differences and instate a "common" language of philosophy. On the other, she rejects what she calls an "ontological nationalism" that essentializes differences between languages and cultures. It is from a third position of multiplicity among languages and multiplicity within a language that Cassin situates the project of a European vocabulary of philosophy.[80] She explains that the term "untranslatable" does not mean a concept that is impossible to translate, but a concept that requires ongoing (re)translation.[81] More generally, Cassin asserts that culture and language are bound together, not deterministically (culture does not determine language's specificities, nor does language give rise to a specific set of cultural differences), but effectively: "A language, as we have considered it, is not a fact of nature, an object, but an *effect* caught up in history and culture, and that ceaselessly invents itself."[82]

What does this notion of language as an effect mean for a French *écocritique*? In the *Vocabulaire européen des philosophes*, Alain Badiou authors the entry for "French," examining the ways in which French philosophy has been informed and affected by the French language.[83] Citing René Descartes's publication of the *Discours de la méthode* (1637) in French rather than Latin, Badiou points to the democratic nature of French philosophical language. By appealing to the "written language 'of the day,'"[84] Descartes set the tone for a "universal and democratic philosophical communication."[85] According to Badiou, French philosophy continues to use "literary language" in order to reach both the general public and the scholarly community. Badiou then looks more closely at linguistic structures that have shaped the ways in which French philosophers have expressed their systems of thought. Examples are given from Louis Althusser, Auguste Comte, Gilles Deleuze and Félix Guattari, Jacques Lacan, and Jean-Paul Sartre to illustrate the specificities of philosophical French, a language of "syntax with little room for semantic ambiguity," a language of verbs and liaisons or successions (not a language of the phenomenon and "descriptive subtlety" like English).[86] Whether the reader accepts this characterization or not (Badiou himself admits that there will always be "poets and writers" who illustrate the exception to the rule), Badiou makes a strong final point that language is a "material *place*" through which philosophical thought must necessarily move to "order its ideas."[87]

This understanding of a "French effect" has multiple meanings for the *écocritique* outlined in this book. First, it underscores the fact that language is not a transparent medium, that it affects the way thinking organizes the world. If I had written this book in French, the critical concepts may have been expressed more effectively using verbs such as *"écologiser la subjectivité," "écologiser la politique,"* or recombining ideas such as *"écologiser et habiter la subjectivité."* Second, Badiou's point that French philosophical thought draws on literary language lends support to my assertion that a French *écocritique* needs to bring French theory and fiction together. The overlap between philosophy and literature has a long history in the French intellectual tradition, from Voltaire's *contes philosophiques* to Sartre's existentialist novel *La Nausée*. Separating the two seems to be in part a product of a 1960s French literary structuralism that sought to define literariness as necessarily distinct from other uses of language. Third, Badiou raises the issue of the politics of language, and reminds the reader that the choice to use one language rather than another is always political.

To some extent, my decision to write in English about what constitutes a "French" effect can be seen as flawed from the start. And yet it is this problem that allows me to flag the politics and histories of national literatures while also questioning the call for a global environmental imagination. The term "French" is a way in which both to construct and deconstruct a sense of culture. On the one hand, as I analyse the particular thinkers and texts in each chapter, the notion of "French" becomes fuzzy – can Bruno Latour, who has given conference papers around the world and now publishes more often in English than in French, be called French? On the other hand, the lack of ecocritical work in France underscores the reality of various sociocultural factors at work. In the end, writing in English but repeatedly using the French word *écocritique* keeps the problem of language's effects on thinking, its embeddedness in culture and history, and its capacity to express difference at the fore of my work. It also speaks to an anglophone readership about the need to contextualize and historicize abstract concepts in the face of calls for a global response to a planetary ecological crisis.

1 Ecological Subjectivity: Guattari and Darrieussecq

L'enjeu écologique, avant d'être scientifique, associative, politique, industriel, est d'abord éthique et esthétique. Il est éthique parce qu'il engage un rapport à l'altérité et à la finitude selon l'ensemble de leurs modalités: humaines, animales, végétales, cosmiques, machiniques ... Les espèces naturelles en peril comme les espèces culturelles en voie de dépérissement ... ne seront sauvées qu'à la condition que soient engendrées des potentialités de vie encore inédites sur cette planète. Donc, pas de repli nostalgique sur un passé irréversiblement balayé par la symbiose humanité-machine, mais production assumée collectivement d'une nouvelle subjectivité, d'une nouvelle socialité et d'une nouvelle "nature."

– Félix Guattari, "La grand-peur écologique (1989),"
in *Qu'est-ce que l'écosophie?* 517–18[1]

While the expression "eco-subject" brings to mind images of environmental practices such as recycling, composting, walking or cycling to work, tending a vegetable garden, etc., the idea of an ecological subjectivity has fewer readily available meanings and associations. In this chapter, I want to elaborate upon ecological subjectivity as expressly that which is not an eco-subject; that which cannot be mapped onto a set of environmental practices; that which is ecological in a much broader sense. As I will illustrate throughout this chapter, the term "subjectivity" avoids the pitfalls of the idea of *subject* often understood as a stable, fixed identity or in opposition to an object. Subjectivity is relational; it cannot be equated with the individual, as it does not have a single centre. It is embodied, but not contained by the body, as it can extend into various social and physical environments. Starting with the concept of ecological subjectivity is a way out of the impasse between two opposing discourses: a humanist belief in the human subject as master and a postmodern embrace of the dissolution of all subject positions. It also opens up a path to the notion of the human as political practice and aesthetic experience.

It is true that structuralism did much to decentre the humanistic self. By making language a central organizing principle, it moved toward a less-anthropocentric perspective. As for poststructuralism, it underscored the institutional, social, and political structures that determine identity, thus putting an end to the notion of an autonomous, self-determining, and rational subject. But this left little room for creating new kinds of subjective becoming. As Félix Guattari explains, "Le sujet s'est trouvé méthodiquement expulsé de ses matières d'expression multiples et hétérogènes. Il est temps, aujourd'hui, de réexaminer ce qu'il en est des productions machiniques d'image, de signe, d'intelligence artificielle, etc., comme nouveau matériau de la subjectivité."[2] In this chapter, I take up the call to trace cartographies of new subjectivities. Whereas categorization fixes things in place and determines their essence, cartography remains open to "un noyau d'incertitude."[3]

North American ecocriticism has argued against the primacy of the human in literary studies, redefining the humanities as being about more than just the human. In his seminal text, *The Environmental Imagination*, Lawrence Buell outlines four criteria of the environmental text, each of which asserts the importance of the natural world and backgrounds strictly human concerns.[4] This approach is meant to counter an anthropocentric reading of texts that focuses largely on human drama and characters. Another way in which ecocriticism has tried to decentre the human subject is by drawing on scientific models and theories from biological and ecological sciences to analyse the representation of human and non-human relationships and interactions as represented in literary texts. Glen Love, for example, calls for a reading of the text in light of how correctly it reflects the "truths" of biological science.[5] While both of these approaches represent a shift away from anthropocentrism, they do so problematically. In Buell's case, the emphasis on non-fiction environmental texts such as Thoreau's *Walden* reduces ecocriticism to a limited set of texts with long descriptions of natural phenomena. As for Love's "practical ecocriticism," it unquestioningly takes science as the objective and authoritative source of knowledge about the real world.

Ecocriticism's endorsement of the natural world stems in part from the work of environmental philosophers. Founder of deep ecology (or what he originally called "Ecosophy T"), Arne Naess was a twentieth-century Norwegian philosopher who developed an ecocentric view of the subject as ceding his interests to those of the greater ecological Self.[6] No longer separate from the physical world, the human subject accepts his or her place as simply a part of a much larger whole. But as Peter Van Wyck notes, deep ecology's melding of self into a holistic Self problematically creates a single human subject position and closes off "the possibility of heterogeneous subjectivities."[7] Moreover, it does not solve the problem of subject/object dualism; it only defers it. Timothy Morton makes a similar point in his discussion of nature writing's treatment of the environmental subject. For Morton, this subject may "yearn to close the gap" between itself and the world, but its very existence depends on such a gap.[8] Van Wyck and Morton's critiques of the ecological Self and the environmental subject respectively suggest that subjectivity and identity are not so easily dissolved into an undifferentiated state of being (in) the world.

Whereas ecocentric views like deep ecology attempt to decentre the human by centring on the natural world, French ecological thought adopts multiple, non-centred positions. Neither biocentric nor ecocentric, it asserts the "*irreducible* diversity of 'natures.'"[9] Environmental concerns are given value in shifting, cultural frameworks; there is no one "nature," just as there is no one single human subject position. As Whiteside notes, French ecological thought develops a strong theoretical engagement with the concept of subjectivities because of its attention to multiple subject positions.[10] By clearing a non-anthropocentric path to humans and natures, French ecological thought offers *écocritique* an approach for considering different kinds of literary texts, those in which human characters are at the fore as well as those in which setting and place play a determining role.

I have chosen to focus on Guattari's *Les Trois écologies* (1989) and *Chaosmose* (1992) in the theory section of this chapter because these texts offer a relevant set of concepts for articulating ecological subjectivity in terms of both a politics and an aesthetics. In addition, they offer an important frame of reference for the concrete developments of ecological thinking in France at the times of their publications. Guattari's involvement in *les Verts* and then his affiliation with *Génération écologie* reflected the splintering of green politics in France during the 1980s and its eventual decline in the 1990s. Guattari's subsequent rejection of these parties also set the tone within French ecological thought for future critiques of environmentalism as a single-issue politics. Finally, Guattari's ecosophy – which examines problems as diverse as North-South inequalities, deforestation, neoliberalism, and consumer capitalism – remains as pertinent today as it was in the late 1980s. As can be seen by the 2013 publication of 500+ pages of Guattari's writings, his ecosophical thinking continues to attract the attention of French scholars.

Darrieussecq's novels *Un bref séjour chez les vivants* (2001) and *Le Pays* (2005) are the object of the literary analysis in the fiction section of this chapter. In the wake of the *Nouveau roman* (1950s) and *l'ère du soupçon*, Darrieussecq's novels continue to engage with writing as formal experimentation. They are not, however, published by *Editions de Minuit*, which is known for its support of minimalist fiction by the *Nouveaux nouveaux romanciers* (e.g., Jean-Philippe Toussaint). Even though the novels offer splintered narrative points of view, they plunge the reader into a world of perceptual experience that emphasizes the materiality of the physical world. They thus point to an ecological aesthetics that does not rely on realism but instead requires the reader to piece together carefully what is in the end a fragmented world. In addition, Darrieussecq illustrates in her work how fiction can take on political issues without being reduced to a soapbox for a single political cause. Particularly interested in the effects of gendering in the French language, Darrieussecq writes in a way that makes evident the subject's construction (and deconstruction) as female within language. At the same time, the content of her narrative experiments highlight the continued role of gender divisions in contemporary society.

If both Guattari and Darrieussecq are taken by the problem of writing about subjectivity, it may in part because of the influence of psychoanalysis on their thinking. Guattari worked at the Borde psychiatric clinic for many years, even though he clearly distanced himself from French thinkers like Jacques Lacan. As for Darrieussecq, she was first a patient undergoing treatment, then a reader of Freud and Lacan for her doctoral thesis, and finally a practitioner herself.[11] It is thus not surprising that Guattari and Darrieussecq write about subjectivity as a continuously evolving process, full of moments of crisis but also potential subversions. At the same time, they both carefully situate processes of subjectivity in a material world. In this way, they illustrate subjectivity as not just relational but also ecological.

Ecocriticism has largely ignored the world of psychoanalysis. Preferring to focus on the physical world, it has paid less attention to the world of the human psyche, and yet the two are intimately intertwined, as studies in environmental psychology are now showing.[12] Starting with the concept of subjectivity in a book on *écocritique* is a way of emphasizing the importance of the concept of the human psyche, especially in terms of French intellectual history. In his doctoral thesis *Violent Signs: Ecocriticism and the Symptom* (2011), Tim Matts outlines some of the reasons why ecocriticism has not yet developed an adequate conceptualization of human subjectivity.[13] Following Frederic Jameson's analysis in *The Political Unconscious* (1981), Matts cites "the cultural and political differences between the French and North American milieus" that "called for very different approaches to political theorising."[14] He goes on to examine the Cold War context, the problem of immanence, and the concept of pluralism as other possible social and intellectual reasons for ecocriticism's resistance to Lacanian theory.

I find Matts's study interesting, but not because we need a psychoanalytic reading of ecocriticism's (at times phobic) reactions to theory. It is true that Matts articulates an original explanation for what many critics have already noted about the beginnings of ecocriticism – that is, its strong opposition to poststructuralist and postmodernist theories. What interests me, however, is the way in which Matts frames his analysis in terms of cultural and intellectual histories in France and North America. Because French literary studies and literature have remained open to Lacanian theory and psychoanalytic approaches more generally, they are fertile ground for developing a notion of subjectivity as entangled in and bounded by specific forms of embodiment, materiality, and sociality.[15]

Theory

Portrait: Félix Guattari

Guattari is most recognized for his collaborations with philosopher Gilles Deleuze. Ecocritics less interested in nature writing, conservationism, and North American environmental philosophy have taken up Deleuze and Guattari's writings to argue for a rhizomatic approach to nature-culture in literary texts. For example, in his introduction to *Deleuze|Guattari & Ecology* (2009), Bernd Herzogenrath outlines the potential of a process-oriented ontology of difference for ecocritical thinking.[16] While drawing inspiration from this work, I am particularly interested in the ways in which Guattari's psychoanalytic perspective gives rise to the notion of ecological subjectivity and how this notion intersects with Darrieussecq's experiments with narrative point of view. Moreover, Guattari's single-authored works have not been the focus of ecocritical work, despite the fact that they offer a more sustained engagement with ecological politics than his co-authored texts.[17]

In France, Guattari's ecosophical thinking has come back into the spotlight with the publication of *Qu'est-ce que l'écosophie?* (2013), a collection of writings, some previously unpublished and others newly edited. In his introduction to the collection, Stéphane Nadaud explains what ecology meant for Guattari: 1) a new politics (in the face of rising disappointment about the socialist left in the 1980s under François Mitterand); 2) a philosophy for rethinking reality, humans, and nature; and 3) a "fonctionnement groupusculaire" or new possible social restructurings and formations.[18] It was on this triadic structure that Guattari constructed an ecosophy that was as pragmatic as it was philosophical: "Il s'agit de concevoir des pratiques d'intervention sociale, y compris politiques, gouvernementales, qui soient cohérentes avec des pratiques sociales de terrain, avec des pratiques dissensuelles, culturelles, analytiques, individuelles et de groupe, et esthétiques et de développer une politique et des moyens, des dispositifs, qui permettent ce caractère dissensuel."[19] Such practices of social and political intervention would address both ecological issues (such as species extinction) and cultural ones (such as declining cultural diversity). Written in the seventies, eighties, and early nineties, Guattari's texts continue to be highly relevant, as they call for "collective involvement in the production of a new subjectivity, a new sociality, and a new 'nature.'" [20]

In her book *Ecopolitics*, Verena Andermatt Conley outlines the ways in which French poststructuralist thinkers have worked to critique the human(ist) subject. Although her focus is elsewhere, Andermatt Conley's book nicely points to a way out of the theory/anti-theory debate that has characterized ecocriticism over the last few years.[21] For Andermatt Conley, poststructuralism grows "from the sociopolitical and environmental awareness of what structuralism has established."[22] She reminds the reader that Jean-François Lyotard, one of the fathers of poststructuralist thinking, wrote an essay, "Oikos" (1989), in which he analyses the war on nature as part of a war waged by the rich on the poor. His essay is a far cry from the high theoretical gesturing and posturing of which poststructuralism has been accused by many first-wave ecocritics.[23] As Andermatt Conley points out, poststructuralism needs to be reassessed as part of an "ecological ethos" that emerged in the wake of *la pensée '68* in France, a differential way of thinking that aimed to undo nature/culture dualism.

More specifically, Andermatt Conley examines Guattari's notion of subjectivity in the context of his ecosophical thinking. She points out the influence of Sartrean existentialism on Guattari's thinking about the subject-object relationship.[24] Building on Sartre's notion of "subjects apprehending an object," Guattari theorizes a "double seizure of 'subject' and 'object,'" that gives rise to "existential territories."[25] Guattari emphasizes the two-way directionality of "existential grasping" where the subject is also acted upon and the existential territory does its own "autopoetic seizing."[26] Moving beyond subject-object dualism, Guattari understands subjectivity in terms of processes of making and unmaking existential territories. Even though Guattari embeds these processes in the material world, he does not use the expression "ecological subjectivity." Instead, he argues (as I do) that the problem of subjectivity must be included in an ecological thinking that goes beyond environmental issues.

Highly critical of consumer capitalism (or what he calls Integrated World Capitalism or IWC for short), Guattari explores alternative subjectivities to that of the reified, individualist, liberal subject. To some extent, his thinking aligns with that of other ecological thinkers who have adopted a multitude of strategies for critiquing the capitalist subject. But Guattari does not propose to dissolve the subject into a larger network of living beings; he chooses a different route for undoing subject/object dualism. As a psychoanalyst, Guattari is keenly aware of the processes that both construct and deconstruct subjectivity. To describe these processes, Guattari proposes a model of thinking transversally that moves away from the static notion of the subject to the dynamic workings of subjectification and desubjectification. Such a shift is at the heart of Guattari's ecosophy whose aim is to articulate subjectivity within three overlapping domains – the mental, the social, the environmental – each of which involves a set of "evolutive processes."[27] As a new perspective for thinking about the human in a larger web of socio-material relations, Guattari's ecosophy outlines a foundation for an ecological subjectivity in opposition to the collective, inactive-induced anesthesia of "capitalistic subjectivity."[28]

Part of the originality of Guattari's ecosophical thought lies in the new "ethico-aesthetic" paradigm that he proposes in response to the following question:

> How do we change mentalities, how do we reinvent social practices that would give back to humanity – if it ever had it – a sense of responsibility, and not only for its own survival, but equally for the future of all life on the planet, for animal and vegetable species, likewise for incorporeal species such as music, the arts, cinema, the relation with time, love, and compassion for others, the feeling of fusion at the heart of the cosmos?[29]

As I will show, Guattari sees literature and the arts more generally as playing a key role in bringing about new subjectivities. Advocating for an approach that combines ethics and aesthetics, Guattari opposes a strictly scientific and rational response to ecological issues. He reminds us of the importance of looking to literature to imagine a future other than the one dictated by consumer capitalism and neoliberalism.

I will follow Guattari's transversal way of thinking toward an ecological subjectivity, first by looking at the **political** possibilities of his theory of ecosophy as outlined in *The Three Ecologies*, and second by examining the **aesthetic** possibilities of his notion of subjectivity as outlined in *Chaosmosis*. Focusing on these two books will allow me to articulate a French ecocritical approach that reads for both politics and aesthetics, one that seeks to fill the gap in thematic readings of literature and ecology, one that destabilizes the paradigm of literary representation, one that reasserts the role of creativity in imagining alternate ways of becoming in the world.

Ecosophy's political possibilities

To develop his ecological politics, Guattari adopts the term "ecosophy," but without ever mentioning Arne Naess, the Norwegian philosopher who first coined the term in the early 1970s. The differences between their ecosophical thinking are, in fact, striking. For Guattari, ecosophy is first and foremost a philosophy according to which there exist three overlapping and heterogeneous ecologies: social, mental, and environmental. If he uses the term "environmental," it is to refer not to a specific set of ecological concerns but to political praxis more generally, one that carefully attends to social problems of difference and responsibility. Ecosophy represents, he explains, "un choix éthico-politique de la diversité, du dissensus créateur, de la responsabilité à l'égard de la différence et de l'altérité."[30] Built on three overlapping and interdependent realities – social, mental, and environmental – Guattari's ecosophical thinking avoids dialectical difference and works toward a politics of multiple diversities.

For Naess, on the other hand, ecosophy is a philosophy of ecological harmony and equilibrium that promotes a holistic view of the interactions of organisms with their environment. Defined as "a total view inspired in part by the science of ecology and the activities of the deep ecological movement," Naess's ecosophy rejects the notion of humans as separate from nature.[31] In *Ecology, Community and Lifestyle* (1976), Naess argues that the ecological Self emerges when the human subject goes beyond narrow human concerns and recognizes itself as part of an ecospheric whole.[32] Through the realization of this greater Self, humans relinquish their place as above or outside of nature. They recognize Earth's intrinsic value and call for an end to modern industrial technology's destruction of Earth's ecosystems.

For Guattari, ecosophy cannot be reduced to the need for more sustainable practices or ways of living with the world. As he explains, "the ecosophic problematic is that of the production of human existence itself in new historical contexts."[33] Moreover, Guattari does not reject outright the use of technology and new media. Instead, he asks how capitalism has used technologies to construct a limited number of homogeneous subject positions. In addition, he asks how media and technology can lead to the creation of new subject-groups. All relations must be viewed, Guattari asserts, through the lens of an ecological logic or an eco-logic that shifts the focus to "the movement and intensity of evolutive processes," an approach "strives to capture existence in the very act of its constitution, definition, and deterritorialization."[34]

To understand fully the political possibilities of Guattari's ecosophy, it is important to examine more closely each of the three ecologies. Although **mental ecology** receives the most attention, it is in no way reduced to the individual's psyche or even the processes of the perceptual; social groups can have mental ecologies as well.[35] Guattari focuses on subjective processes that cultivate dissensus and a singular formation of existence. Derived from a "pre-objectal and pre-personal logic," these processes escape the logic of the rational mind and instead constitute an "ecology of the phantasm ... that requires the drafting of an expressive framework that is both singular, and more precisely singularized."[36] Guattari cites specific literary examples (Joyce, Goethe, Proust) to explain how these mental ecologies bring subjectivity into existence. I will come back to Guattari's understanding of aesthetics in the next section. For now, I want to underline the fact that Guattari's ecosophy makes a place for literature not as a way of "reconnecting" with the natural world, but as a site for creating and imagining new subjectivities.

Guattari's **social ecology** moves beyond the dualisms of nature and culture, biology and technology, the organic and the machinic, by examining "the interactions … [between] ecosystems, the mechanosphere and the social and individual Universes of reference."[37] Transversalist thought examines biological phenomena like "superbug" bacteria created by an overuse of antibiotics alongside cultural phenomena like that of self-replicating cultural memes created by television and mass media. Biological and cultural "bugs" coalesce in a network of human, social, and biological vectors and assemblages. Proposing a return to the past would be "absurd," insists Guattari. Instead, we need to ask how we can construct a "social movement *under today's conditions.*"[38] Again, Guattari points to some potential sites of contestation where social groups oppose capitalism's market-value exchange system.[39] Without proposing a "ready-made model of society," Guattari posits that we need new ways of defining "collective interest" and new aesthetic and social practices.[40]

When discussing **environmental ecology**, Guattari makes it immediately clear that he is not using the term "environmental" in the North American sense of a return to nature and increased care for the non-human world. Guattari critiques the reduction of ecology to concerns about preserving nature: "Ecology must stop being associated with the image of a small nature-loving minority or with qualified specialists. Ecology in my sense questions the whole of subjectivity and capitalistic power formations, whose sweeping progress cannot be guaranteed to continue as it has for the past decade."[41] Guattari's critique reflects a commonly held view in France that perceives environmentalism – often unjustly so – as a reductive single-issue politics. When a member of *les Verts*, Guattari argued for a wide spectrum of issues that ecological politics had to address, from social inequalities to environmental destruction. It is this more "generalized ecology"[42] that Guattari attempts to outline by connecting the environmental to the social and the mental.

Present- and future-facing, Guattari envisages an environmental ecology that anticipates the "worst disasters" as well as the "most flexible evolutions."[43] This does not mean, however, falling prey to the kinds of apocalyptic rhetoric that have proved to be equally problematic in environmentalist discourse. Guattari acknowledges that we have modified our ecosystems on a global scale and are now responsible for ensuring that the Earth remains habitable for the greatest number of humans. As Guattari notes, this epistemic shift in our relationship to the Earth means that environmental ecology must also be a "machinic ecology," that is, an understanding of the techno-scientific infrastructures in which biological life is bound up.[44] Rather than opposing technology and ecology, Guattari imagines future evolutionary changes made possible by machines and calls for an "ecosophical ethics adapted to this terrifying and fascinating situation."[45]

Ecosophical ethics are both theoretical and pragmatic, as Guattari had hoped to demonstrate if elected a member of the French political party *les Verts*.[46] He explained in a short article at the time: "L'engagement dans une telle perspective n'est pas seulement affaire d'idées et de communication, mais également, et peut-être avant tout, de renouvellement des pratiques."[47] Guattari targets the way democracy is practiced more generally, calling for a renewal of politics that will infuse all political programs and agendas with ecological thought.

He admonishes French ecologists for not being more involved in issues related to all three ecologies, such as urban life, education, health, and new media technologies. Guattari's article had a lasting effect on French green parties. In 2006, *les Verts* redefined their political platform as a "démocratie écologique conviviale," citing directly from Guattari's earlier text.[48] As Chantal Asp and Marie Jacqué point out, thinkers like Guattari were highly influential in the development of French green politics and policies, even if they remained critical of French politics in general.[49]

Near the end of *The Three Ecologies*, Guattari opens up his discussion of ecosophical politics to the role of the creative imaginary. He urges the reader to tell stories about the "permanent recreation of the world" as a way of countering the reduction of information in the media.[50] To support this call for storytelling, he cites Walter Benjamin: "'Storytelling … does not aim to convey the pure essence of a thing, like information or a report. It sinks the thing into the life of the storyteller, in order to bring it out of him again. Thus traces of the storyteller cling to the story the way the handprints of the potter cling to the clay vessel.'"[51] Benjamin's metaphor of the potter and clay reminds the reader of the materiality of storytelling, of the way in which it, too, is bound up in physical processes. Guattari goes on to describe his tri-ecological vision as "bringing into being other worlds beyond those of purely abstract information" and "engendering Universes of reference and existential Territories."[52] Guattari's description of ecosophy's creative practices clearly includes the literary text's ability to bring to life possible worlds and plunge the reader into alternate subjectivities.

Subjectivity's aesthetic possibilities

How do literary texts imagine new subjectivities? What kinds of subjectivities emerge from art more generally? How does the reader or spectator experience these subjectivities? What aesthetic possibilities follow from ecological subjectivity? Published in 1992, three years after *Les Trois écologies,* Guattari's *Chaosmose* (as it was originally titled in French) focuses on the question of subjectivity, while also developing further the aesthetic possibilities of ecosophical thinking. It thus offers a complementary perspective for outlining an ecological subjectivity in the context of Guattari's ethico-aesthetic paradigm. As Guattari explains in the first few pages of his book: "My professional activities in the field of psychotherapy, like my political and cultural engagements, have led me increasingly to put the emphasis on subjectivity as the product of individuals, groups, and institutions."[53] Working with patients at the Borde psychiatric clinic brings Guattari back to what is most at stake in his philosophical and political project: "the development of a new kind of subjectivity."[54] In the face of increasing individualism and capitalist production, Guattari asks what subjectivities contain the possibility of new openings to the socius and the cosmos. He argues for a complex, multiple, relational subjectivity that follows from an "eco-logic." By this, Guattari means a heterogenic logic of the machinic, virtual, and chaotic, one that produces multiple existential refrains and territories. In order to tease out the aesthetic possibilities of this subjectivity, I will move more slowly through Guattari's arguments and examples in *Chaosmose.*

To define subjectivity, it is necessary "to decentre the question of the subject … traditionally … conceived as the ultimate essence of individuation, as a pure, empty, prereflexive apprehension of the world, a nucleus of sensibility, of expressivity – the unifier of states of consciousness."[55] To trouble dualist thinking that posits the world as "out there" and the subject as "in here," Guattari proposes to map subjectivity as a set of relational processes, as "the ensemble of conditions which render possible the emergence of individual and/or collective instances as self-referential existential Territories, adjacent, or in a delimiting relation, to an alterity that is itself subjective."[56] Subjectivity is not, then, simply a subject whose boundaries have become less definable; it is instead a situation in which specific circumstances give rise to temporary assemblages (or a coming together) at individual and collective levels. But if individualism has triumphed as the dominant contemporary subjectivity, how is it then possible to imagine new subjectivities?

One way in which Guattari responds to this question is by considering the role of art in contemporary society. He begins by outlining three aesthetic paradigms: 1) the aesthetics of ritual and religion that embeds creative practice in specific social and material activities ("a particularised axiological reference"); 2) the aesthetics of modern society that defines art in terms of transcendent values such as Beauty, Progress, and more recently, Capital; 3) a new processual paradigm that shifts responsibility from a transcendent entity – God, the system, etc. – to multiple assemblages, be they collective, institutional, or different machinic interfaces. To create new subjectivities, the new aesthetic paradigm does not propose a return to rituals and religions (first aesthetic paradigm) or a reversal of capitalism's standardization of subjectivity (second aesthetic paradigm). Instead, it enacts a "different type of re-enchantment of the expressive modalities of subjectivation" by way of "processes of creation that auto-affirm themselves as existential nuclei, autopoietic machines."[57] Drawing on the convergence of biology and technology, Guattari asserts that these "autopoietic machines" generate their own new Universes of infinite meaning.

Chaosmosis is central to this creative process. It is both chaos and complexity, or more precisely, the double movement of a complex system collapsing into chaos and chaos giving birth to new complexities. According to Guattari, creative forces necessarily plunge into chaos to increase complexity, but they can just as well disappear into chaos.[58] The relationship between chaos and complexity is reciprocal and not dualist. Chaosmosis does not oscillate "between zero and infinity, being and nothingness, order and disorder"; it "rebounds and irrupts on states of things, bodies, and the autopoietic nuclei it uses as its support for deterritorialization."[59] As a creative force before it is applied to specific works (scientific, philosophical, literary, etc.), chaosmosis is the world of infinite virtual entities and possible Universes of reference. Intensities build upon previous intensities, unbinding creative forces from the logic of capitalist production.

Although Guattari calls for a new ethico-aesthetic paradigm, he does not subordinate art to a predetermined ethics, and most certainly not to a well-defined environmental ethics. As Gary Genosko succinctly notes: "Ecology is not art's prop; neither is art ecology's secret weapon."[60] Guattari envisages creative processes that are not limited to artistic practice and an ecology that is not bound to a single ethics. Art can become the site of new assemblages, but it can also fall into the trap of simply reproducing capitalism's uniform consumer subject position. Guattari nevertheless holds on to a hope for a "different deployment of aesthetic components" in the face of "the immense crisis sweeping the planet – chronic unemployment, ecological devastation, deregulation of modes of valorisation, uniquely based on profit or State assistance."[61] In other words, art's eco-potential does not reside in its representation of the natural world or its expression of an ecological message; it resides in the way creative forces enact and enable new subjectivities.[62]

How can literature more specifically participate in a new ethico-aesthetic paradigm? Guattari does not respond to this question, but he does open his book with an epigraph from Marguerite Duras's novel *The North China Lover* (1992). In the cited passage, the play of light and shadow over the course of a day on a ship at sea is described as "'an unreadable and wrenching script'" that "'takes shape and destroys itself at the same slow pace ... and then, unceasingly, lives again.'"[63] Similar to the quotation from Benjamin, this description collapses the distance between the written word and the physical world. But it also reminds the reader of the ways in which the circulation of ideas in a text or the processes of the natural world resist interpretation. As an "autopoietic machine," the literary text simultaneously creates and destroys meaning. Integral to these processes, the reader participates not as pure consciousness, but as embodied subjectivity. As Guattari explains, the body can be "conceived as [an] intersection of partial autopoietic components, with multiple and changing configurations, working collectively as well as individually."[64] Like the body, literature becomes the site of "many existential territories linked by the same transversal chaosmosis."[65]

Guattari also draws on literature to elaborate the notion of "existential refrains." As John Tinnell explains, existential refrains are "crucial sites through which subjectivity is produced, negotiated, and learned."[66] On the one hand, they can simply reinforce the production of capitalist subjectivity, as when an advertising song plays over and over in our heads.[67] On the other, they can "resingularize serialized ensembles" when the detached fragment becomes part of a polyphonic subjectivity. As an example of a resingularizing existential refrain, Guattari points to Marcel Proust's repeated descriptions of the madeleine cookie. If literature becomes a privileged (but not unique) site of existential refrains, it is in part because poetic texts can "both transmit a message or denote a referent while functioning at the same time through redundancies of expression and content."[68] When they create polyphonic and plural subjectivities, literary texts counter capitalism's tendency to impose one system of value on multiplicity.

While ecocriticism has emphasized realism's ability to close the gap between word and world, Guattari points literary studies in a different direction. By citing Duras and Proust, but also Beckett and Joyce, Guattari reveals the eco-logical potential of literature that plays with language, that ambiguously uses formal and linguistic repetition, and that troubles the relationship between word and world. In this way, his ecosophy provides an ethical framework for re-reading modernist, non-realist, and experimental texts. At the same time, his ecosophical aesthetics breaks down the distinction between biological and technological, conscious and unconscious, material and immaterial. As autopoietic machines, creative processes participate in the material world while still retaining their self-organizing capacities. Existential refrains detach from the text and attach to the reader becoming part of a new temporary assemblage. Yet even this description introduces too much stability into the decentring affects and percepts of the aesthetic experience that Guattari describes in the following way: "I am swept away by a becoming other, carried beyond my familiar existential Territories."[69] In the end, Guattari's ecosophy provides fertile ground for cultivating an *écocritique* whose ethics encompass mental, social, and environmental ecologies, and whose aesthetics engage with the complex, material processes of the creative imaginary.

Fiction

Portrait: Marie Darrieussecq

Well-known contemporary author Marie Darrieussecq was born in the town of Bayonne in the French Basque Country. This may at first seem like an insignificant biographical detail, but when one considers the relationship to place in her novels, this detail takes on importance. Darrieussecq does not write regional literature; on the contrary, her novels are set around the world, in places ranging from Australia to the Antarctic, Paris to Buenos Aires. They illustrate a sense of place, but one that extends from the local to the global. Darrieussecq refuses to be categorized as a "French writer" and prefers the adjective "European." She could be called cosmopolitan except that she also identifies with the particular situation of the Basque Country in France and recognizes the importance of writers publishing in the Basque language (although she herself writes in French).[70]

In many ways, Darrieussecq's novels challenge the notion of being French, and so represent an excellent starting point for examining the idea of "French" critically. She refuses the kind of French nationalism that remains blind to the internal heterogeneity of the nation-state. Even when writing about a place as culturally prominent as Paris, she decentres the reader's view of the cosmopolitan city by describing small city squares and street corners. Writing all her texts in French (essays, plays, novels, short stories), Darrieussecq is keenly aware of the ways in which language shapes our experiences and perceptions of the world.[71] Openly critical of gendering in the French language, she quotes feminists such as Monique Wittig who refuse to follow grammar rules and who purposely write "quelqu'une" instead of "quelqu'un" and "une autre" instead of "un autre."[72] In her novels, she experiments with multiple narrative voices, typography, and *autofiction*, reminding the reader of writing by *nouvelles romancières* such as Nathalie Sarraute. She works and publishes in France, writes in French, but uses language to subvert notions of nation and culture. In short, Darrieussecq's novels trouble the notion of a "French literature," revealing what is a socio-historical construction rather than a given.[73]

A more traditional ecocritical approach, one that is looking for environmental texts that foreground the non-human world and clearly promote an environmental ethics, would be less interested in Darrieussecq's novels. Even if they do refer to nuclear power plants, water and air pollution, Darrieussecq is not critiquing destructive human practices. Yet it would be a mistake to reject these texts as purely humanist endeavours that reassert the dominance of the human over the environment. Darrieussecq's novels are deeply engaged with what it means to be a living being in a material world that includes minerals, plants, and animals, as well as immaterial beings. Because her stories pay careful attention to new ways of being and becoming in the world, while also exploring new forms and genres for expressing such embodied processes, they lend themselves well to ecocritical analysis. Rather than fit these novels into the category of environmental literature, I will illustrate their relevance and importance in terms of a further understanding of the notion of ecological subjectivity.

All of Darrieussecq's novels explore becoming in and with a world very similar to that of the contemporary, globalized, neoliberal West.

While Darrieussecq has written some novels in imaginary futures (*Truismes*) or very near to our own present (*White*), I have chosen *Bref séjour chez les vivants* (2001), translated in English as *A Brief Stay with the Living*, and *Le Pays* (2005), not yet translated into English, because they represent a complementary set of themes related to place, landscape, and embodiment. While the first novel, *Brief Stay*, explores the global possibilities of ecological subjectivity, the second, *Le Pays*, examines its more local significations. In the first novel, three daughters and a mother narrate their daily life from three different places around the world – Buenos Aires, Paris, and the family home in the French Basque country. In the second novel, *Le Pays*, the main character, Marie Rivière, moves back to her childhood home after living many years in Paris. Her objective is, she explains, to give her son a landscape beyond small Parisian city parks. Preparing for the birth of her daughter, Épiphanie, she also returns to the *pays* in order to write a novel entitled *Le Pays*. Both novels weave elements of Darrieussecq's life into the textual fabric of the fictional worlds in order to undo the boundaries between the real and the imaginary.[74]

In addition to layering elements of her own life into her novels, Darrieussecq experiments with narrative form as a way of destabilizing a fixed subject perspective. In *Brief Stay*, the fragmenting of a family still haunted by the memory of a little boy drowned in the ocean many years before is mirrored in the narrative voice that abruptly shifts from one character's thought processes to the next without any transitions. This form is also taken up in *Le Pays* where two narrative voices echo each other to tell the story of the main character after her return to her home near the town of Bayonne in the French Basque country. In this case, the narrative form reveals the splitting of a psyche into two points of view, one first person, the other third person, but that also overlap as they echo each other's phrasing, expressions, and descriptions. Both these novels emphasize the extent to which the question *qui suis-je*? is intimately and necessarily related to the questions *où suis-je*? and *d'où viens-je?*

The (dis)placement of (female) subjectivity is a recurring theme in Darrieussecq's novels. In her analysis of *Le Pays*, Catherine Rodgers outlines the ways in which Darrieussecq explores the "limits of the self" alongside the limits of the world and the limits of language.[75] Similarly, Helena Chadderton identifies the self, society, and language as the three pillars of Darrieussecq's textual worlds.[76] My analysis will build on these previous studies, but will move away from the notion of the self and toward the notion of subjectivity. To examine the political and aesthetic possibilities of ecological subjectivity, I will examine Darrieussecq's two novels in terms of 1) how they "bring into being other worlds beyond those of purely abstract information"; 2) how they "engender Universes of reference and existential Territories" that resist capitalism's anesthetizing effects; and 3) how they "confront the vertiginous Cosmos so as to make it inhabitable."[77] Darrieussecq's fiction aligns well with Guattari's three ecologies and with his ecosophical thinking more generally, but it also underlines the difficulties of sustaining subjectivities that are just as often unravelling as they are (re)assembling.

Writing the processes of (de)subjectification

In her most innovative experiment with form, Darrieussecq uses multiple narrative voices in *Brief Stay* to tell the story of four related women.[78] This immersion in multiple processes of subjectification reminds the reader of the role of sexualized and gendered bodies. Without reducing the body to a particular set of female experiences, Darrieussecq explores various stages in the lives of her four female characters: the divorced and remarried mother, coping with the death of her son many years earlier and still living in the family home in the Basque Country; her cosmopolitan oldest daughter, Jeanne, living in Buenos Aires, who is married and trying to become pregnant; the middle daughter, Anne, a research assistant in Paris, desperately looking for friendship and love; and the youngest daughter, Nore, living at home and exploring her newfound adolescent sexuality. Representative of white, middle-class society, the four narrators illustrate problems that are fairly typical of women living in the Western world. And yet the novel's form forces the reader to enter a world less familiar, leaving behind the stability of easily identified subjects and embarking on waves of polyphonic subjectivity.

According to Chadderton, Darrieussecq's novel creates an impression of thought processes swirling about in an immaterial world of consciousness, foregrounding time and memory. She adds that the multiple narrative voices in the novel create a sense of fragmentation that mirrors the workings of memory and its linguistic construction.[79] As for Simon Kemp, he makes the more general assertion that "the workings of the mind, and of the conscious mind especially, have been the central theme of all Darrieussecq's work from her second novel onwards."[80] It is true that the reader gets to know the four main characters of *Brief Stay* through their thought processes. Yet the notion of "mind" maps too quickly back onto a disembodied humanistic self. The novel continuously underlines the problem of mind/body dualism, illustrating the difficulties of a subjectivity that is solely immaterial or linguistic.

Coming back to Guattari's three ecologies is useful for understanding the processes of (de)subjectification in the novel. The most mentally dispersed and disassembled of the three sisters, Anne, does not know what to do with her body: "Put my body someplace, be in charge of myself, as though of the mothership … The problem is the habitat. Especially at night, more than ever, you float around your body, not knowing what to do with it."[81] Mental ecology intertwines with the machinic, setting in motion processes that are more often desubjectifying than subjectifying. Anne's corporeal disconnection is amplified by her connection to what she calls the "worldwide consciousness." She imagines herself as a receiving and transmitting node of the "world's encephalic field"[82] and describes "surfing over the network of the worldwide brain."[83] In Anne's case, the capacity for connecting to the noosphere or the world of ideas that are constantly circulating in a globalized world leaves her bereft of a sense of her own body. She does not hide, moreover, the increased surveillance that comes with these telepathic capacities; she speaks of being recruited by agents into a worldwide organization, revealing the cracks in her psyche and the dangers of a global ecology of interconnected ideas.

Discussing the conjuncture of mental and social ecology, Guattari describes family traditions, local customs, and judicial law as examples of collective subjectivities that are capable of resisting Integrated World Capitalism, and that offer sites of resistance to disembodied, immaterial realities. In Darrieussecq's novel, the family acts, however, less like glue holding the members together and more like a centrifugal force driving them apart. The first time a missing family member is mentioned is when Anne remembers sharing a secret moment with her older sister, Jeanne, but not with Pierre "who was too small for us to talk to" and "then no one to talk to at all."[84] The loss of a family member represents a deep psychological trauma that characterizes all of the female subjectivities in the novel. Pierre also acts as a (dis)organizing principle of the text's ecology, as he is first mentioned in the novel with no indication of who he might be. The reader is given a hint when the women's mother mentally counts and accounts for her children, a practice she does regularly to make sure she knows "where" they all are: "My first is Jeanne, my second is Anne, my third is Nore and my answer is … One missing."[85] The reader is left to piece together the parts of the story that refer to a young boy on the beach in red swimming shorts, a body washed up on the shore several months later, and the mother's refusal to get out of bed for months. To come back to Guattari's notion of collective subjectivity, Darrieussecq makes it clear that dead family members play as important a role as the living in social ecologies. As the title of Darrieussecq's novel – *A Brief Stay with the Living* – indicates, the actual lived life represents only one way in which realities are imagined, forged, and remembered.

The third sphere to consider in terms of the processes of subjectification in Darrieussecq's novel is environmental ecology. It is important to note once again that environmental does not mean a return to the natural world or a set of eco-practices. It means reinventing, rethinking, and reimagining our relationship to the physical world in its many modifications. In the novel, the effects of toxicity and radiation are clearly portrayed, for example, when Anne imagines the bodies affected by the radioactive material shipped from elsewhere in the world to Marie Curie in France.[86] The novel does not condemn technological advances or scientific research, but outlines instead the porosity and vulnerability of human bodies.

According to Cynthia Deitering, toxic consciousness emerges when we realize that nature – long appreciated for its healing and aesthetic qualities – may in fact be extremely dangerous.[87] This awareness can be seen in some of the mother's musings in the novel. As a gardener, the mother interacts frequently with the green, vegetal world; the novel opens with a scene of her pruning roses, early in the morning, flooded with a feeling of "happiness so huge and liquid."[88] This feeling is, however, short-lived, and a sense of foreboding and unsettledness colours the rest of the mother's musings. Back in her garden later in the afternoon, she notes the dangers that might be hiding in the dew and the grass. She thinks of Chernobyl and the radiation that infiltrates bodies, causing cancer.[89] Her ex-husband has moved to Gibraltar to start a wind farm, convinced of the need to shift to renewable resources,[90] while the mother does not know what to think of nuclear power.[91] Like Anne, she does not reject scientific advances, but she is clearly aware of their sometimes-harmful effects on bodies.

Darrieussecq's portrayal of this toxic consciousness reflects a more general attitude toward nuclear power in France. According to Michael Bess, "France was arguably the world's pioneer in nuclear research, the Paris laboratory of Marie and Pierre Curie performing some of the earliest and most path breaking experiments on radioactivity and its causes."[92] Bess goes on to explain that the French population's reaction to the creation of reactors was largely neutral because these reactors were, according to the government, an example of France's world-leading technology; in the seventies, to be French meant to embrace nuclear power.[93] It was not until the Chernobyl disaster that the environmentalist movement in France found the momentum needed to form a critical mass in opposition to nuclear reactors.[94] An example of such thinking can be found in Guattari's work when he notes that "the proliferation of nuclear power stations … threatens, over a large part of Europe, the possible consequences of Chernobyl-style accidents."[95] Guattari is not, however, willing to endorse the anti-nuclear movement, not because he does not see the risks, but because he is wary of "reductionist, stereotypical order-words which only expropriate other more singular problematics."[96] Similarly, Darrieussecq's novel avoids reducing environmental ecology to a single issue, outlining instead the effects of new technologies on bodies.[97]

Permeability extends ecological subjectivity beyond the living body. The novel reminds the reader that even after death, the body continues to harbour living organisms. When Pierre's body washes up on the shore after three months in the sea, it has become a habitat for marine creatures: "A coral body, fauna growing all over it, and … those *opernes*, with their pincers and antennae, a Spanish delicacy."[98] The description breaks down the belief in the human body as sacred, emphasizing the becoming-edible of human flesh and the cycles of life and death (the body becomes food for the sea creatures who become, in their turn, food for humans). What kind of subjectivity is possible, however, when the body is no longer home to consciousness but continues to participate in environmental ecology?

Given that subjectivity is not equal to thought or mind or consciousness, it is possible to trace the continued effects and affects of bodies, their circulation in mental and social ecologies even after a human being's death. In the case of Pierre's body, he continues to influence the familial relations of the members left behind. But his effect extends into the material world, undoing the opposition between the real and the supernatural. When Jeanne and Anne would play in the living room in front of a painting of the sea, Pierre's body would reappear, smelling of the sea, "one side of his head … a huge mollusc, his own flesh transformed by the sea into a shell of himself."[99] Both human and sea creature, both spectre and flesh, Pierre's body is part of a world of material hybridity.

The novel's ending reinforces the role of death in the undoing and (re) assembling of ecological subjectivity. As Jeanne's car slowly descends into the Tigre river with her trapped inside, she takes stock of the watery world around her. She worries about whether her underwear and bra are matching, whether she should have gone on a diet, and what the reactions of her family members will be. Fragments of songs, memories, conversations, and sensory perceptions bubble up arbitrarily as she slowly loses consciousness. As the ellipses increase and the words dwindle, the reader experiences her death as a transition rather than an end. An image of Pierre that briefly appears in front of Jeanne reminds the reader that she too will become habitat for marine animals. There is no final revelation about death. Instead, we are brought back to the other family members' realities at the end of the novel: Anne awakes at dawn screaming without knowing why, and her mother heads out to her garden to tend roses. Social ecology (familial relations), mental ecology (Anne's telepathic connection to events in the world), and environmental ecology (Jeanne's transition into body as material matter) all come together, leaving the reader with a sense of quiet loss.

To elaborate further the eco-potential of Darrieussecq's novel, it is necessary to consider more closely the characters' relationships to space and place. To frame my analysis of *milieu* in Darrieussecq's novel, I will draw on Ursula Heise's ecocritical work in *Sense of Place, Sense of Planet* (2009). As Heise notes, environmentalism has often asserted a sense of place as a way of countering globalization's nomadism and capitalism's emphasis on mobility. She adds, however, that a sense of place can and has led to forms of ruthless nationalism, and even fascism in the case of Nazi Germany.[100] In addition, Heise points out that an emphasis on local attachment and belonging denies the reality of immigrants displaced for any number of reasons from their places of origin. Arguing for a sense of planet, Heise offers a definition of eco-cosmopolitanism as "an attempt to envision individuals and groups as part of planetary 'imagined communities' of both human and non-human kinds."[101] This question of a (lack of) sense of place and a (growing) sense of planet will serve as an initial framework for looking at the *milieux* in which ecological subjectivities evolve in Darrieussecq's novel.

The novel is set in different places around the world. The mother and Nore are the most sedentary, residing in the Basque country. Staying in one place does not, however, necessarily translate into a sense of place. The mother goes through life as if "centrifuged out to the edge of the world forever" after the drowning of her son Pierre.[102] Jeanne, on the other hand, is presented as the most nomadic, leaving home at age seventeen, travelling to the Philippines, Africa, and Australia, before finally settling in Buenos Aires.[103] She describes her sense of planet in terms of the effects of globalization, which has made French croissants and baguettes as available in a cosmopolitan Latin American city as in Europe: "Here, in Buenos Aires ... you're in France more than anywhere else, where we're all in Italy, in Germany, in Spain, in the Basque country, in Sweden, in Europe."[104] In the case of both the characters who never leave home and the one who never comes home, a sense of *milieu* clearly does not map onto a single local, regional or national identity.

As Kemp notes, Darrieussecq's characters are often world travellers who have a complicated relationship with their homeland. He concludes that they must learn to develop an identity that is independent from geographical belonging: "Trouver un terrain neutre – littéral ou figuratif – pour se construire une identité indépendante de toute appartenance géographique paraît être la clef du problème."[105] While I agree with Kemp's observation about the exiled state of Darrieussecq's characters, I argue that they do have an attachment, not to a single geographical place but to certain kinds of landscapes. As Rodgers explains, the sea plays a key role in Darrieussecq's novels.[106] Watery landscapes create a sense of place. This is clear in *Brief Stay* when Jeanne lists the characteristics of what would be for her the "right place to live": "a) a European capital with Europe at the other side of the world; b) water, a river, canals, the sea; c) the countryside just an hour and half's drive away."[107] No longer mapped onto a single geographical reality, a sense of place can lead to a sense of planet; many different regions around the world can be near water and not too far from the countryside, familiarly European and yet far from Europe.

The importance of water is also clear in Jeanne's sense of her body as habitat or as an ecology of intersecting "partial autopoietic components, with multiple and changing configurations, working collectively as well as individually."[108] Waking from a dream, she tries to orient herself in space and time. She then opens up her thinking to a watery imaginary, describing "everything all at the same time, herself, this body, and the atolls and arms and the whale's body, the animal forming a cyst in her leg, both the tropics and Europe, this city and over there, the temperate zone of her birth."[109] The body contains an eco-cosmopolitan community, home to non-human animals and geographical formations. Water becomes the connecting fluid, the common element of the human body and the planetary body. In this way, Darrieussecq illustrates that ecological subjectivity is also and always material.

Even though the middle sister, Anne, has difficulty coming to terms with her own embodiment, she imagines the planet as more than just a noosphere or world of ideas. She wonders what it would be like to view the earth from a spaceship and get a glimpse of "the blue sphere through the porthole."[110] Rather than commenting on how this "Blue Marble" image conveys a sense of the biosphere's fragility, Anne is simply reminded of her own incapacity to connect to her body.[111] Later in the novel, she again imagines the astronaut's view of planet Earth from space, but this time in more detail: "Australia's sheepish head, Europe's nose, Panama's bellybutton, Africa's skull, China's gut and the three genitalia, Tierra del Fuego, the Cape of Good Hope and Tasmania, then the oceans' blue-green eyes opening and closing, eyelids, head turning."[112] Anne gives the earth material form, tracing a cartography of interconnected body parts. Whereas Jeanne's sense of planet comes from an understanding of her own body as habitat, Anne remains an orbiting satellite, viewing the planet from afar, disconnected from her own corporeality.

For the youngest sister, Nore, seascapes are a place of discovery, but also an important place for cultivating a sense of something much larger than herself. She returns again and again to the beach, without always knowing why. She meets a man who eventually becomes her lover, but from whom she feels curiously detached. The shifting sands and rolling waves at the beach mirror her own changing body as she explores her sexuality. But her interest in the sea goes beyond human sexual development. Although she does not make Jeanne's human-body-as-watery-world connection nor Anne's biosphere-as-body connection, Nore develops a sense of planet by opening her imagination up to a geological deep time when viewing the sea:

> White lines rolling onwards, in the back-to-front film, at the beginning of time, rolled up again like a rug, perhaps we would see the sea recede, empty itself over the horizon, run down the back of the sky from where, what would happen? Lava, flowing back towards gases, fire – gone, the first dinosaur's wagging tail, after the arrival of the first fish, the first seaweed – the vaporized earth falling apart, flowing back to the primordial explosion, the big bang.[113]

The earth's *longue durée* makes Nore's nineteen years of life appear inconsequential. Yet she goes on to assert the importance of trying to give words to an experience of the sea, in terms of both images and sounds. She concludes by pointing out that there will always be more sea to describe, "endlessly."

In the end, Darrieussecq's novel points to the need not only for a sense of place and a sense of planet, but also a sense of body. Her emphasis on the female body with its leaky, porous boundaries and its openness to watery landscapes illustrates that subjectivity cannot be contained or centred. Moreover, ecological subjectivity pushes against the boundaries set by language. For Darrieussecq, one of the main problems with narrating in the first person about the female body is the way in which French genders nouns and pronouns. In her article "Je est unE autre, ou pour qui elle se prend,"[114] Darrieussecq explains that the masculine gender dominates in French because of rules of agreement. She adds: "J'ai la sensation récurrente de devoir imposer à mon corps de femme une langue d'homme ... ou de devoir imposer ce corps de femme à cette langue d'homme, le français."[115] While objecting to the idea that her writing is militant or feminist, Darrieussecq calls for a language that is more in keeping with the contemporary world, "un monde de femmes."[116]

For Stacy Alaimo and Susan Hekman, French feminists like Monique Wittig have pursued a "flight from nature" that has made it difficult to come back to material reality or to construct what they call "material feminisms."[117] Yet Darrieussecq folds French feminist thought into her writing project, which is meant to provide readers with a renewed sense of the real world. As she explains during an interview:

> Le monde est aussi fait d'électrons, de microbes, d'ondes, de planètes ... bientôt sans doute de clones, d'OGM, de nouveaux sons, de nouvelles odeurs ... etc. ... Je participe au mouvement permanent des défricheurs. Je veux ouvrir des yeux sous les yeux des lecteurs, des oreilles sous leurs oreilles, une nouvelle peau sous leur peau. A quoi sert un livre qui ne propose pas de voir le monde comme s'il se dévoilait pour la première fois? Pour ce travail, il faut des phrases nouvelles, des formes nouvelles, de nouvelles postures d'écriture.[118]

In many respects, Darrieussecq articulates a literary project that clearly overlaps with new materialism and counters the notion of French psychoanalytic feminism as anti-matter or anti-nature. In addition, her description of the material echoes the ideas I have been developing in this chapter: 1) ecological subjectivity does not distinguish between "natural" nature, on the one hand, and "unnatural" nature, on the other (matter includes electrons, viruses, waves, planets, GMOs, etc.); 2) ecological subjectivity is necessarily embodied (sight, smell, and touch are part of the way in which a literary text creates new subjectivities, new Universes of reference); 3) ecological subjectivity is embedded in an aesthetic experience that decentres the reader in terms of both content and form.

Writing the body in/out of place

Published four years after *Bref séjour chez les vivants*, Darrieussecq's novel *Le Pays* problematizes the possibility of "coming home" in a globalized and interconnected world.[119] After spending several years in Paris, the main character returns "home" to the place where she was born, a fictional country called Yuoangui.[120] Given that the main question the novel asks is what it means to return to a place, an ecocritical approach is particularly relevant. But a purely thematic reading of the novel would be problematic. Darrieussecq continues to experiment with form, using *autofiction* and two narrative voices *en écho* to create multiple layers of fictionality. The novel covers a period of approximately a year – from shortly before the moment when the main character discovers she is pregnant to shortly after she gives birth to a baby girl – but simultaneous and repeated accounts of past and present create multiple temporalities. It is through this multi-narrated, multi-temporal lens that the reader comes to know a life that is and is not based on that of the author, Marie Darrieussecq.

Autofiction is a hybrid genre that first emerged in the French literary setting in the late 1970s.[121] In response to the structuralist work of Philippe Lejeune and Gérard Genette, Serge Doubrovsky published *Fils* (1977), a novel in which a homodiegetic narrator is also the main character and has the same name as the author. Some of the historical dates and places in the novel are based on the author's life, while others are fictionalized, so that the text complicates what Lejeune has called *le pacte autobiographique*. The reader remains unsure of what overlaps in terms of the author's life and the fictional events of the novel. Since the publication of Doubrovsky's novel in the seventies, *autofiction* has become an important genre in French contemporary literature.

In *Le Pays*, Darrieussecq is experimenting with *autofiction*, naming her main character Marie, but giving her the last name Rivière.[122] After many years of living in Paris, Marie Rivière decides to move back to her home in Yuoangui, a fictional counterpart to the Basque country, where Darrieussecq herself grew up.[123] Whereas the French Basque country remains a department of the French state, Yuoangui is its own nation-state. Centred on an extremely charged political issue – the Basque country has been demanding independence for many years – the novel does not endorse nationalism. On the contrary, it examines the problematic construction of nation along many different lines (language, landscape, culture, etc.). The *autofiction* genre allows Darrieussecq to set the novel in an easily recognizable place – and so reassert the importance of a real geographical referent[124] – but also to fictionalize this reality so that the questions raised about nation, state, and country are not limited to one geographical place.[125]

To further complicate the relationship between reality and fiction, the main character Marie Rivière is writing a novel entitled *Le Pays* that is a similar story of a writer returning home. The use of the *mise-en-abyme* places Darrieussecq's novel in line with other key texts in French literary history, such as André Gide's *Les Faux-monnayeurs* (1925). At the same time, Darrieussecq develops her own style, using two font types to distinguish between the first-person narrative of Marie Rivière telling her own story and the third person narrative that also tells Marie Rivière's story. The narrative *dédoublement* creates a fragmented lens through which the reader views and experiences the character's world. This view is further broken up by the novel's use of "j/e" (an English equivalent might be "I/me" or "m/e") that splits the first-person pronoun in two. It is through this kaleidoscope that the reader catches glimpses of the author not as a fully formed subject but as one of the multiple subjectivities that nourish the fictional world of the text.[126] Rather than leading away from the world, Darrieussecq's use of *autofiction* illustrates subjectivity's complex relationships within social, mental, and environmental ecologies.

Even though Darrieussecq's novel is clearly *l'aventure d'une écriture* (an adventure in writing), it is also *l'écriture d'une aventure* (writing about an adventure).[127] *Le Pays* is a richly satisfying read. The opening passage immediately draws the reader into the world of the first-person narrator, Marie Rivière:

> Je courais, ignorante de ce qui se passait. Je courais, *tam, tam, tam, tam,* sentiment, à mon rythme. Ça montait dans mes jambes, mes genoux chauffaient,

l'attache des muscles gonflait. Je m'étais mise à courir depuis que j'étais arrivée ici. Ignorante de ce qui se passait. J'enfilais mes chaussures et hop, je courais. J'avais le sentiment de faire quelque chose. Comme quand on fume, ou quand on écrit: le temps passe. On le sent physiquement s'écouler. On sent le flux.[128]

Marie's description brings to life the body's movements in a physical world: the use of onomatopoeia creates a rhythm that is echoed in the simple, short sentences and sentence fragments. The repetition of keywords immerses the reader in the flow of the text. Guattari provides a useful description for this kind of writing when he speaks of a "pseudo-narrative" that "deploys repetitions that function, through an infinite variety of rhythms and refrains, as the very supports of existence."[129] The term "pseudo" is used here not to mean a "false narrative or story" but one that "nullifies the play of distinctive oppositions at the level of both content and form of expression."[130]

Emptying her mind yet completely present in her body, Marie opens up to the landscape around her. The "j/e" becomes road, tree, country: "S'absorber dans, absorber le paysage, c'était une partie de la pensée."[131] Rather than a subject unilaterally grasping an object, Marie experiences a sense of being apprehended by the landscape. Guattari describes this as "a kind of relationship of uncertainty" that can only be articulated by "a pseudo-narrative" that has as its "ultimate goal a dispositional *mise-en-scène*."[132] No longer an "I" at all, Marie has become a "what" (*ce qui*) from which sentences emerge: "Ce qui avançait sur la route c'était des sphères jouant les unes autour des autres, un équilibre de chutes et de rebonds, un ensemble de sauts. Ni moi ni autre ni personne. Air, paysage, course. J/e ne pensais à rien et dans le rien perçaient les phrases, de plus en plus vite."[133] Ecological subjectivity creates the conditions for the text to write itself, an autopoietic machine working at the intersection of mental, social, and environmental ecologies.

Kemp explains that Darrieussecq's formal experiments are strongly influenced by cognitive science, which "rejects Cartesian dualism to figure mind and brain as a single, physical 'substance.'"[134] Analysing the different narrative modes in Darrieussecq's novels – psycho-narration, narrated monologue, quoted monologue – Kemp offers a useful model for understanding Darrieussecq's representation of thought processes. But Kemp's emphasis on the mind (even as physical brain) does not fully articulate the materiality of matter in Darrieussecq's novel.

Mental ecology necessarily opens up to environmental and social ecologies, illustrating the kind of "praxic opening-out" that is, according to Guattari, the "essence of 'eco'-art."[135]

This is particularly clear in the novel's descriptions of Marie's experience of her porous body. On one of her visits to the country's coast, the third-person narrator describes the exchange of matter that is characteristic of the kind of ecological subjectivity I have been mapping out in this chapter: "Vos molecules se mélangent au ciel et à l'eau, la solitude se diffuse. Les mots et les choses s'écartent, la pensée ne suit plus, les signes se désamarrent; et le moi devient une grande béance pleine d'eau salée."[136] The watery, molecular body refuses to come together in an autonomous, self-determining, rational subject. Rather than this being an "abnormal state" of "coming undone," it is the way in which Marie experiences her connection to place on numerous occasions.

Writing is not an opportunity for Marie to find the self or work toward a fixed sense of identity. On the contrary, the creative imagination starts with an emptying of the subject and an opening out to the world: "J'aimais le globe sur mon bureau et j'aimais ce promontoire sur la mer parce que j'avais besoin, souvent, de renouer avec la sidération comme un point d'origine de l'écriture."[137] Although not used in everyday speech, the term "sideration" literally means being planet- or star-struck and can be used to describe a general disturbance of the psyche.[138] Immersing herself in processes of desubjectification, Marie allows words, phrases, and images to emerge on their own. Darrieussecq describes a similar feeling when discussing her own writing practices: "Pour dire le monde il faut être dans une rêverie proche d'une sorte d'extase dans la langue, où on sort de son moi privé."[139] The echoes between these two descriptions reveal an interesting paradox: it is in the experience of writing as an erasure of self that Darrieussecq herself appears most present in the novel.[140]

Dissolving a sense of self does not, however, dematerialize experience. To write about *le pays*, Marie asserts the need to return to Yuoangui. Rejecting nationalist sentiment, she explores the multiple realities of a country in terms of its geography, culture, history, and language. In the first section of the novel, entitled *Le Sol*, Marie explains her reasons for leaving Paris and moving her family back to Yuoangui: "Je voulais un paysage pour Tiot … Je voulais proposer un pays pour Tiot."[141] Marie wants her son to experience the land, but also a language, set of cultural traditions, and histories. As for her own connection to Yuoangui, Marie struggles to feel at home. Landscape (*paysage*) ends up playing a key role in her attempts to connect with the country (*le pays*) as land (*le pays/le sol*).

Yuoangui's geography is rooted in the physical reality and topography of the French Basque Country. Bordered by the Atlantic Ocean to the west and a mountain range to the east, Yuoangui has a natural beauty that is, Marie explains, both "un cliché et une nostalgie."[142] She highlights the fact that landscapes are often represented in order to satisfy the city dweller's desire for "beauté, bon air, mer."[143] At the same time, landscapes are also a way of getting to know the land as a country: "Le pays est fédéré par le paysage vu depuis la Corniche."[144] Although socially constructed, landscapes are not static; they change with time. As Marie notes, the landscapes no longer correspond with her memory of the land: "Elle était rentrée au pays mais elle avait beau l'arpenter, user semelles et pneus contre sa croûte et dans ses sables, tout lui échappait. Le pays n'était pas le pays du souvenir. Tout était semblable et tout était différent, les temps ne se juxtaposaient pas, les paysages laissaient du jeu."[145] Disoriented by the gap between the "paysage pratiqué" and the "paysage remémoré,"[146] Marie nevertheless begins to construct a connection to the land as physical reality.

Landscape is often defined as a large expanse of land viewed by a single, immobile observer. Critical of such a definition, Gary Nabhan asserts that seeing land as landscape is a luxury afforded only to those who do not live and work off the land.[147] To some extent, this is true in Marie's case, as she visits seascapes at her leisure in an attempt to understand "comment on fait, avec ce pays."[148] But Marie's experiences are neither purely aesthetic nor purely visual. Her opening up to the water and sky reveals an ecological subjectivity that undoes the problematic division between viewing subject and constructed landscape. Moreover, it is through this experience of "becoming-molecule" that Marie understands how she can write a book about *le pays*. She must start with the feeling of being dispersed in a landscape: "Écrire: 'je suis de là', elle ne savait pas bien ce que ça voulait dire. Il fallait tenter l'expérience, placer un sujet dans un lieu, étudier les lieux communs des personnes et des pays. Ça commençait comme ça, paysages et questions."[149] Landscape is not, then, a static view of the natural world; it is a place of interaction and exchange where the subject opens up to trees, land, water, but also molecules, air, atoms. Nature/culture and material/immaterial binaries break down as the body emerges in and with the world.

While the novel clearly illustrates ecological subjectivity in the case of Marie's experiences of opening up to the cosmos, how does it portray a more collective subjectivity? For Guattari, nationalism does not lead to new subject groups because it so often reduces difference to one subject type.[150] Darrieussecq's novel similarly questions nationalism and nationalist sentiment. Marie Rivière refuses to become a spokesperson for Yuoangui culture even though she is writing about *le pays*. Unable to speak the native language, Marie also questions the alignment of language, culture, and the nation-state. She chooses to write in French but sees herself as a European writer,[151] pointing to a transnational collective subjectivity. In addition, her geographical references are clearly cosmopolitan. During conversations on the phone with a friend in Paris, she names cities around the world and then concludes: "Où habiter, voilà leur conversation préférée avec Walid. Quelle ville peut remplacer le monde, puisqu'on ne peut habiter le monde entier? Eux, parmi les Terriens les mieux lotis, passeport, argent, santé, temps, ils ne se lassent pas, Walid et elle, d'établir la liste raisonnée des villes."[152] Even while intimately experiencing place, Marie cultivates a sense of planet.[153]

Critical of mass media's "ossification" of family and married life,[154] Guattari asserts that ecosophy will develop new practices for "group-being" that experiment "as much on a microsocial level as on a larger institutional scale."[155] He avoids providing a blueprint for new social practices and strongly opposes reductive Oedipal explanations of the family. At first glance, Darrieussecq's novel appears to propose a traditional nuclear family: Marie Rivière, her husband Diego, their son Tiot, and the yet-to-be-born daughter Épiphanie. Cracks appear, however, when Marie reveals the presence of the dead, missing, and displaced who continue to inhabit her mental and social ecology: her brother Paul stolen from his baby carriage; her adopted brother Pablo now in a psychiatric home; her dead grandmother, her Amona. These spectral beings – Paul and Amona – literally continue to take up time and physical space because of Marie's frequent visits to the House of the Dead, where visitors can recreate images and voices of lost loved ones using hologram technology. Unique to Yuoangui culture, these rituals of mourning connect Marie to a larger social group: "Le *nous* me venait spontanément quand j'évoquais nos traditions funèbres, par une sorte de solidarité indigène."[156] A collective subjectivity of the living and the dead, a *socius* in which ghosts play key roles, provides Marie with a sense of connection to the country.

Her association with the dead, however, presents certain dangers. In the fourth section of the novel, entitled *Les Morts*, Marie returns over and over again to the House of the Dead. But she is brought back to the world of the living by the increasing needs of her pregnant, growing body in the final section of the novel, entitled *Naissances*. She imagines her body as part of much larger and smaller ecosystems, ranging from the universe to amniotic bubbles: "Ça fait un joli emboîtement, l'Univers, la Terre, l'Europe, le Pays, une voiture, un corps, un utérus, et des petites bulles qui tournent."[157] No longer one, but not yet two, the pregnant body challenges the logics of dialectical difference. Marie describes her womb as an environment not just for the fetus but for other animals as well: "Je suis pleine d'une nombreuse faune. Je suis un paysage rempli d'animaux, je suis un pays amniotique."[158] The pregnant body's leakiness spills out when Marie goes into labour. Arriving at the hospital, she discovers that she understands the nurse speaking in Yuoangui, using the word *Ur* for water to indicate that Marie's waters have broken: "J'entendais la vieille langue sans y penser. Je buvais la langue. Je nageais dedans."[159] Swimming in the language that she resisted for so long, Marie discovers her birthing body as an opening toward the larger social body.

In the end, collective subjectivity emerges both from porous bodies becoming landscape and a *socius* in which the living and the dead circulate. As the novel's ending explains, "Les fantômes ne rôdent pas dans les limbes. Ils n'existent que dans la rencontre … Ils ne sont que pour nous."[160] This final *nous* places the question of the collective at the heart of the novel's exploration of what constitutes a sense of belonging. At the same time, Darrieussecq is clearly avoiding the exclusionary practices used to identify and define new collectivities. As she explains during an interview, *Le Pays* is not "la défense d'une patrie" and yet it is "un livre très utopiste qui imagine une planète de petits pays."[161] But would a world made up of much smaller nations give rise to more cultural and linguistic diversity? Would it counter globalization's homogenizing forces and allow a different kind of cosmopolitanism to emerge? Writing about the possibility of new subject groups to counter capitalism's grasp on the *socius*, Guattari suggests that "particular cultures should be left to deploy themselves in inventing other contracts of citizenship" and that "ways should be found to enable the singular, the exceptional, the rare to coexist with a State structure that is the least burdensome possible."[162] Even if Darrieussecq's novel refuses to be categorized as representative of a single culture, it asserts the necessary existence of such cultural singularities.

I do not want to reduce the novel, however, to a politics of new collectivities. Although the novel's title underscores the role of the land/

country as the main narrative thread, Marie's experiences are the lens through which the reader encounters this theme. Without mapping her experiences on to a (problematic) universalizing female experience, it is important to recognize the function of the body as central to my point about ecological subjectivity. Marie describes in detail her particular female body as it harbours another, smaller female body. The corporeality of both these bodies is made to matter over and over again. When Marie's daughter, Épiphanie, is born at the end of the novel, her embodiment is emphasized. She is described as "logée dans un corps," she has "consentie à rassembler dans cette chair-ci (et aucune autre) le corps qui la faisait apparaître."[163] The notion of "lodging in a body" evokes once again the temporariness of such a coming together or assemblage. Occupying this body (for now), Épiphanie may or may not experience the becoming-landscape that characterizes her mother's subjectivity. It is because of its corporeality that her subjectivity remains open to the *socius* and the physical world.

Conclusion: Aesthetic perspectives and new subjectivities

According to Guattari, "[W]e will only escape from the major crises of our era through the articulation of: – a nascent subjectivity; – a constantly mutating socius; – an environment in the process of being reinvented."[164] Darrieussecq's narrative worlds introduce the reader to such an ethico-aesthetic paradigm. While *Brief Stay* underscores the processes of desubjectification that undo becoming in and with the world, *Le Pays* outlines the possible conditions of ecological subjectivity as it emerges through the experience of landscape, the body, life and death, but also through the (dis)assemblage of writing, language, and becoming (an) other. As Guattari notes, literature and art can bring about change, not because they have an inherent political message, but because they place the reader in the position of co-creating new worlds, new subjectivities, and new practices.

The aesthetics of Darrieussecq's novels are essential to this process. In *L'Autofiction et les femmes. Un chemin vers l'altruisme?* Annie Richard objects to the critique of *autofiction* as a genre centred on the self and the ego.[165] She develops the thesis that it focuses instead on undoing the self and on "being an/other" in the world. Because it constantly undermines the strict division between fiction and reality, *autofiction* develops an ambiguous reading contract with the reader. Rather than trying to confirm the events of the story, the reader is invited to construct the story world with the author/narrator. Darrieussecq's novels illustrate this relationship, never telling only the story of her characters, raising larger questions about how to construct a mental ecology in a world of communication technologies and world citizens (*Brief Stay*), how to integrate family tragedies into a larger social ecology (*Brief Stay* and *Le Pays*), how to rethink an environmental ecology on the basis of the body's experience of the land(scape) (*Le Pays*).

Emerging from Darrieussecq's novels, the reader has participated in a world in constant formation and transformation. Her sense of self has been challenged by the novel's insistence on the processes of subjectification that include the physical and psychic worlds. What she then does with this experience cannot be determined in advance. As Nathalie Blanc and Jacques Lolive explain, art can give rise to cosmopolitical subjectivities – or ecological subjectivities – when it aims to "créer un monde commun habitable," when it embraces "une perspective vitaliste et creative, parfois exubérante," and when it comes to terms with "la globalité du vivant."[166] Leaving behind the realm of predetermined ideals, as Darrieussecq's novels do, aesthetics emerge from the creative processes of the chaosmosis and the (often destabilizing) encounters with the living/non-living world.

2 Ecological Dwelling: Serres and Lafon

Animal en mouvement, il [*homo sapiens*] s'arrête et habite un bâti végétal; comme un oiseau dans le nid, comme un nid dans des branchages. Debout, animal-végétal, il habite des maisons arborescentes comme lui. Voilà pour son habitat local ou pour le lieu du locataire.

Voici maintenant pour l'habitat global, le globe terrestre. La Terre n'a pas tout à fait la forme d'une sphère. Boule qui se déplace en translation, comme une bête en mouvement, elle tourne sur elle-même autour d'un axe nord-sud, verticale alors comme une plante. Enflée à l'équateur, plus aplatie aux pôles, arbre en rotation; animal en translation.

Animal-végétal, *Homo sapiens* habite un globe végétal-animal. Une chimère petite habite une chimère grande; cet amphibie grand recueille des amphibies petits, nous.

– Michel Serres, *Habiter*, 170[1]

Understood as a place to live, the term "dwelling" evokes a long evolutionary history of humans finding diverse ways of protecting themselves from the natural elements, ranging from the tree houses of early *homo sapiens* described by Michel Serres in this chapter's epigraph to the urban skyscrapers of today's megacities. In response to the size and density of our contemporary dwellings, we either marvel at human ingenuity or lament the increasing ecological footprint we leave on the planet. But this is not how I will be using the term in this chapter. Rather than referring to a specific structure or type of building, I am using the term "dwelling" as a present participle of the ongoing action of the verb "to dwell." The French equivalent *l'habiter* clearly conveys the dynamic nature of dwelling as a collection of living practices and processes. As the infinitive form of the verb, *l'habiter* differs from *l'habitation* or *l'habitat,* which are both noun derivatives used to refer to a specific place. As Mathis Stock explains, *l'habiter* means "faire avec de l'espace" (making with space) and not "être dans l'espace" (being in space).[2] In opposition to definitions of dwelling as a state of being or a place of residence, I will develop further the notion of dwelling in terms of the practices of living in specific habitats.[3]

What, then, does ecological dwelling mean? Green structures whose ecological footprint is reduced by using recycled materials and integrating geothermal and/or solar energy, for example, are often given the name "ecological dwelling." While such endeavours are laudable, I am using the expression to explore human practices and interactions rather than a kind of building. As in the previous chapter, I am not using the adjective "ecological" to refer to a set of environmentalist policies or principles. Instead I am using it to ground the notion of dwelling in the physical processes, exchanges, and interactions of bodies in place. This emphasis on material matter breaks down the division between "natural" and "unnatural" dwelling. Instead the practices of dwelling are ecological when they take into account the materiality of the space being made. Does this mean that all places are livable or dwell-able? Can we "make with" post-industrial waste sites as well as we can with community garden spaces? As can be seen by a quick Google search, the term *habitabilité* (or "live-ability") is clearly at the heart of French political ecology. There is, however, no one place that is heralded as the most *habitable;* a place may be completely toxic to one kind of living being and yet an ideal home for another. Moreover, a creature can adapt to a place and so learn to live in what was formerly a dangerous environment. Even though *habitabilité* has largely been defined in terms of how liveable a place is for human beings, the notion of ecological dwelling requires one to ask what other beings find a place liveable. The association of ecological dwelling with practices of living undoes the thesis of human exceptionalism and opens up these practices to the largest possible number of living beings.

Ecocriticism has continually engaged with the notion of dwelling. In his book *Song of the Earth,* Jonathan Bate draws on Martin Heidegger's philosophy to articulate an ecological poetics that models "a certain kind of being and of dwelling" and "provides an image of ecological wholeness which may grant to the attentive and receptive reader a sense of being-at-home-in-the-world."[4] While critical of Heidegger's ecological thought,[5] Greg Garrard includes the notion of dwelling as one of the key tropes of ecocriticism in his Routledge introduction to ecocriticism.

According to Garrard, dwelling can be defined as the "long-term imbrication of humans in a landscape of memory, ancestry and death, of ritual, life and work."[6] Both Bate and Garrard theorize dwelling more in the conventional sense of being-in-place rather than doing-with-space. It is true that Garrard enumerates activities that characterize dwelling – ritual and work, for example – and that his chapter looks in depth at the many practices of rural and georgic dwelling. But I am proposing an understanding of dwelling as practices that evolve over both short- and long-term periods, and that include change and transformation, and not just traditions and memory. In this way, I am responding to Garrard's call at the end of his chapter for ecocriticism to take up the "interpretation and critique of the various inflections of dwelling."[7]

It may seem surprising that I am focussing on the rural in this chapter given the reality of contemporary life, which is more and more urbanized. According to UN reports, 86 per cent of developed countries and 64 per cent of developing countries will be urbanized by 2050. In light of these statistics, why focus on the rural, which has often been associated with a nostalgic turn to the past? This chapter proposes to complicate the association of the rural with the past and the binary country/city opposition. Drawing on the philosophy of Michel Serres and the fiction of Marie-Hélène Lafon, I will consider the rural as a way of imagining a global relationship to planet Earth and understanding a *milieu* that is constantly undergoing change and transformation. More importantly, I have chosen to focus on rural practices and ways of living for this chapter because of their continued importance in the French contemporary imaginary.

According to Jean-Pierre Le Goff, France's national identity is still largely associated with the rural: "Dans l'imaginaire national, la France reste encore associée à un univers rural et villageois."[8] After having returned to the same village year after year, Le Goff comes to the conclusion that the French *paysans* are undergoing a state of slow and agonizing death, one that began shortly after the Second World War when France underwent strong economic growth and modernization. In the last thirty years, the *paysan* has been replaced by the *agriculteur* as small family farms have been taken over by large-scale industrial farming.[9] Le Goff's sad lament for the figure of the *paysan* is characteristic of the way in which the rural is often imagined in France today – as the end to a particular French history, culture, and mode of living.

But if rural living has come to an end in France, why focus on it as a possible example for ecological dwelling? What can this model offer if it can only be the story of the "last survivors"?[10] As I will show in this chapter, rural living is far from dead in France. True, farming has undergone and is undergoing deep and profound transformations, but framing this change as a definitive "end" is problematic. In her analysis of the ways in which the general public has imagined and described the rural in France over the last fifty years, Nicole Mathieu reveals a set of shifting perceptions and representations.[11] She points out that the most major change has been the separation of the rural from the agricultural. In the minds of the public, "agriculture" is associated with destruction of the landscape, while the "rural" has come to mean a closer relationship to nature and the land.

At the same time, there has been, Mathieu notes, a progressive diversification of rural activities, with the promotion of hiking, tourism, *ferme-auberges*, and ecotourism, that require different skill sets and a different working population than traditional farming communities. In the final section of her analysis, Mathieu highlights once again the dangers of imagining rural places as culturally homogeneous: "Les représentations qui font de la campagne un milieu homogène comme celles qui définissent des différences par les termes de 'rural profond,' 'rural désertifié,' voire même 'campagnes vivantes' sont très décalées par rapport à la complexité des différenciations économiques réelles des espaces ruraux."[12] Mathieu concludes that the radical transformation of the rural has led to more diversified economics and politics in some cases, but in others to a reified, aestheticized countryside of "neo-villages" in which the rich play the role of "gentleman farmer." She makes no predictions for the future, but her analysis points to some of the possibilities of a "post-industrial" rural characterized by a "pluriappartenance à des lieux habités de façon variable dans le temps et dans l'espace."[13]

I begin with Mathieu's analysis because it outlines competing representations of the rural in France over the last fifty years. On the one hand, the idea of a disappearing way of life gives rise to a narrative of loss that leaves little hope for the future. In this narrative, the *paysan* plays a key role because his disappearance creates a void that can never be filled. His end is definitive, with no possibility for transformation. On the other hand, the socioeconomic reality of the rural illustrates that the end of the *paysan* has given rise to a multiplicity of other figures like the *agriculteur* and the *écologiste*. Rather than positing the rural as a remedy to urban living or as a place of escape from contemporary consumer capitalist society, I will examine the rural as a place where material and corporeal conditions are carefully negotiated alongside socioeconomic realities, as a living ecosystem in which new practices emerge and others disappear.

In this chapter, I focus on a philosopher, Michel Serres, and a novelist, Marie-Hélène Lafon, who offer two angles from which to view the pressing question of how a French environmental imagination can or cannot still be associated with the figure of the *paysan* and rural living. For Serres, the story of the *paysan* is first a narrative of loss because of the drastic reduction in the number of farmers in France over the last fifty years. But Serres goes on to draw inspiration from this figure, asserting that the *paysan* can serve as global model of a more symbiotic relationship between humanity and planet Earth. For Lafon, the end of the *paysan* does not mean the end of rural life; on the contrary, her novels illustrate the necessity of transforming rural practices in light of changing socioeconomic realities. Moreover, Lafon's novels highlight the problem of exclusionary practices that resurface in rural settings because of these changing realities. Ecological dwelling emerges not in the figure of the *paysan* but in the practices of other beings and bodies who are learning to "make/create space" in rural settings. Whereas Serres retains the figure of the *paysan* to move in the direction of a planetary eco-consciousness, Lafon's *autofiction* brings the reader back to the local practices of embodied experiences of place. At the same time, both Serres and Lafon are committed to writing the rural: Serres in light of contemporary ecological issues, and Lafon in light of her own personal experiences growing up in (and then leaving) the Cantal region. In addition, they are keenly aware of the ways in which language can contribute to the *habitabilité* of a place when it reveals the many material, embodied traits of dwelling.

As I did in the previous chapter with Guattari and Darrieussecq, my reading of Serres's philosophical concepts will be brought to bear on my analysis of Lafon's *autofiction*, but not as a way of "testing" the novels nor of applying the philosophical concepts. Instead, the theory and the fiction will allow me to explore the larger concept of ecological dwelling that I am articulating in this chapter. Neither Serres nor Lafon uses this exact expression. Nevertheless, their works lend themselves well to an ecocritical approach because of the ways in which form and content are so carefully bound together therein. Even though Serres writes philosophy and Lafon *autofiction*, they are both careful stylistic writers, drawing on the semantic riches of the French language while also playing with and transforming its syntactic rigidity. In this way, they clearly illustrate the possibilities of the "French effect" for thinking and writing about the *paysan* and rurality.

Theory

Portrait – Michel Serres

According to Bruno Latour – a former student of Michel Serres – Serres's philosophy stands apart from other well-known theories and philosophies such as poststructuralism or postmodernism. For Latour, Serres models humanist thinking in the sense that he casts his intellectual net far and wide while also avoiding confrontation and critique.[14] Because he writes about science, art, literature, religion, myth, and technology, to name a few of his many interdisciplinary crossings, Serres is difficult to classify. And he seems to prefer it that way. He asserts that he does not want to be associated with a school of thought, nor does he want to be the creator of a new branch of philosophy. Instead, he aims to forge an interdisciplinary path that works to construct rather than deconstruct, one that clearly illustrates philosophy's debt to literature and science.

Serres discusses many different contemporary issues, such as the capitalist economic crisis (*Temps des crises*), the new Internet generation (*Petite Poucette*), the need for ecological thinking (*Le Contrat naturel*), the communication age (*Hermès*), the rise of biotechnologies (*Hominescence*), and the social function of pollution (*Le Mal propre*). His writing draws from literary traditions of metaphor, image, and narrative as much as from the philosophical toolbox of argumentation, logic, and analysis.[15] Moreover, Serres is an extremely prolific writer, having published over fifty books since finishing his doctoral thesis on Leibniz in 1968. Because of this diversity and complexity, it is necessary to choose a specific thread when exploring Serres's "ecology of knowledge."[16] My focus will be on the figure of the *paysan* and the concept of the *contrat naturel*, but this will allow me to include a range of Serres's texts (from *Détachement* [1983] and *Les Cinq Sens* [1985] to *Hominescence* [2001] and *Habiter* [2011]), and to outline his ecological thought more generally.[17]

As Latour notes, language is for Serres "the very material on which to experiment," a way of creating new meaning and new perspectives on the world.[18] This does not mean, however, that Serres follows the "linguistic turn." On the contrary, he is critical of philosophies that adhere to the notion of language as the only way to experience and organize reality. In early texts like the *Hermès* series (1969–80), Serres calls readers to leave the stark walls of academia behind and experience the solidity of the real world. In *Les Cinq Sens* (1985), he develops a realist empiricism in contrast to poststructuralism's and postmodernism's emphasis on linguistic and political structures. In *Éclaircissements*, Serres explains that philosophy is driven by a desire to answer simple questions asked during childhood about our bodies, our skin, the senses, the sea, the sky, trees, animals, cities, justice, law, rights, and love.[19] He adds that answers to these questions can be found not in books, but in "a direct, often painful, experience of the state of things themselves."[20] It is from empirical experience that Serres constructs his understanding of language, not as a prison house, but as one of the material worlds in which we learn to dwell.[21]

Serres's writing points to the political possibilities of an ecosophical aesthetics discussed in the previous chapter. To take but one example, his book *Genesis* (a text about the emergence of meaning from a background of noise) begins in the following way: "A flight of screaming birds, a school of herring tearing through the water like a silken sheet, a cloud of chirping crickets, a booming whirlwind of mosquitoes … crowds, packs, hordes on the move, and filling with their clamor, space; Leibniz called them aggregates, these objects, sets."[22] Fauna, flora, but also human bodies and beings, physical objects, are the matter with which Serres thinks. Philosophy does not view the world aerially, floating above in the ether of ideas; it has its feet (or hands) solidly planted on the ground. In addition, there is no distinction made between natural matter on the one hand and cultural on the other. Like Guattari's ecosophy, Serres's philosophy is ecological in this sense of undoing nature/culture dualisms and proposing a way of engaging with the world that goes beyond environmental issues.

In this way, Serres's philosophy reflects more generally the characteristics of French ecological thought. Even if Serres's thinking cannot be reduced to one particular cultural perspective – he has taught on both sides of the Atlantic, alternating between the Sorbonne and Stanford for many years – his work remains firmly rooted in the French language.

Unlike Latour, he does not publish in English, and relies on translations to reach a wider audience. Serres mines the French language for less commonly used words, draws on etymology in his arguments, and plays with polysemy in his explanations, making the work of his translators quite difficult. In many ways, Serres's eco-thought cannot be separated from its expression. For Serres, language does not remove us from the material world; it is part of this world, as the water in which thinking swims. Ecological dwelling, thus, necessarily includes the practices of language.

The figure of the paysan: *Writing on/of the land*

Descending from a long line of *paysans*, Serres freely admits the importance of this figure in his way of thinking about the relationship between humans and the physical world. I use the term "figure" because Serres weaves the *paysan* together using concrete particulars and abstract concepts, personal experiences, and cultural generalizations. Philosophy is, for Serres, a way of creating not only concepts, but more importantly, figures and characters.[23] His own writing includes tales, *exemplum*, apologues, anecdotes, and stories, and has been described as lyrical and extremely rich. While the *paysan* is central to Serres's eco-thought, it is also representative of the way he writes (about) the world and constructs a philosophical system. To illustrate the double role of the figure of the *paysan*, I will work chronologically through the texts in which Serres discusses in most depth this historical and symbolic character. A clear picture of the philosopher following the traces left on the land by the *paysan* will emerge from this first part of my analysis.

Published in 1983, Serres's book *Détachement* carries the subtitle "apologue" which, in literary terms, is a moral fable that may or may not include talking animals. Yet none of the book's four chapters ends with a clear moral lesson, nor do they present any imaginary creatures. Instead, they blend Serres's own personal experiences with socio-historical analysis and so demonstrate more generally his approach to reading and interpreting the world.[24] In the chapter entitled "Paysan," Serres adopts a cross-cultural perspective, comparing agricultural practices in the East (China) and the West (France). His main premise is that agricultural practices inflect the way in which knowledge emerges in different cultures. Chinese rice paddies that flood the land and have no bordering forests are indicative of a culture in which knowledge comes from the openness of the sky and the wind. In France, on the other hand, brush and forests that surround farmed fields are left uncultivated; knowledge arises from the irrational, the unstable, the unpredictable.[25]

While this summary may appear overly reductive in its portrayal of cultural differences, Serres is not setting one culture above the other. Rather, he is using the comparison to situate his own philosophical project in a larger and longer cultural history: "Je sème des lettres et je plante des mots, j'ensemence de signes les lignes."[26] Even if Serres is not a farmer, he sees his philosophical writing as a continuation of (agri)cultural practices in the West, and in France more particularly. He is writing not to dominate, but to construct a system of knowledge that leaves ample room for the unknown, the chaotic, the fallow. In this way, Serres follows in the footsteps of his ancestors who wrote their contract with/on the land. A sort of *paysan-philosophe,* he treads carefully on the subjects he discusses, moving between disciplines without claiming mastery or authority.

Serres further develops the concept of writing on/of the land in *Les Cinq Sens* (1985), another text that is difficult to categorize. In this text, Serres argues for an empirical philosophy in opposition to the linguistic turn of the seventies and eighties. He examines and explains the interaction of the senses in corporeal and material experience. Rather than separate each of the five senses, Serres describes the land as a body in which smell, taste, sound, sight, and touch mingle together to create an empirical experience of the world. This act of creation is better expressed using Serres's terminology as an act of composing. The receptive body *com-poses* or "makes with" the world through its layers of skin:

> The body is constructed as books are composed, its pages come together like pieces and patches. Entirely sewn from skin, at first, naked in its closed bay, as though it had been dressed a sheet at a time … by an assemblage of pieces of skin or a juxtaposition or stack of assorted garments, sewn together, overlapping, but leaving gaps, because some places repel each other. Skin is no synthesis, but basting, collage or patchwork.[27]

In response to the (over)emphasis on the closed world of language, Serres outlines a *com-posing* body that experiences the world not as a whole, but as a collection of constantly changing conditions.

Describing the earth's body as composed of patches and bits, ragged garments sewn together *pagus* by *pagus* (this word means both a piece of the countryside and a page), Serres comes back to the role of the *paysan*. Working furrow by furrow, the *paysan* creates a patchwork and transforms the countryside into landscape.[28] Serres explains that we must stop asking how we can see this landscape (so that we may arrive at a view of the whole) and start asking how we can compose our own garden (and so learn to work with diverse pieces and places). While we can take Serres's advice literally, following the example of urban agriculture and local food movements, the word "compose" suggests a general relationship between the local and the global. On a figurative level, composing a garden means learning to piece together bit by bit, and always only contingently, experiences, activities, events, so that identity is never stable, but instead remains fluid and open like the body and the countryside: "This is what the countryside is, the moving totality of its real fragments, paved with hybrid pages."[29] Serres imagines the earth in terms of its geological skin, which has undergone many different transformations since the beginning of time, a multitude of "variations on the theme of variety."[30] Imagining a passage from the local to the global, Serres begins to anticipate the concept of the natural contract and the need for a new relationship between humanity and the globe in its entirety.

Before examining more closely the politics of Serres's eco-thought, it is worth summarizing briefly how these practices align with ecological dwelling. First, engaging with place or "making with space" (whether these be cultural or agricultural practices) must leave room for the untended, the fallow, the disorderly. Serres is wary of totalizing views of the world because they impose the same, homogeneous order on all things, suppressing the creative processes that arise from the unknown, the chaos of noise. In terms of ecological dwelling, this means acknowledging the unknowable, the unattainable, in our practices of making space. It means recognizing that it will not be possible to map out the conditions of live-ability for all beings in a particular place. Second, Serres's philosophy of mixed bodies can be used to articulate the role of the senses in ecological dwelling. While sight has dominated the way in which humans make space (most often in terms of perspective), Serres emphasizes the role of smell, touch, hearing, and taste. Drawing on Serres's notion of the com-posing body, ecological dwelling can be understood as embodied, sensorial practices that are inseparable from changing material and physical conditions. This means opening up to circumstances over which we do not have control and possibly learning new practices related to other sense-building.

The natural contract: Ecological dwelling in/with the world

Published in 1990, *Le Contrat naturel* lays the theoretical foundations for learning to live more ecologically with the earth.[31] The figure of the *paysan* appears only briefly in the text, but it represents a local example of the natural contract and so is key to Serres's arguments. At the heart of the book is the question of a new relationship between global earth and global humanity. Drawing on Rousseau's notion of a social contract, Serres explains that humans have also always had an unsigned contract with the land, the terms of which differ from one culture to another. In the West, the figures of the *paysan* and the *marin* have been most representative of the natural contract because they have lived in close and intimate contact with nature as a set of constantly changing local conditions. The question is, Serres asserts, how we can move from these local conditions to a set of global conditions and still maintain a natural contract.

In the first pages of the book, Serres asks a series of key questions that anticipate the issues of climate change and were, to some extent, far ahead of their time when the book was published in 1990:

> Is it possible to describe, calculate, even conceive, and ultimately steer this global change? Will the climate become warmer? Can one foresee some of the consequences of such transformations and expect, for example, a sudden or gradual rise in sea levels? What would become, then, of all the low countries – Holland, Bangladesh, or Louisiana – submerged beneath a new deluge?[32]

We now have the answer to some of the questions that Serres asks. Two of the regions Serres names here – Bangladesh and Louisiana – have been especially hard hit by extreme weather conditions that are a result of global warming. Whether we can "steer" global change in the right direction remains to be seen. For Serres, it is a matter of following Pascal's wager: we must take action now without knowing whether the worst case scenario will ever come true. This is the reason Serres begins to develop the notion of the natural contract.

Before looking at the many metaphors, figures, and anecdotes used to illustrate the natural contract, it is helpful to consider the words "natural" and "contract" separately. Serres is not referring here to the natural as the opposite of cultural or artificial. He does not imagine the natural world as wild or pristine. For Serres, nature is "l'ensemble des objets, ces formes à l'état naissant et qui transforment cette forme."[33] Rooted in Serres's earlier work on science, this definition of nature refers to the epistemological conditions necessary for the birth of objects and beings. Nature, then, is not an unchanging set of objects or processes that exist outside of culture. Instead, it is a function of specific socio-historical contexts. This means that today's nature is very different from the nature of fifty years ago or a hundred years ago, before the rise of information technologies, scientific advances, environmentalist thought, etc. In short, the adjective "natural" refers to a changing collection of forms with which we co-create, coexist, and co-evolve.

As for the term "contract," Serres is referring to the conditions, attachments, and connections that bind us to the physical world. He examines examples from the past in which science and the law intersect in the search for knowledge; he cites Galileo's exclusion from the scientific community as an example, but also underlines the vocabulary used in science regarding the "laws" of nature. He concludes that our relationship to the physical world is built on the association of science and law. Discussing the rights of the earth to thrive and survive is another example of this association. But Serres does not spell out a set of legal rules and laws for living ecologically. Instead, he aims to invent a new way of discussing and imagining our multiple relationships to the physical world. As Paul Harris notes, "Serres's conception of the natural contract clearly does not espouse simple championing of or return to 'nature,' but points the way towards a new kind of ecological discourse."[34] The power of Serres's natural contract lies not in its legal applications, but in its capacity to generate alternative ways of imagining our relationship to the earth.

Given the creative potential of Serres's natural contract to imagine a symbiotic relationship with the earth, why is this concept not better-known? One of the reasons is, of course, the context of French philosophy in the early '90s. In *Le Nouvel Ordre,* Luc Ferry lambasts Serres as a deep ecologist and an anti-humanist who aims to undermine long-standing traditions of French philosophical thought. This misreading of Serres's careful attention to the ways in which nature and culture are intertwined is not the most surprising element of Ferry's critique. What is most noteworthy is the way in which Ferry polices the gates of philosophy, arguing that if the natural contract is a "literary metaphor" then it cannot also have philosophical weight.[35] Ferry is, however, not the only thinker to question Serres's use of figures, metaphors and anecdotes to illustrate the natural contract. For John Clark, the figures, illustrations and stories in *The Natural Contract* are examples of Serres heading off "in the wrong direction" on "his intellectual flights of imagination."[36] But I argue that it is because the natural contract is both literary metaphor and philosophical concept that it holds so much creative power.

Despite other attacks from French thinkers and polemicists,[37] Serres has continued to develop the concept of the natural contract. In subsequent texts, he has described other figures and stories for outlining a more symbiotic relationship with the Earth. For example, he adopts the example of park guides who patiently observe the interactions of flora and fauna.[38] For this more contemporary figure of the natural contract, Serres draws on his experience of national parks in the American West, but also on his visits to the Pyrenees. He imagines the relationships in parks along the lines of a political ecology in which organisms interact in a complex web that extends out to the planet in its entirety. Yet Serres has not forgotten the figure of the *paysan*, coming back to the example of a local natural contract that profoundly altered the landscape, creating a fragmented patchwork that can still be seen today from the sky (or by using Google Earth).

Serres's natural contract serves as a model for ecological dwelling for three main reasons. First, it underscores the need to take into account the ways in which science has articulated a relationship to the physical world. This does not mean that ecological dwelling must follow science as the voice of authority about climate change. Rather, as part of its practices of making (with) space, it must be informed by scientific thought – for example, weighing conservation biology's models of baseline and novel ecosystems. Second, the natural contract offers a way of framing our responsibility and accountability to the physical world in terms of attachments and connections. The images of a mountain climber "bound to" a sheer rock face illustrate that attachment and responsibility go both ways. Ecological dwelling adopts the principle of connections as part of its politics of *habitabilité*. Third, Serres asserts the importance of attending creatively to the eco-political. New concepts, figures, and metaphors are needed in ecological thinking to help us imagine what may be very different future scenarios.

The end of the paysan*: Future(s) for ecological dwelling*

Around the same time Paul Crutzen was proposing the term "Anthropocene" to refer to a new era in which humans have left their imprint on the earth's atmospheric and geological systems, Serres published *Hominescence* (2001), the first in a series of texts about our contemporary human condition. Serres invents the word *hominescence* to refer to a crucial turn in the history of hominization, a turn that is characterized by a new global relationship between humanity and planet Earth, a new biotechnological relationship with our bodies, and a new communicational relationship with others. While these changes may not be as drastic as learning to walk upright or inventing fire, they are nevertheless, Serres contends, radically transforming our notion of the human. They are thus part of the ever-ongoing process of hominization, or becoming human. But Serres is careful to add that there is no single set of human traits; instead, the human is "that which we construct in time by our acts and thoughts, collective and individual."[39] There is no universal human nature that transcends time and place. In addition, Serres underscores the fact that we do not know what type of human our present acts will produce, but that this is the question philosophy needs to be asking urgently: What kind of humans do we want biotechnology, cognitive science, geoengineering, etc. to produce?

The end of farming and agriculture as the most common occupation in Western culture is the most important event of our present stage of hominization, according to Serres. He adds, however, that humans are now responsible for an increasing number of species and ecosystems. We have shifted from a local form of domestication to a global one, leading to the creation of a "cosmoculture."[40] Such a change is not good or bad in and of itself, Serres writes, but it requires us to imagine multiple future scenarios of a global habitat, a global *habiter*. Serres uses the term "biosom" to describe our "common home" on planet Earth or the world of living beings that we are constructing together.[41] The practices included in this *habiter* stem from both the sciences and the humanities. Optimistic about the possibility of this convergence, Serres writes: "La pluralité des langues et le multiculturalisme cohabitent avec la diversité du vivant, aussi brillante de la variation des corps individuels que dans les chaînons de l'ADN où se reproduit, comme une image, dans et par un alphabet d'éléments simples, la diversité des langues."[42] Cultural diversity and biological diversity become inextricably woven together.

As our common home evolves, Serres reflects on the changes in terms of processes of subjectivity. Stable identity and a sense of being no longer characterize our experience of becoming in virtual and real spaces. He writes: "Je fluctue, percole et ne suis pas."[43] Serres comes back to his own experience of multiple displacements, asking how this may lead to a new relationship with the land that is based less on belonging and more on processes and practices of hybridization: "The wanderer, the exile, adapting to and travelling across all manners of waters ... accumulates in his body passages, landscapes, customs, languages, and mixes them."[44] In this way, Serres posits a possible future for a new relationship to the earth that incorporates mobility, movement, and mingling. The story of the end of the *paysan* is, then, one of both loss and transformation for Serres. As the descendant of a disappearing figure in human history, Serres works to inscribe on the page what the *paysan* inscribed on the land; at the same time, he recognizes the need to make the passage from the local to the global, following not the straight line of Cartesian rational thought, but the contingency of mixed bodies.

As a writer-philosopher, Serres strives to inhabit both language and the world. He works from individual pages, places, and experiences, to construct a larger view that remains full of hope and even joy. In *Biogée* (2010), Serres recounts his experiences of mountains, rivers, wind, weather, fauna and flora, sometimes with other human beings and other times alone. Rooted in autobiography, such a text moves beyond philosophy, reaching toward literature and reasserting the poetic force of language. It clearly illustrates ecological dwelling as an act of composing, in the etymological sense of practicing and creating with the living world. In this way, the emphasis shifts from dwelling as a noun to dwelling as a verb, similar to living and inhabiting. There is, then, no one ecological place to live; instead, ecological dwelling happens in those places that make possible the practices of composing with the living world.

The issue then becomes: How can we dwell ecologically in a living world that is also undergoing the sixth greatest wave of extinctions in the planet's history? Even if bacteria will no doubt continue to survive on Earth for millions of years to come, can this still be called a "living planet"? At what point does the living world become a dying one with which humans can no longer make space? Serres's figure of the *paysan* serves as a useful example for responding to these questions. The end of this way of life can be framed as a narrative of loss or as a narrative of transformation. In the first case, we mourn the end of an era and have little hope for the future. In the second, we recognize change and work toward new practices of ecological dwelling. Serres indicates a way of doing both: he emphasizes the historical mark the figure of the *paysan* has made in our relationship to the land in the West. He then uses this figure to imagine a global *habiter* that accounts for multiple displacements and processes of hybridization that date back to *homo sapiens* building "arborescent houses like himself." As the epigraph to this chapter notes, we are still "animal-vegetal" beings living on a "vegetal-animal globe"; we are still "small amphibians" inhabiting "a large amphibian." In the end, Serres inscribes the legacy of the *paysan* in future imaginings about the planet, in future transformations of becoming human, so that a narrative of loss becomes one of continuity and adaptation.

Fiction

Portrait: Marie-Hélène Lafon

Whereas the pastoral fell out of style in French literature in the nineteenth century, the figure of the *paysan* reappears time and time again in well-known French novels of the last two hundred years. In opposition to the pastoral's celebration of nature, nineteenth-century realist writers such as Honoré Balzac and Émile Zola painted a picture of the difficult labour conditions of peasant and village life. In the twentieth century, authors like Paul Claudel, Bernard Clavel, Jean Giono, and Maurice Genevoix highlighted regional differences in their stories about villages and farms in France.[45] More recently, in the later part of the twentieth century, a different breed of writers has emerged, using non-fiction to describe the transformations of the French countryside and life in small villages. As Sylviane Coyault explains, writers like Pierre Bergounioux, Pierre Michon, and Richard Millet are not celebrating a return to nature; instead, they are drawing on their own experiences of *la province* as a way to examine further the relationship between writing and reality.[46]

Deeply influenced by her own childhood, growing up in the countryside, Lafon highlights the individual stories and experiences playing out in the Cantal region in her novels.[47] As Lafon explains, autobiographical elements serve as the backbone of her novels.[48] The figure of the *paysan* plays a key role in the three novels I will analyse in this chapter: *Les Derniers Indiens* (2008), *L'Annonce* (2009), and *Les Pays* (2012).[49] These novels are very much inspired by the work of contemporary French authors who focus on changing socioeconomic and geographical characteristics of *la province*.[50] Lafon's writing differs, however, from that of her contemporaries who also write at length about life in rural areas around France. First, Lafon avoids the first-person narrator-author, inventing fictional characters to tell the stories of these places. Even in *Les Pays*, the clearest example of *autofiction*, Lafon gives her main character a different name from her own. Second, her writing remains rooted in storytelling so that description does not dominate the narrative flow. Plot and character development are central to the story. Even when setting is brought to the fore, it is experienced as part of a character's embodied practices of making space.

Lafon writes about the rural as a place inhabited, imagined, smelled, recited, and sensed.[51] Fiction becomes a conduit for bodily and sensory experiences of a concrete, material world. Readers experience the character's world of smell and touch, they "pass through" the character's worlds in her novels: "Il faut que tout s'incarne," she asserts.[52] To give expression to sensory experience, Lafon develops a writing style that reminds the reader of the role that breathing and the senses play in comprehending the world.[53] The lists of nouns, adjectives, and past participles reveal the complexity of a world in which experiences accumulate without necessarily being categorized or ordered. Her novels immerse the reader in shapes, sounds, shadows, and movements, leaving them with a visceral sense of the materiality of the real world.

Although Lafon is often compared to writers like Pierre Michon and Pierre Bergounioux, her realist aesthetics are also influenced by Raymond Depardon's cinematography and photography. First, there is the careful, almost ethnographic portrayal of farming communities that does not remove the observer from the frame but instead imbues the image with the writer or photographer's subjectivity. Both Depardon and Lafon grew up in farming communities, left them, and work to recreate a sense of these *milieux* through their own particular experiences. Second, their portraits of rural settings are neither idealizing nor nostalgic. Depardon speaks of wanting to capture rural life in his documentaries in such a way that twenty years later, "une tendre humanité" still emerges from the screen.[54] For her part, Lafon does not judge her characters' at-times cruel treatment of others but instead presents the complex interactions of humans and animals without romanticizing these practices.

Given Lafon's careful attention to the natural world, could her writing be described as eco-fiction? As I already noted, Lafon does not use the first-person pronoun, and writes fiction (with the exemption of her prose essay, *Album* [2012]). Moreover, her writing does not raise environmental issues such as the destructive practices of agriculture or the struggle against GMOs in France. In general, Lafon's characters develop intimate relationships with objects and beings in rural areas. But intimate does not mean harmonious. Intense might be a better word to describe the characters' experience of a world that is very present, very concrete, a world that includes kitchen tables, chairs, and silverware as well as cows, dogs, storms, and trees. Moreover, the rural is not synonymous with nature in Lafon's novels. "Rural" presents an ensemble of physical conditions that the body may experience similarly to or differently from those of urban spaces. It thus seems misplaced to characterize Lafon's writing as eco-fiction or to align it with the work of French writers like Giono or American nature writers like Thoreau.

Each of the three Lafon novels discussed here develops a different perspective on the interactions that are possible with others, bodies, and the non-human. Yet they have a certain *air de famille* about them, or what Lafon calls a "lien de filiation."[55] *Les Derniers Indiens* (2008) asks how one can continue to live in the country when one has never left it, when one has never known anything different; *L'Annonce* (2009) asks how one can move to the country to start a new life, to find a new home, when one has never before lived in the country; and *Les Pays* (2012) asks how one leaves the country to move to the city, how this affects relationships to others, to the body, and to the world more generally. Taken together, the three novels provide a complex picture of the rural as a place undergoing radical transformation, but that nevertheless has an important role to play in imagining future practices of ecological dwelling.

Dying and evolving practices of place

The first novel, *Les Derniers Indiens*, portrays the difficulties of a small rural community from the perspective of Marie Santoire, a woman in late middle-age who lives with her older brother, Jean, on what was formerly a well-run farm in Cantal. The novel's title comes from an expression used by Jean and Marie's mother when she was still alive: "Les Santoire vivaient sur une île, ils étaient les derniers Indiens, la mère le disait chaque fois que l'on passait en voiture devant les panneaux d'information touristique du Parc régional des volcans d'Auvergne, on est les derniers Indiens."[56] For Marie's mother, the shift from farming to ecotourism is a tragedy because it represents the end of the *paysan*. But Marie's own attitude is much more ambiguous. There is no documenting of lost customs of cultivating the land and no lamenting the loss of traditional values in Marie's narrative about her life with her brother Jean. In reality, neither of the two works the land, living off the small inheritance they received after their elderly mother's passing. Moreover, they rarely visit with others, and lead a solitary, isolated life.[57]

But the novel does not merely tell the story of Marie and Jean, whose lives as former *paysans* are fading away; it also describes the life of their neighbours, who are adapting to the new socioeconomic conditions of life in the country. The stifling environment in which Marie and Jean live is contrasted with the flourishing, bustling lives of their neighbours. The novel's first few pages carefully describe the old table and chairs in the Santoire family home, which have remained the same for at least two generations – according to Jean, "changer est inutile."[58] But rather than emphasize the value of such chairs as symbols of the way things were, Marie prefers to describe in detail the colourful, cheap dresses hanging on the next-door neighbour's clothesline. While her mother and brother refuse any interactions with that noisy, procreating group because of their social class, Marie is envious of this vibrant example of life evolving and adapting next door. By telling the story largely through Marie's eyes (but in the third person), the novel creates a tone that recounts the end of the *paysan* and the emergence of new modes of rural living without nostalgia.

Nicole Mathieu's analysis of the transformation of the notion of the rural is helpful here. The neighbours' activities very much reflect the type of socioeconomic diversification that Mathieu discusses in her article. First, they industrialize and modernize their farm, buying up land from the Santoire family, increasing their production of the local Saint-Nectaire cheese;[59] next, they transform some of their buildings into *gîtes* and *auberges*, following the shift to green tourism, attracting people from the city to enjoy life in the country for a week or two.[60] While Jean reacts negatively to the neighbours' embrace of agricultural modernization, Marie describes a relationship that goes beyond differing values, traditions, or even economics: "Ils étaient différents et semblables, on ne concevait pas le monde sans eux, l'autre côté de la route sans eux, on respirait leur air, on buvait leurs bruits, on les inventait, on s'en occupait."[61] Marie's relationship to the neighbours is one of vital functions – breathing, drinking, imagining. For life to go on in rural areas, it must grow, reproduce, and change, something Marie recognizes but that her brother Jean refuses: "Chez Santoire on n'était pas affairé, pas adapté, on ne le serait plus."[62]

The novel does not cultivate sympathy for the Santoires while describing their slow decline into isolation and bitterness after their mother's death. Jean's xenophobic diatribes are related in lengthy, two-page sentences without quotation marks. Class politics are evoked in the Santoires' former relationships with the men who worked on their farm. Without being explicitly critical, the novel illustrates that this conservative politics has no future as more and more "outsiders" arrive in Cantal, renting homes for a week or two to enjoy the country, diversifying the population, even if for only a short time. In the final pages of the novel, Marie predicts that the neighbours will buy their house after she and Jean pass away and that they will use it to create another *gîte* for ecotourists.

The theme of death is further developed in the novel by Marie's references to the murder of one of the neighbour's girls, Alice, thirty years earlier. The reader initially interprets these references as Marie's way of asserting the presence of tragedy and death even in the midst of life. But the unsolved murder takes on larger dimensions as Alice appears in Marie's dreams: "l'Alice était un comble, une ligne impossible, un fil tendu vibrant au-delà d'elle il ne pouvait rien y avoir, rien se produire, rien arriver, on ne comptait plus, ça ne comptait plus."[63] Alice represents, to some extent, Marie's own wasted life as a passive observer rather than an active participant. In the novel's final paragraph, this sense of wasted life is further reinforced when Marie reveals what she had found in the upstairs wardrobe several years before: the belt of the coat Alice was wearing when she disappeared. The reader is left wondering whether Jean is the murderer. In the end, the slow decline of the *paysan* is overshadowed by the tragedy of the murder of a young girl, and there is little room left for sympathizing with the last of the "survivors."

While regionalist literature in France has at times naively embraced and promoted the value of country living over that of the city, Lafon avoids this position in *Les Derniers Indiens*.[64] The rural is portrayed ambiguously, in all its contemporary complexity. There is certainly a sense of bitterness in Jean's remarks and observations, but Marie's point of view is more ambivalent. The novel offers less a bitter memory of times and customs gone by and more an ethnographic account of the present interactions of objects, beings, and people in rural areas. The contrast is striking between the *paysan* as a dead and dying species, and the rural as a place of changing practices where the key to survival is adaptation and transformation.

If ecological dwelling appears in the novel, it is not in the practices of farming or living off the land. While suffering their own personal loss with the death of Alice, the neighbours have found a way to continue living. They have learned to "compose with the world," to use Serres's expression, not just in the sense of adapting to change but also in the sense of experiencing the world as bodies in a material environment. Marie often remarks on the way the members of this family interact with each other, through touch, their strong smells, their noisy laughter.

> Là, au bord de la petite route, sur le terre-plein, entre les deux maisons, les pieds dans l'herbe grasse, sous la pluie de novembre, dans la torpeur d'août ou les gelées blanches d'avril, sous la neige, dans le vent cru, elles sentaient. Elles creusaient autour d'elles un puissant sillon de fragrances chiffonnées; c'était sucré, c'était mâle, c'était vert, chaud, changeant, piquant, âcre, âpre, animal, parfois vinaigré, toujours radical et renversant.[65]

Even though she is part of the disappearing *paysans,* Marie has not completely lost the connection to her own sensing and perceiving body. She is keenly aware of the neighbour's smells, which traverse categories, combining sweet and spicy, warm and sour. As Marie gets older, she realizes that maybe the *mélange* so despised by her mother in terms of social classes would have been better than the emptiness of a home abandoned to the shadows. The capacity to adapt, to diversify, and to hybridize are integral to ecological dwelling.

To some extent, the practices of ecological dwelling can be compared more generally to the processes of evolutionary adaptation. In both cases, it is a question of organisms learning to change in response to socio-ecological conditions. But whereas the latter occurs over longer periods of time (even sociocultural evolution refers to changes over a longer cultural time period), the former can happen in a single lifetime. Moreover, ecological dwelling pertains to eco-cultural and not genetic changes. Marie and her neighbours have the same general biological capacity to compose with the world, to practice a making of place, and to participate in the materiality of the world. Yet they inhabit different socioeconomic realities, with Marie refusing to participate in social life while the neighbours cultivate family relationships and work to diversify the economy. Overall, the rural community has increased its capacity to survive.

But has it increased its *habitabilité*, at least for the humans concerned? The novel ends with a description of Alice's belt, which Marie has found in her brother's armoire: "Elle l'avait reconnue. La ceinture d'Alice. Pliée, propre, verte."[66] Evolutionary theory has in the past emphasized competition, the survival of the fittest, as a driving force of natural selection. But Jean's murder of Alice does not fit with this explanation: the disappearing *paysans* are the weaker, less-adaptable group in the novel. Another possible explanation is that Jean's killing of Alice reflects the kind of "désir mimétique" that René Girard claims gives birth to culture.[67] But again, Jean's life will soon end, and the neighbours will take over his family home after Marie dies. I would like to suggest a different angle for understanding the murder of a young girl by the older son of a farming family. In the light of the concept of ecological dwelling, the murder symbolizes the problematic cutting of ties and attachments, the refusal to integrate into mixed communities, and a denial of accountability to an/other.

Composing landscapes and bodies

Lafon explains that she writes about the rural world, or what she describes as "un monde qui n'en finit pas de finir et de se réinventer," because that is where she was born; her books have inherited the legacy of her biographical life.[68] At the same time, she insists that she is not chronicling an ending, but rather a transformation: *L'Annonce* (2009) is about the possibility of inventing something new, she explains.[69] Compared to *Les Derniers Indiens*, it is true that *L'Annonce* paints a brighter picture of adaptation, diversification, and *mélange* in the rural setting of Cantal. The book is largely a love story about Annette, who is from a small industrial village in the north of France, another region under economic stress, and Paul, who is a farmer running a small milking business with his sister and two uncles in Cantal. The book recounts the story of their life together after Annette responds to a personal ad that Paul has placed in a local newspaper (hence the title of the novel, *L'Annonce*).

For the most part, the story is told through the eyes of Annette, but the omniscient narrator also reveals from time to time the thoughts of Annette's young son Éric, and those of Paul and his sister Nicole. At first, it seems like the characters in *L'Annonce* take up the positions laid out in *Les Derniers Indiens*: Nicole and the two uncles act as the bastions of a former way of life (very much like Jean in the previous novel), and

Paul serves as a bridge between an old and a new world (something like Marie, but more open to social and personal interactions with others). Annette and Éric do not, however, represent a separate, evolving sphere like the neighbours do in *Les Derniers Indiens*. Their multiple interactions and relationships have a deep and lasting effect on the dynamics of Paul's family. Paul, Annette, and Éric represent the possible future of the rural as a place *recomposé* in response to a new set of social, economic, and material demands.[70]

While Annette is not from the country, she is not from a large urban centre like Paris either. The novel avoids the city/country binary opposition and instead maps out an industrial North/agricultural South geography specific to France. Paul and Annette first meet face-to-face in the middle of France, so that neither of them is on his or her own territory and each must recreate the place from which he or she comes. Interestingly, Annette says almost nothing about her industrial village in the North, while Paul spends much time talking about his farm in Cantal. Annette realizes that she must come to terms with this place to which Paul is so intimately connected, yet she has no preconceived notions about the country either as "nature" or as "backwards." She answers Paul's ad not because she "likes the countryside" – even if this is part of what Paul indicates he's looking for in a woman in the ad's text – but because she wants to start a new life, far from her alcoholic ex-boyfriend. She explains: "La campagne, pourquoi pas. Ailleurs. S'arracher."[71] Her move to the countryside, then, is a move away from a place more than a move to a place. This creates a sense of disorientation when she first arrives in Cantal, as she must learn to "reconnaître le pays."

To do this, Annette engages in a set of practices that map more generally onto ecological dwelling as I have been defining it in this chapter. Standing before the three large picture windows of the second floor that she shares with Paul and Éric, Annette has a view of the fields, the farm buildings, and the neighbouring village. Her initiation into the land begins with learning the shifting tones of light and dark in the countryside: "Elle apprenait la lumière qui réveillait chaque chose, l'une, l'autre ensuite, visitée prise nimbée; les prés, les arbres, la route en ruban bleu, les chemins tapis, les vaches lentes et les tracteurs matinaux, cahotants, volontiers rouges."[72] Experiencing the landscape through sight is the first way in which Annette begins to "recognize" the land. To learn to "make space" in Cantal, she must come to terms with her body, which slowly comes alive again after many years of being suppressed: "Les corps aussi; les corps surtout. Pas réapprendre, pas recommencer; inventer."[73] Inventing a new sexuality and coming to know the landscape as felt, smelt, and experienced, Annette learns to dwell as a mingled body in a recomposed place.

According to Serres, we need to learn to compose with the material world by way of an immersive experience in which taste, touch and smell converge, sight and smell are heightened: "We return yet again to mixture and to the concept of variety, both immediate in the rich, complex, vibrant experience of the senses."[74] Serres emphasizes the need to move beyond words as categories, beyond our ordering and categorizing instinct in order to appreciate more fully the material world as an ever-changing landscape. Lafon's insistence on the reader's experience of a smelled, tasted world while reading her novels attests to a similar desire to materialize language. But Lafon also draws attention to the web of social relationships in which composing takes place, to the everyday practices that are integral to ecological dwelling. As Annette explains: "Composer signifiait tout, le jour la nuit, la lessive l'entremêlement, la nourriture et l'étreinte."[75] Making *habitable* means interweaving the mundane (laundry and food), the cyclical (day and night), and the highly physical and emotional (sexual relations). The use of enumeration in the sentence enforces the sense of gathering things together without imposing an order on them.

Similarly to *Les Derniers Indiens*, *L'Annonce* outlines the transformations that farmers are undergoing because of difficult socioeconomic conditions. Paul becomes the spokesperson for these issues, critiquing his neighbours' decision to embrace large-scale industrialization and then becoming caught in the stranglehold of debt.[76] He refuses this course of action and maintains a small milking business that he knows has no future because he has no children: "Rien ne serait transmis, continué, perpétué."[77] The sadness of this statement is tempered by the fact that Paul never wanted to be a *paysan* in the first place. Abandoned with his sister on his uncles' farm as an adolescent, Paul had no choice but to follow in their footsteps, despite the fact that he would have preferred to be a mechanic.[78] Lafon complicates again the story of the *paysan* as the narrative of the end of long-term traditions and customs. Instead, she emphasizes the practices of learning to compose with others (human and non-human) in a changing economy.

For those who have moved there from elsewhere, the rural community presents multiple opportunities for interacting with the non-human world and practicing ecological dwelling. Annette does not take up farming duties; instead, she rediscovers her body as a way of knowing the land. Her eleven-year old son Éric also learns how to dwell in this particular socio-ecological community. Upon arriving at the farm, Fridières, he immediately establishes a close relationship with the farm's dog, Lola, conversing with her, claiming to understand her thoughts, and surprising everyone with "l'alliance indéfectible qui s'était nouée, sous les yeux de tous, dès que l'enfant étranger avait fait irruption."[79] Éric's friendship with Lola stands in sharp contrast to the relationship Paul's sister Nicole has with the farm's animals. She purposely kills and skins farm-raised rabbits in front of Éric in order to rid of him of his idea of animals as companions.[80] And yet Éric refuses her view and continues to interact with animals as thinking and feeling beings.[81] In terms of practices of ecological dwelling, Éric illustrates a greater sense of accountability and responsibility than Nicole, even though she is meant to represent the "traditional" attitude toward farm animals.[82]

In light of the novel's use of the word "alliance" to describe Éric and Lola's relationship, it is useful to come back to Serres's notion of the natural contract. For Serres, cohabiting with animals, living together under one roof in places where smells and bodies mingle and mix, was part of our earlier *domos* or home.[83] He then asks if this *domos* can exist on a global scale as a way of extending the relationship of care and cohabitation between humans and animals: "Ainsi l'association d'humains, de vivants et d'objets, requise aujourd'hui, par et pour le *Contrat Naturel*, reprend la *familia* latine et la ferme rustique, en une *paysannerie généralisée*, sous des espèces globales, *sub specie mundi*."[84] Whether we are capable of human-animal accountability and responsibility on such a global scale is not clear. Lafon's novel illustrates that, even locally, the relationships between human and non-human beings remain complex and often contradictory. At the same time, Serres and Lafon both illustrate that ecological dwelling necessarily includes practices of making space with non-human animals who have their own habits, customs, and cultures for socio-ecological adaptation.

The expression *faire maison* appears on multiple occasions in Lafon's novel, even though it is not an expression commonly used in French.[85] One possible English translation is "to make a house." But Annette and Paul already have a home in which they live with Éric, on the floor above which Nicole and the uncles reside. The expression clearly refers to something other than constructing an actual building. Understood metaphorically, the expression *faire maison* can refer to the ways of interacting with others so as to "make home" together. This is how Annette first uses the expression to describe "cette périlleuse acrobatie du couple rassemblé, pièces et morceaux."[86] In terms of the reassembling of bodies, the notion of *faire maison* points to the very real, material movements that are necessary when adapting to the contours of a new space. The expression resurfaces in the novel to describe Paul's appreciative attitude toward the practices of piecing together: "Il prévoyait, voulait et se donnait tout entier pour que autour de lui à Fridières, pieces et morceaux s'assemblent et fassent maison. Il aimait ces mots, faire maison, et en usait volontiers pour les familles qui continuaient à se tenir plus ou moins fières dans les bâtisses trâpues disséminés à Fridières, au Jaladis, à la Fougerie."[87] For Paul, making a home refers, as for Annette, to the assembly of disparate pieces. But it also refers to the continued resilience of the farming families in the community.

Key to these practices of ecological dwelling is not, however, preserving farming customs and traditions, or conserving one way of knowing and interacting with the land. Despite the fact that the milking business was doing well, that Paul's sister and his uncles continued to help him on the farm, something was missing in Paul's life. As he explains, he placed a personal ad in order to find someone outside of the community with whom he could *faire maison*. For rural life to remain resilient, it must be open to "corps étrangers, tombés d'ailleurs, du nord du monde de la ville" as Annette and Éric are first described when they arrive on the farm. As these two *corps étrangers* modify the other bodies in the rural habitat, as they "make space" together, they become a vital part of the landscape: "la femme et l'enfant, les recueillis, faisaient désormais partie du paysage, avaient creusé le sol sous eux, pris corps et racine."[88] The organic metaphor of bodies taking root emphasizes once again the material processes that are part of ecological dwelling.

The novel does raise, however, the question of how many other outside bodies can come to participate in the practices of *faire maison*. Éric asks his mother and Paul if his maternal grandmother, who still lives in an industrial village in the North, can move to Fridières as well. He realizes that his grandmother will face much resistance from Nicole and the uncles, and yet he seems to recognize that these *corps étrangers* are needed. The rural has a future, not as a return to the past, but as a mix of new, reassembled bodies and pieces. While Serres envisions a *paysannerie généralisée* as a possible global model for ecological dwelling, Lafon outlines a more local and provisional solution that depends on learning to recognize rural landscapes, integrating *corps étrangers*, and treating non-human animals as feeling, sensing, thinking beings.[89]

The novel ends with a description of the photographs that Paul and Annette brought with them the first time they met in a restaurant in the middle of France. While Annette only briefly displays her photos, Paul describes his in detail: first, his First Communion photo; second, a photo of him at twenty years old, sitting on his first tractor; and third, a photo of Nicole with their uncles when she first received her driver's license. The influence of Raymond Depardon's photography is most present in these final pages. The photographs capture moments in time, revealing the tension between change brought about by modernization (the tractor) on the one hand, and, on the other, rural traditions as upheld by the two uncles who appear in the final photograph, "devant la porte de l'étable, fichés en sentinelles dans la pierre grenue, grise et rugueuse à l'oeil, fondus en elle, émanés du bâtiment, crachés par lui, et voués à sa garde vigilent pour les siècles des siècles."[90] An image of the "long-term imbrication of humans in a landscape," the photograph of the uncles' timeless rootedness contrasts with the story of the change and transformation that characterize Annette and Paul's relationship. The reader is left with the question of how photography and storytelling recount and represent rural life. What needs to be conserved and preserved in fixed images? What needs to be critiqued and troubled? How do fixed images of dwelling as tradition, custom, ancestry, and memory encounter stories of mingled bodies and reassembled places?

Ecological dwelling in urban environments

In *Les Pays* (2012), Lafon asks the question of how one moves to Paris, the cultural and intellectual centre of France after growing up in a small farming community, how one becomes an urban dweller while still maintaining a relationship with the rural. At first glance, the novel appears to take up the well-known plot of a young person moving from *la province* to Paris in order to have access to "l'univers intellectuel, qui seul permet l'accès à la conscience de soi."[91] But the novel manages to avoid the country/city binary by carefully outlining the traces of place on bodies and the practices of dwelling that are carried from one place to another. At the same time, it acknowledges the continued challenges faced by farming communities and the difficulties of bridging urban/rural differences. In the end, the novel represents both environments as places that can be fully experienced – emotionally, psychologically, sensorially – by certain bodies.

Les Pays is the clearest example of *autofiction* in Lafon's collection of novels. The story is about a young girl, Claire, who moves to Paris to take up the study of Classics at the Sorbonne, leaving her family behind on the farm. Even though the novel does not adopt the defining characteristic of *autofiction* (the main character and the author do not have the same first and last names), it includes many biographical elements: Lafon left Cantal at a young age, studied in Paris and eventually became a Classics teacher. And yet by creating Claire as a fictional character, Lafon diffracts her own experience so that it is impossible to read the novel as a blueprint of the author's life. Lafon carefully structures the novel in three sections, adopting different narrative points of view to complicate further *autofiction*'s relationship to reality. Although less formally experimental than Darrieussecq, Lafon similarly requires the reader to engage with the poetics and aesthetics of her writing rather than look for biographical correspondences.

The first section of the novel is told largely from the point of view of Claire's father, the *paysan*, and so emphasizes the difficulties of the encounter between country and city. The opening scene in the novel describes the sense of jarring unfamiliarity (literally in French *dépaysement*, or without the feel of country) that the *paysan* feels upon arriving in Paris. The young daughter Claire, her brother, and her father are visiting the father's niece, Suzanne, and her husband, Henri, in the Parisian suburb of Gentilly. They take the train from Cantal to Paris, even though the father would have preferred to drive. The impossibility of navigating Paris by car when one is used to country roads reminds the reader of tropes of the hopelessly lost country cousin.

This initial reading is, however, challenged by the example of Suzanne, the niece whom Claire's family is visiting in Paris. To adapt to urban living, Suzanne has learned, not to forget her rural roots, but to carry traces of the land with her, in her way of walking, speaking, and moving through space: "Suzanne, par le jeté du corps, la voix, le pas, les mains, appartenait à ce bout de pays élimé, à cette vallée de la Santoire derrière elle laissée loin."[92] Moreover, she returns to Cantal with her husband to visit the family on the farm every summer. During these visits, she converses with her uncle, Claire's father, about the future of farming in France. While he underlines the agonizing end to a former way of life – "l'inévitable agonie" – Suzanne asserts the need for change – "l'adaptation, l'innovation, l'invention."[93] It is, of course, easier for Suzanne to imagine new beginnings for rural living given that she does not deal with this reality on a daily basis. And yet the novel suggests that the perspectives made possible by people like Suzanne are necessary for reimagining rural life.

By far the longest of the three sections, the second part of the novel tells the story of Claire's integration into city life a few years after her initial visit to Paris with her father and her brother. The body becomes a central theme as Claire discovers and experiences what it means to live and study in the city. On the one hand, Claire emphasizes the definitive nature of her move – she does not go back to the country to see her parents in the summer, she only calls them every two weeks, and she talks very little about her childhood with friends or acquaintances. On the other hand, Claire carries with her the smells from the countryside: "Elle avait une mémoire aiguë des odeurs et savait par coeur les bois nus de février, les granges vides à la fin du printemps ou la Santoire grosse de neige fondue."[94] Moreover, she first experiences the urban environment through her sense of smell. She can quickly identify the distinct odours of the amphitheatres, the buses, the metro stations, even though the streets of Paris leave her somewhat perplexed: "Quelque chose de trop volatil lui échappait; elle avait pensé les premiers mois que ça puait, carrément, que Paris puait, sans nuances, sauf dans le quartier chinois de la lessive où s'entassaient sur les trottoirs des sacs de victuailles, d'herbes, de fruits sans nom."[95] She eventually becomes accustomed to these street smells and even admits to a friend that when she wakes up to the sound of a rooster crowing (in the Chinese quarter of Paris), she almost feels like she is back home.[96] Through her body, Claire continues the practices of dwelling that she had learned growing up in the country while also making a place for herself in the city.

Despite having very few friends during her four years at the Sorbonne, Claire develops social relationships that diversify her understanding of the rural. The daughter of a bourgeois, upper-class family, Lucie Jaladis invites Claire to her Normandy home. But this rural setting is not one Claire recognizes, even though Lucie's ancestors were also *paysans* at one time. Claire quickly discovers that that there is not one *province* in opposition to Paris, but that there are many different rural settings and traditions in France. She comes to a similar understanding about nature. Upon visiting another friend's childhood home in the Fontainebleau forest, Claire notes that she has trouble connecting with this nature, that in fact "nature" is not a word she would have used back home on the farm: "Tant de faste et de vertical munificence heurtait ce qu'elle gardait en elle d'organique connivence avec les hêtres et les frênes du pays premier."[97] In addition to undoing a representation of rural nature as homogeneous, this description highlights the novel's stylistic particularities.

Even though the narration adopts the perspective of a teenage girl, the vocabulary is rich (with terms like *faste* and *munificence*) and the diction is extremely poetic (as with, for example, the inversion of adjective and noun in the expression *organique connivence*). Similarly, when Claire meets Mme Rabot, who is from an area close to the village where she grew up in Cantal, she speaks of her "fibre agricole" and of her stories as the "saga paysanne incongrue."[98] Language allows Claire to continue to inhabit places that were left behind. Moreover, Claire's way of inhabiting rural spaces through language and stories is not disembodied. On the contrary, she comes to terms with a very visceral emotion when listening to another friend, Alain, talk about his desire to return to Cantal:

> Pour la première fois ... quelque chose s'était incarné qui lui serrait la gorge, le centre, et réclamait d'elle un travail muet d'ajustement, de raccord ... elle apprivoiserait et apprendrait à aimer et rechercherait cette singulière émotion suscitée en elle par l'apparition d'un corps, d'une voix, de paroles exhumées du monde premier, ancien, antédiluvien.[99]

Her sentiment is not one of nostalgia or homesickness, but an emotion that she can only describe in terms of its physical effects. Embracing this emotion, even seeking it out, is clearly in line with Claire's attentiveness to smells, sounds, light, seasons, and weather in the city: "En elle, dans son sang et sous sa peau, étaient infusées des impressions fortes qui *faisaient paysage* et *composaient le monde*, on avait ça en soi, et il fallait élargir sa vie, la gagner et l'élargir."[100] The practices of "making landscape" and "composing a world" start with the body, "in the blood and under the skin"; they are what allow Claire to "make space" in the city.

The third section of the novel describes Claire's life twenty years later, teaching Classics and still living in Paris, divorced, a well-settled urban dweller. Yet Claire maintains a connection to the rural, by spending summers at her country home in Cantal. This final section begins by describing the transition she makes as she readjusts to being back in the city:

> Elle respire la ville aimée, sa seconde peau, elle hume le fumet familier qu'elle ne parvient pas tout à fait à démêler; c'est tout entassé, machine et chair, rouages et sueurs, haleines suries et parfums fatiguées sur poussière grasse, c'est animal et minéral à la fois; c'est du côté du sale et elle se coule dans cette glu, elle prend place s'insère dans le flot ... La ville s'apprend par le corps et se retrouve par lui.[101]

The machine, animal, mineral smells of the urban environment break down rigid category distinctions. Claire's body inhabits both the urban and the rural environment like an animal inhabits its burrow; she has "un terrier dans la ville minérale" and "un terrier des champs."[102] This coexistence does not collapse difference – the country and the city remain "deux pays" and "deux temps"[103] – but they can be bridged by the embodied practices of ecological dwelling.

For Claire's father, who remains in Cantal, the possibility of dwelling in the city remains closed. Bringing his grandson with him to visit Claire in Paris, the father is again uncomfortable and disoriented, as he was during the long-ago visit when Claire was just a young girl. He is *dépaysé* – again, literally, country-less – first when his grandson shows him his own farm using Google Earth on Claire's computer, and then again when, as he is gazing at the computer, Claire puts on a television documentary about life in Cantal: "Perplexe, vaguement égaré entre grand et petit écran, film et documentaire ... il opinait et répétait dans sa gorge ... C'est nous c'est nous on est comme ça c'est nous."[104] The *paysan* recognizes his way of life, and yet the representation on the screen creates a sense of otherness. Like the photographs described at the end of *L'Annonce*, the documentary records a moment, but also captures it in time, as if the rural communities in Cantal were already relegated to the past, no longer evolving and adapting.

Lafon's novels raise the problem of representation, asking how literature can portray without capturing, depict without fossilizing. Because they refuse to idealize or romanticize life in the country, they create the sense of an ongoing story that has continued relevance in an increasingly urbanized French society. No solution is given for rural exodus; instead, the novels illustrate the necessary and difficult processes of transformation in rural communities. Writing almost exclusively about one single rural region in France,[105] Lafon may not attract a large readership. Yet her carefully crafted literary style is garnering more and more attention because of its capacity to render a sensually rich world of smells, sounds, images, and movements.[106] Although her novels represent rural life through a realist lens, they develop a style that loosens the rules of syntax, accumulating sense perceptions without imposing order on them and reminding the reader of language's origins in embodied experience.

Conclusion: Inhabiting language as ecological dwelling

As the planet becomes less inhabitable for humans and other species, we can ask how representations of the rural can shed light on current and future relations between humans and the non-human world. The point is not to reduce literature to a political cause, but to bring literature into dialogue with a multitude of political, social, and historical issues. Moreover, Lafon's texts are not an example of *littérature engagée;* they do not try to convince the reader of a political message about rural communities. Rather, they create a world of experience that the reader works to integrate into her own understandings of the world. Serres's philosophy, on the other hand, calls for living differently in the world, and yet his writings about the rural cannot be reduced to a single political message either. While he points to the figure of the *paysan* as an example of a more symbiotic relationship with the world, he is not advising that we all take up farming. Instead, he adopts this figure to imagine new, global relationships between humanity and Earth that are rooted in care and attachment rather than preservation practices.

Both Serres and Lafon clearly illustrate the importance of embodied experience for representing and understanding ecological dwelling. Serres's philosophy of mixed bodies articulates processes of interaction and exchange that take on new forms, nuances, and expressions in Lafon's novels. When fully open to the environment, the human body composes landscapes (with) smells, tastes, sounds, touch, and sights. Serres reminds us that the earth, too, is a body whose patchwork crust – very much like our own human skin – bears the traces of the passage of time.[107] The connection to the global can be made by way of this analogy, so that we begin to imagine the earth as a body that is constantly exchanging matter with the environment, a body that is self-monitoring and self-maintaining, and yet highly vulnerable. Whereas Lafon emphasizes the local body, Serres addresses the need for stories about the Earth-as-body that go beyond Earth systems science – stories that create new metaphors, concepts and figures for ecological dwelling on a planetary scale.[108]

Telling stories is rooted in the practices of language, not as disembodied text, but as ecological experience. As Serres explains, the French language is also a habitat: "Langue: lit, cuisine, atelier, mon lieu, mon jardin, mon pays, je veux dire ma maison. *Ibi patria.*"[109] Refusing the notion of national belonging, Serres describes language as his home, his kitchen, his workshop, his garden. Similarly, Lafon emphasizes the materiality of language as a world we inhabit when speaking, reading, and writing, and develops a poetics that delves into the unordered flux of percepts and affects. Immersed in Serres's and Lafon's worlds, the reader becomes aware of the richness of the French language, its ability to go beyond abstract and universal concepts and describe the thick viscosity of the real world without necessarily imposing order on it. In this way, Lafon and Serres model practices of ecological dwelling in their writing.[110]

3 Ecological Politics: Latour and Rufin

So, to study is always to do politics in the sense that it collects or composes what the common world is made of. The delicate question is to decide what sort of collection and what sort of composition is needed.

– Bruno Latour, *Reassembling the Social*, 256–7

Les partis qui se réclament de l'écologie politique n'ont pas à s'engager sur un programme, mais sur la mise en place d'un État de discussion et de négociation des associations légitimes et illégitimes entre les intérêts multiples des humains et des non-humains. Ils ne *savent* pas. Ils ne sont pas "pour" ou "contre." Ils s'engagent à garantir que la représentation sera recherchée, explorée en commun, et que la décision sera considérée comme légitime par les parties prenantes.

– Bruno Latour, "Cosmopolitiques, quels chantiers?!" 18[1]

The epigraphs above nicely highlight two understandings of the term "political": first, the broad sense of the political as making decisions that necessarily include some beings and exclude others; second, the narrow sense of the political as government parties whose voice is heard because of already instituted decisions. While both notions of the political will be evoked in this chapter, I begin with the practices of "collecting and composing" that are at the heart of human activities, including literary studies. As Latour asserts in the first epigraph, "to study is always to do politics." While contemporary French thinkers such as Jacques Rancière assert that all literature is political, many literary scholars still hold to the idea that the study of literature transcends politics. As I explained in the book's introduction, political readings of texts, whether in the form of queer studies, animal studies, or postcolonial studies, continue to be met with suspicion in French literary circles. My objective in the introduction to this chapter is to make clear the decisions that are inherent in ecocritical readings rather than pretending that literary study is somehow disconnected from the sociopolitical sphere.

This also means responding to the notion of eco-politics mentioned in Latour's second epigraph. Too often eco-politics are associated with a set of green environmentalist policies and principles, such as respecting and preserving nature. But this alignment tends to obscure the ways in which such principles are built upon previous inclusionary and exclusionary practices (e.g., what is taken as nature is a given). As I have been doing in previous chapters, I will develop the notion of the ecological as a way of examining the assumptions made about the environment and undoing the notion of environmentalism as a homogeneous movement. At the same time, I will ask what the limits of an ecological politics are in terms of composing and collecting. How large a tent can eco-politics be? How much dissension should be part of the process of building this tent? What critiques of environmentalism need to be heard as part of the process of developing an ecological politics?

Environmental awareness and environmentalist politics are at the heart of what ecocritics do and why they do what they do. Activism has played an important role in defining ecocritical approaches, with some arguing that an ecocritic must necessarily adopt more sustainable practices and ways of living.[2] For others, there is no praxis without theory, and so it is problematic to argue about the kind of (hybrid) car one should drive without touching on the deeper ideological issues of an environmental consciousness, for example.[3] Whatever position is taken on the nexus of theory and praxis, ecocriticism works from the premise that cultural texts must be read politically. This assertion glosses over, however, some important (and at times irreconcilable) differences within ecocriticism. First, there is no one single ecocritical politics applied to the text; indeed, there are many different political orientations, ranging from deep ecology to ecosocialism, from environmental justice to ecofeminism. Second, there has been a wide array of understandings of how to read a text politically. Some ecocritics evaluate the text in terms of whether it is a "good" or "bad" response to the current environmental crisis. Others consider instead the ways in which the text subverts, critiques, and reimagines dominant social discourses about nature, ecology, the environment, and the non-human world. Third, literary texts are only one component of how an ecocritic decides "what sort of collection and what sort of composition is needed" to arrive at a common world. It is in this third sense of the political that ecocriticism and *écocritique* overlap the most.

Where the two diverge is when ecocriticism is used to refer to a narrow set of environmentalist politics. In opposition to the linguistic turn of the 1980s that posited reality as textual, early ecocriticism called for a return to the materiality of the real world, and in particular to "real nature" as experienced outside of urban spaces. This countercultural, counter-(post)modernist stance was often rooted in a North American environmentalist politics that asserted the importance of wilderness. Nature writing in particular was taken as an exemplary environmental text because it foregrounded the non-human in this encounter with nature. But the notion of wilderness and the literary genre of nature writing are often shored up by a problematic nature/culture dualism. In addition, they are not widely referenced outside of New World literary histories (never mind the fact that "wilderness" in North America refers to a very different geographical and socio-historical reality than "wilderness" in Australia). My point in outlining ecocriticism's cultural specificities is not to refute the possibility of reading French literature politically, but to assert the need for multiple understandings of the eco-political and the importance of practicing what Donna Haraway calls "situated knowledges."[4]

Bruno Latour's work and Jean-Christophe Rufin's novels illustrate the ways in which ecological politics have been played out and are playing out in France. Latour has been building a political ecology for many years now, one that offers a strong theoretical framework for understanding the place and role of non-human agents in the social sphere. His contribution to ecological politics may not take the form of environmental activism, but it paves the way for a shift to a "progressive composition of the common world."[5] Rufin's novels first appear to be in direct opposition to Latour's eco-politics. In the first novel, *Globalia* (2004), environmental and animal ethics have been institutionalized in a dystopian world. The extremes of this futurist society illustrate a dark side, the controlling power of environmentalism when it aligns with totalitarianism.[6] The second novel, *Le Parfum d'Adam* (2007), narrates the workings of an ecoterrorist group planning to use a new strain of cholera to wipe out a large percentage of the human population. But while highlighting the dangers of radical ecology, Rufin also pushes the reader to reflect on alternative forms of ecological politics. For Rufin, the issue of socioeconomic inequalities always comes into play when trying to "compose a common world." It is from this perspective of the relationship between developed and developing countries that Rufin works to define a new humanism.[7] While Latour works positively to construct a political ecology that includes the non-human world, Rufin works negatively, denouncing the excesses of ecologism.

Why pair Latour and Rufin in this chapter if their ecological politics only contain contrasting features? It is true that my goal is to offer a wide range of contemporary responses to environmentalism in France. But Latour and Rufin converge in some respects as well. First, they are both highly critical of a certain "save-nature-save-the-planet" environmentalism. For Latour, such a position simply upholds the nature/culture dualism; even when it does take up the issue of overpopulation, it still posits nature as other-than-human. For Rufin, such a view risks erasing social inequalities, as it considers humans to be a homogeneous group threatening the future of the biosphere. Second, both Latour and Rufin illustrate the continued positioning of ecological politics with respect to Luc Ferry's earlier text, *Le Nouvel Ordre écologique* (1992). Contrasting Ferry's idea of the human as detached from the state of nature with Serres's notion of humans and nature as co-constituting, Latour sides more with the latter than the former.[8] Yet even for Latour, the problem of humanism is a necessary starting point for ecological politics. As for Rufin, he explicitly references Ferry in the postface of his novel *Le Parfum d'Adam* as one of the few French intellectuals aware of the underlying ideological dangers of deep ecology. Like Ferry, Rufin associates deep ecology with an Anglo-Saxon thinking that runs the risk of undermining a (French) philosophy of universal humanism. Finally, Latour and Rufin illustrate the extent to which French ecological politics continues to carry the traces of a sense of difference with respect to North American environmentalism. While Latour moves easily between linguistic communities, developing a cosmopolitan identity that extends far beyond French borders, Rufin largely addresses a French-speaking public, using his fiction to warn readers of the deleterious effects of (American) globalization. Bringing Latour and Rufin together in this chapter will allow for further explorations of cultural comparisons and additional critiques of a reified notion of French ecological politics.

Theory

Portrait: Bruno Latour

Bruno Latour is a well-known thinker outside of France. In ecocriticism, he is often seen either as representative of what is distastefully referred to as "French Theory" or as an important figure in the development of non-dualistic ecological thinking. These reactions to Latour's work follow two waves of ecocriticism – the first wave working to bring nature writing in from the margins of canonical literature, to reassert the importance of activism in the classroom, to bridge the gap between the text's world and the biological world, to counter some of the excesses of postmodernism and poststructuralism; and the second wave working to contextualize terms like nature and environment, to pay more attention to cultural differences, to shift attention toward multiple types of environment, and to bring identity politics related to race, gender, and species difference together with environmental concerns.[9] As ecocritics have argued, Latour's thinking can play a key role in moving ecocriticism toward a greater engagement with science studies, political ecology, and comparative anthropology.[10] While building on this work, my approach will examine Latour's political ecology in additional ways, asking how Latour continues to engage in dialogue with the humanism and universalism that are so deeply ingrained in French intellectual history.

Much like his former teacher Michel Serres, Latour is an extremely prolific writer, having published over thirty books and a hundred articles since *La Vie de laboratoire* (1979).[11] Given the scope of Latour's work, which covers a wide variety of contemporary issues while also drawing on a number of disciplines to develop a broad anthropological and epistemological framework, it is difficult to offer an overview of his work. Rather than take on such a mammoth task, I will focus on three specific conceptual nodes to get at the heart of Latour's ecological politics. The first thematic group – *nature/ecology* – may seem like a logical place to start given environmentalism's emphasis on the human destruction of nature. And yet Latour is very critical of the idea of preserving or conserving nature. I start with these terms because they offer an initial view of the differences between Latour's ecological politics and North American environmentalism. The second thematic group – *collective/globalization* – shifts the focus to the larger scope of

Latour's ecological politics. Latour opens up the political arena to non-human entities in order to articulate a common world. He is aware of the dangers of universalism, and yet holds to the idea that in a time of global ecological crisis, we need to work toward making the universal (I will come back to this emphasis on "making" later in my analysis). The third thematic group – *democracy/diplomacy* – brings the focus back to the reality of implementing such a far-reaching political ecology, by outlining first the components of a new democracy and then the processes of diplomacy. To conclude, I will consider how Latour draws on his own biography as a citizen of the French Republic and a cosmopolitan intellectual to outline political ecology. In many ways, his work illustrates the productive tension between the personal and the universal, the concrete and the general, the anecdotal and the analytic that is key to addressing contemporary environmental issues.

Latour's relationship to the development of ecological politics in France is worth looking at more closely. Latour does not engage with well-known thinkers of ecology like Serge Moscovici, "France's most prescient green thinker,"[12] nor with Emmanuel Mounier and his personalist ecologism, nor with Alain Lipietz and his ecosocialism. The one ecological thinker to whom Latour makes reference on multiple occasions is Michel Serres, but Latour does not take up the concept of the natural contract, preferring to develop his own theoretical framework for closing the gap between science and nature. In terms of Latour's initial interest in ecological issues, he appears to have been most affected by Pierre Lascoumes's critique of ecological movements and their integration into official governmental politics and policies. In *L'Éco-pouvoir. Environnement et politique* (1994), Lascoumes argues that we have lost the ability to debate environmental issues because we take scientific fact as absolute truth. This leads to what Lascoumes calls an *éco-pouvoir* that has the last word when issues such as pollution are brought to the political table. Latour picks up where Lascoumes leaves off and attempts to construct a new political ecology capable of debating such issues, including the question of the role of science as authoritative voice in such matters.

Latour's political ecology does not map onto a set of concrete policies or regulations, nor does Latour get involved in Green party politics. He has been in dialogue with political ecologists in France, and has published articles on various occasions in the journal *Écologie & Politique*, a scholarly journal founded in 1992. During an interview with Denis Chartier published in that journal in 2010, Latour made it clear that he maintains a certain distance with respect to green politics, asserting that *les Verts'* vision of politics, science, and society does not go deep enough.[13] Much like Serres, Latour attempts to build his own ecological politics from the ground up, looking at science and epistemology as already part of the sociopolitical sphere. Given Latour's critique of ecologism and *les Verts*, it is not surprising that his thinking has at times been less than well-received in France.[14]

Why, then, choose Latour's political ecology to lay the groundwork for a distinctly French *écocritique*? First, Latour's emphasis on nature as social matter rejects the nature/culture binary that characterized early North American environmental philosophy. Second, even if Latour has not participated in green politics in France, his thinking on democracy and his desire to compose a common world is clearly in dialogue with the long intellectual history of French universalism. Third, Latour raises the issue of the continued relevance of humanism, but refuses Ferry's dichotomy between humanism and anti-humanism when it comes to ecological politics. In this way, his thinking resonates with various chords in contemporary intellectual France, even though his political ecology cannot be reduced to a single cultural context.

Making nature(s) matter

The title of Latour's book *Politics of Nature* (2004 [1999]) nicely illustrates the difference between ecological thinking in France and American environmental philosophies. Latour is politicizing nature in his book, asking how the concept of nature outside of culture has shut down thinking about ecological thinking in many instances; he is not developing a politics of nature as if this latter held some foundational truth from which to construct a politics, as if politics existed objectively within nature. Borrowing from Serres, Latour explains that nature, science, and politics all occupy the same social sphere.[15] Nature is one way of ordering humans and non-humans, among others. This is why Latour uses the plural term "natures" or multinaturalism to remind the reader that other cultures have constructed other collectives.[16] He asserts the existence of an ever-changing external reality in which non-humans and humans are mobilized, domesticated, socialized, and brought into the collective under different circumstances.[17] Latour also redefines society so that it is no longer seen as human-constructed in opposition to a natural given. For Latour, the social is an association, a collection that is immersed in a pluriverse or exteriority that has not yet been called into the social sphere.[18] In other words, he shines the same critical light on the idea of society as he does on the idea of nature; this is what he calls a comparative anthropology, one that takes nothing for granted, one that reveals the work, scientific and political, involved in creating a collective.

Although he has been accused of social constructivism, Latour does not deny the reality of the material world.[19] Nature and the natural are very much a part of the Western world's understanding and perception of reality, but they are assemblages, explains Latour, that have gone through the process of hierarchy and institutionalization to become full-fledged members of the collective.[20] If Latour is so wary of the terms "nature" and "natural," it is because of the heavy political work they have been made to do in the past, as some sort of absolute measure for establishing a political position. He mentions the concept of the laws of nature that has been used to justify political agendas such as racism and to defend economic systems such as capitalism. There are no market/natural laws that exist outside of the social fabric; there is no reality that exists as some unchanging background in front of which the drama of science, politics, and history plays out. He summarizes his idea thus: "We no longer have a society surrounded by a nature, but a collective producing a clear distinction between what it has internalized and what it has externalized."[21] For Latour, a politics that engages with nature as always and already social matter is in fact in a much better position to develop an ecological politics, a politics of due process that asks: How many are we? Can we live together? How do we arrive at a well-formed collective?

The objective of *Politics of Nature* is to develop a political ecology that is built on a new constitution that does not distinguish between subjects and objects, facts and values before the democratic process has even taken place. Because his objective is to get to the root of the problem of dualist modern thinking, Latour is extremely critical of environmentalist agendas that are limited to the cause of preserving or conserving nature.[22] Political ecology is not and cannot be, he writes, a "défense de la nature." Instead, political ecology must get to the heart of our way of knowing and organizing the world. For Latour, this perspective holds much promise:

> We can benefit from the fundamental discovery of the ecology movement: no one knows what an environment can do; no one can define in advance what a human being is, detached from what makes him be. No power has

> been given by nature the right to decide on the relative importance and the respective hierarchy of the entities that compose, at any given moment, the common world. But what no one knows, anyone can experiment with, so long as he or she agrees to take the path of testing, while respecting the procedures that specifically avoid shortcuts.[23]

Optimistic about the potential of truly thinking ecologically, Latour calls for a constitution that is capable of dealing with the world in all its strange complexity. This new constitution works to recognize as many agents (human and non-human) as possible in social networks and refuses to categorize them as (passive) object or (active) subject.

In opposition to the long history of modernizing and modernization in the West, Latour invents the terms "ecologizing" and "ecologization" to describe the broad objective of learning to listen to the voices of an increasing number of agents.[24] We are living in a collective of more and more attachments, more and more assemblages. This obviously complicates immensely the possible political agenda of the Green party. But this is Latour's point. Political ecology must become a way of thinking embraced by all political parties; it must get to the epistemological heart of the matter. I will discuss later whether this is a utopian view or not. For now, it suffices to say that Latour is both outlining a future political ecology and describing what he sees as some of the current practices at summits on global warming.

For those who find Latour's ideas too theoretical, too abstract, it is important to point out that Latour is drawing in part on his work with the French Ministry of the Environment in the 1990s. His studies with the Department of Water revealed the extent to which water issues are a complex combination of institutions, values, spokespeople, and tools. According to Latour, this department should in reality have been called the Department of Fish, Air, Scientific Organizations, NGOs, etc.[25] He underlines the fact that the Ministry of Environment was poorly equipped to deal with such issues because of its reliance first and foremost on scientific facts.[26] Because of this hands-on consulting work, Latour arrived at the conclusion that a much wider understanding of environmental issues and concerns was needed.

At the same time, Latour warns against ecology's claim to some sort of global vision of the world: "Accepter que l'écologie porte sur la totalité des liens, ce serait donc perdre deux fois l'humanité de vue, d'abord au profit d'une unité supérieure aux hommes, ensuite au profit d'une technocratie de cerveaux supérieurs aux pauvres humains."[27]

A socio-eco-political controversy may include many actors, human and non-human, but its many threads do not offer a clear passage from the local to the global. There is no way of arriving at some coherent or holistic whole. This makes Latour's political ecology an open project that is impossible to reduce to a set of environmental policies or initiatives, and that offers powerful conceptual and practical tools for addressing issues that are never just environmental, but also social, economic, and political.[28]

Composing collectives in/and a common world

While critiquing a total, unifying vision of ecological interrelatedness, Latour is nevertheless very interested in the processes of unification, that is, the processes by which a collective is composed. This does not mean a "joining of man and his environment," nor a "reunifying of objects and subjects," nor an "adding together of man and nature."[29] "Man," "subject," "nature" all presume the existence of an entity that precedes the processes in which Latour is so interested. To avoid predetermined notions, Latour uses the term "collective" to mean "a set of procedures for exploring and gradually collecting [a] potential unification."[30] And he acknowledges that forming a collective is always experimental,[31] so that a collective could always have been or could be composed differently.[32]

The term "compose" is key to Latour's understanding of how human and non-human actors come together in the world. This may be due in part to Serres's influence on Latour's thinking, given that Serres elaborates the concept of composition in *The Five Senses* (see previous chapter). An important difference is that Serres articulates the practice of composing to describe the receptive, human body in a changing landscape, whereas Latour is interested in composition as a practice of the social and political body: "Il faut *composer* dans tous les sens du terme. Cela définit un programme politique, aussi bien qu'un programme scientifique ou esthétique."[33] Insisting on "composition" as an alternative to "construction" is also a way for Latour to differentiate his work from that of social constructivists who aim to critique and deconstruct rather than compose and create: "It thus draws attention away from the irrelevant difference between what is constructed and what is not constructed, toward the crucial difference between what is *well* or *badly* constructed, *well* or *badly* composed."[34]

In his "compositionist manifesto," Latour explains that the verb *to compose* refers to the idea of things being put together "while retaining their heterogeneity."[35] He likes the word's multiple meanings in various areas of artistic creation and expression, science, and politics, and concludes that "to compose with" is "to compromise, to care, to move slowly, with caution and precaution."[36]

Despite being keenly aware of the difficulties of bringing this ideal of composition to fruition, Latour does not adopt an apocalyptic view of the current global ecological crisis. Instead, he focusses on the possibility of a collective that fully acknowledges the processes of inclusion and exclusion, the role of diplomacy, the role of the pluriverse as exteriority. He avoids utopianism by describing the need for a *good* common world that is not a prescription for the *best* of all possible worlds. Moreover, he asserts that he is describing processes that are already taking place *in part*, but that have gone unnoticed because of the lack of theoretical terms and concepts.[37] This means that the *good* common world is an extension of the way we are already composing the world.[38]

Composing a common world does not mean, however, that there exists one single, "right" collective. The modern Constitution represents one type of collective and our contemporary condition another, yet there are many other possibilities.[39] In other words, Latour develops a notion of plural collectives that is similar to his notion of plural natures.[40] At the same time, each collective should be working toward a universal that it is "built from utterly heterogeneous parts that will never make a whole, but at best a fragile, revisable, and diverse composite material."[41] He insists that even if we can never compose with the entire world, this should be the aim of a political ecology. It is in this way that Latour's universal differs from Ferry's universalism. Latour is not constructing a universal ethics built on the notion of human rights or human nature or human qualities; he is instead questioning the supposed stability of such terms as "human," "rights," and "quality," arguing that they already exclude certain beings (often non-human) from the collective. He shifts emphasis to the act of making the universal, so that the processes of working toward a collective are what become the most important.[42] On an individual level, he speaks of becoming aware of the many, many ways in which we are attached to the non-human world locally, nationally, and transnationally.[43] On an institutional level, he outlines a new democracy in which diplomacy plays a key role in negotiating among collectives in a globalized world.

Democracy and diplomacy, or redistributing humanism

In *Ecological Politics and Democratic Theory*, Matthew Humphrey examines the ways in which environmentalism has been perceived as compatible or incompatible with democracy.[44] In the first section of the book, he focuses on radical environmentalist groups such as Earth First! that reject the tools of democracy for bringing about change, and in the second section, he explores some possible ways for bringing democracy and ecological politics together. Latour would no doubt agree with Humphrey that democracy and ecological politics are compatible, but he forges a very different path from the one outlined by Humphrey. He is not interested in reforming current Green parties or tweaking democracy here and there. For Latour, political ecology must start by undoing the separation of politics and the sciences to build a new constitution. It must promote a democracy that includes many more attachments, obligations and entities, that brings many more humans and non-humans into the *polis*. In short, Latour upholds the democratic process, but only once it has been rebuilt from the ground up.

Latour starts by outlining a procedural democracy that starts with the following questions, asking not just once, but over and over again: Who is speaking? Who is acting? Who is able?[45] He then describes the two-house structure of this democracy. What distinguishes his bicameralism from that of other democracies are the types of questions and powers attributed to each house. The upper house has the power to discuss and negotiate the question, "How many are we?" while the lower house has the power to order and categorize, asking, "Can we live together?" Since the acts of speaking, negotiating, discussing and consulting – in short, speech acts – are all a crucial part of this procedural democracy, the reader wonders how non-humans are able to participate. Latour responds by redefining speech in terms of propositions instead of statements. We are not sitting across from polar bears in the lower house and asking them to answer the question of how many we are. Instead, scientists, politicians, moralists, and economists represent non-human actors who have played a role in shaping the kinds of propositions that can be used to say something about them. Latour uses the expression "speech impedimenta" to convey this notion of being bound or attached to the non-human agent about which one is speaking. He rejects the idea of the scientific experts first knowing all the facts and bringing them to the politicians who then make a value decision based on these facts. For Latour, such a democracy is not a democracy at all, since it does not recognize the interactions and attachments of humans and non-humans in the composition of such facts, or the many other procedures that inform such values.[46]

Including non-humans in procedural democracy does not mean according them a set of predetermined rights.[47] Latour asks how we can know what rights are if we have not first looked at the processes that give rise to the collective. This means not accepting human rights as a predetermined category either, and instead examining the ways in which the human is "delegated, mediated, distributed, mandated, uttered."[48] Latour is not shirking the issue; he is instead thinking about morals that are not dictated by a moralism that claims to know in advance what constitutes a "right," a "human" or a "responsibility."[49] For Latour, the key lies in articulating a democracy that takes into account the greatest number of entities. A chimpanzee, a mountain range, a beetle, a fossil fuel, a mineral, a rainforest, a virus can all become part of the collective.[50] Even if he continues to use terms like "human" and "non-human," Latour does so with the understanding that these are contingent categories dependent on attachments that differ from one collective to another.

Latour is not, however, doing away with all things human. His thinking has been described as an "ahumanism" because it avoids the humanism/anti-humanism binary that plagues Luc Ferry's thinking about ecological politics.[51] Recognizing Latour's debt to Enlightenment philosophy, Whiteside speaks instead of a renewed humanism that characterizes French political ecology more generally: "Ecological humanists strive not so much to propagate a new environmental ethic – one which relocates the center out of which all value radiates – as to promote certain collective, pragmatic shifts in the nature-humanity nexus."[52] Latour himself reminds the reader that humanism has always included non-humans, even if we have been blind to their presence as agents in our collective.[53] Redistributing humanism becomes a matter of acknowledging and acting on these previous and currently forming attachments.[54] Instead of searching for the essence of human nature (as involving perfectibility, autonomy, free will, etc.), Latour's humanism reallocates agency across the board of beings and things, machines and organisms, humans and non-humans.

For discussion, negotiation, and consultation among different collectives, Latour looks to the diplomat, whose role is to learn the habits and properties of these collectives. He calls such people "ecologist diplomats," not because they endorse environmental ethics, but because they speak "the language of dwellings."[55] What Latour means is that the diplomat learns the language of the common house, or the *oikos*, by making articulate other collectives. Not surprisingly, Latour sees the ecologist diplomat as following in the steps of the anthropologist who works comparatively across plural natures and plural cultures.[56] These diplomats do not exist outside of a collective, but rather within as many different collectives as possible. Their experiences range across as many natures and cultures as possible so as to retain the complexities inherent in composing a common world.

For a more concrete understanding of the work of the ecologist diplomat, it is helpful to look briefly at Latour's own biography. Although he studied as a philosopher and wrote a doctoral thesis on the Gospels, Latour quickly became interested in anthropology during his time teaching in Abidjan on the Ivory Coast.[57] Living outside of the Western world, he became aware of the ravages of capitalism, colonialism, and industrialization, and began wondering if the tools of ethnography and anthropology could be used to analyse Western society as well. He started to develop a comparative anthropology that focussed on work being done in science labs in the USA and France.[58] He was then invited to take part in Shirley Strum's study of baboons in Kenya, and encountered a very different way of interacting with the non-human world than the one he had studied in science labs.[59] This led to the publication of various books on actor-network theory, which Latour has since defined as one mode of existence among others.[60] At the heart of Latour's thinking is an anthropology that takes the history of modernization, the philosophy of the modern world, as one world view among others and not as the way the world "really is" and against which all other world views must be measured.[61] Working across disciplines (science, philosophy, anthropology, primatology), as well as across cultures (France, USA, Ivory Coast), Latour has been forging the path of the ecologist diplomat for many years.

Latour's most recent project illustrates the limits and possibilities of the work of diplomacy. *Enquête sur les modes d'existence* (2012) opens channels of discussion with other collectives that have not followed the path of Western industrialization and that are coming to terms with modernization in the age of ecological crisis. While Latour is the author of this "inquiry," he makes his diplomatic project available to a much larger number of participants by way of the online digital version of the book, which can be commented on and discussed by users around the world.[62] This process of commenting, negotiating, and consulting is meant to model the processes of democracy outlined in *Politics of Nature*.

While any user can create a profile, comments do not appear automatically; they must first pass through a review process, and are accepted or rejected by a smaller group of selected editors and reviewers. Democracy does not mean that all voices are present, and so conflicts arise during the review process. As Latour explains, composing a common world includes dealing with difference, hiatus, and incompatibility: "Pour ma part, je vois plutôt dans l'entreprise diplomatique un aiguisement des conflits, du moins dans un premier temps."[63] He then adds: "Ce qui m'intéresse dans la figure du diplomate, c'est précisément qu'il n'y a pas d'autre arbitre qui permette de définir la paix."[64] Latour's own work clearly illustrates the diplomat's capacity both to stir the pot – for example his role in the science wars – and work toward peace – for example, his work in comparative anthropology.[65]

Coming back to Latour's comment that what counts is what comes after the ideas and the theorizing, I will conclude by asking what has come of Latour's political ecology. It is true that Latour has been involved in projects on the ground, working with different French government agencies and ministries and helping to run the French university known popularly as Sciences Po. In this sense, his ideas have had an impact on these real-life situations. Even if his bicameralism has not been officially instituted, it is fair to say that his thinking about democracy and diplomacy has influenced environmental policy in France. It is also true that Latour's theories and ideas have been taken up by scholars around the world, in disciplines ranging from architecture to law, literary studies to science studies, and of course, sociology and anthropology. In my case, I am drawing on Latour's ecological politics to construct an *écocritique* that is rooted in the political, but not bound to one single political agenda or platform. To read ecocritically, I adopt a critical stance toward the idea of nature, as Latour does, but also look more specifically at literature's participation in the collective, democracy, and diplomacy: how does the literary text integrate non-human voices? To what extent does it participate in democratic representation? How does it contribute to a common world in terms of diplomacy (negotiating among collectives) and creativity (imagining alternate worlds and futures)?

Whereas Guattari and Serres both underscore the role of stories and the arts more generally in ecological thinking, Latour has given much more attention to the sciences. In recent articles and conferences, he has, however, been using the term "geostory" as a way of engaging with the notion of the Anthropocene.[66] To tell the story of the earth as Gaia, we need, Latour asserts, to include as many different non-human agents and involve as many storytellers as possible: "novelists, generals, engineers, scientists, politicians, activists, and citizens – getting closer and closer within such a common trading zone."[67] He cites Richard Powers's best-selling novels and scientist Pieter Westbrook's *Life as a Geological Force* (1992) as examples of texts that "do justice to … *the agents* of geostory."[68] Latour's insistence on the need for a new geostory in the face of the Anthropocene echoes what many ecocritics have been saying about a new environmental imagination. Yet I would argue that literature and the arts more generally contain many stories about non-human agencies, but on micro- rather than macro-levels. So even if I admire Latour's optimism about the telling of a common geostory, I prefer to come back to individual texts and their thematic and formal specificities. As Guattari notes, literature can create new subjectivities at the level of the sentence or even the word in the form of existential refrains. As ecocritics, we need to lend an ear to such refrains before they are lost in the bellowing of a notion as grand as the Anthropocene.

Fiction

Portrait: Jean-Christophe Rufin

Despite being awarded the most prestigious French literary prize, the *Prix Goncourt*, for his novel *Rouge Brésil* (2001), Jean-Christophe Rufin has not yet attracted the attention of many literary scholars. He is regarded as a best-selling author with an important French readership, but he is not mentioned in literary overviews of French contemporary literature, such as Viart and Vercier's *La Littérature française au présent*.[69] He freely acknowledges his desire to write for the general public and make his novels as accessible as possible. One of the founders of *Médecins Sans Frontières* and now a French diplomat, Rufin is not the kind of novelist who participates regularly in the French literary scene. This may be one of the reasons why his novels have received less scholarly attention than they might otherwise have done. Another reason may be that Rufin does not show any particular affiliation with French literary traditions. While his novels range from historical fiction to future dystopias and ecological thrillers, his style is that of a storyteller, using dialogue, setting, and suspense to engage the reader. Moreover, it is clear that Rufin has a political message that he wants to convey in his novels. He does not hide the fact that he uses fiction to warn his readers of contemporary ideological trends. Both of the novels I will analyse in this chapter – *Globalia* (2004) and *Le Parfum d'Adam* (2007) – include a postface in which Rufin explains his authorial intentions as well as the political nature of his writing:

> Ce livre est né d'un désir d'unité. Jusqu'ici, j'avais tenu séparées deux formes de productions littéraires: d'une part des essais consacrés au tiers monde, aux relations nord-sud, aux questions humanitaires; de l'autre des romans dont l'action se déroulait ... dans l'Histoire lointaine. À mes yeux, les deux étaient liés et ce que je mettais en scène dans le passé n'était qu'un exemple particulier d'une question plus générale et toujours actuelle: la rencontre entre les civilisations et les malentendus, les espoirs, les violences qui en procèdent.[70]

For Rufin, writing fiction is an extension of his other political work, that of diplomacy and humanitarian aid. His novels offer an interesting counterpoint to Darrieussecq and Lafon's more literary-inspired texts, as they clearly challenge the notion of literature as separate from politics.

Rufin's novels fit generally into two main categories: 1) historical fiction – *L'Abyssin* (1997), *Sauver Ispahan* (1998), *Rouge Brésil* (2001), *Le Grand Coeur* (2012), and *Le Collier rouge* (2014); and 2) political fiction – *Les Causes perdues* (1999), *Globalia* (2004), *La Salamandre* (2005), *Le Parfum d'Adam* (2007), *Katiba* (2010), and *Check-point* (2015). Even if all of Rufin's novels raise political questions, the ones in the category of political fiction examine more specifically the problem of relations between developing and developed countries in a globalized world.[71] In *Globalia* and *Le Parfum d'Adam*, environmentalist policies, beliefs, and practices are an integral part of the way in which the North controls the global South. Environmentalism's "save nature" or "save the planet" modes of intervention take on unsettling proportions, becoming an instrument used to keep people in line (*Globalia*) or eliminate the less "desirable" (*Le Parfum d'Adam*). These two novels thus illustrate another important element of ecological politics in France, one that remains wary of environmentalism's slippery slope toward misanthropy, racism, and xenophobia.[72] At the same time, both novels open up the question of the collective, reasserting a humanist philosophy deeply concerned with social justice and the devastating effects of Western capitalism. In many ways, these two novels highlight the difficulties of putting into practice what Latour calls the common world. They emphasize the dangers of democracy and globalization, leaving the reader with a darker vision of our possible future than Latour's ecological politics.

If a French *écocritique* were only interested in environmentally oriented literature, it would have no time for Rufin's work. But this is not the ecocritical approach I have been developing in this book. Even novels that are highly critical of environmentalism can be examined in terms of how to form human and non-human collectives and whether democracy and diplomacy continue to work politically. Rufin's novels are clearly participating in such a discussion. At the same time, it would be a mistake to consider them only in terms of their themes. Both novels use storytelling for didactic purposes, and adopt well-known generic forms to do so. Moreover, as I have already explained, they openly work to undo the division between storytelling on the one hand and political issues on the other. A dystopian futurist novel, *Globalia* tells the story of Baïkal, a young protagonist who rejects the political propaganda produced by the state of Globalia, a not-so-disguised version of a United States of America that has taken over the world.[73] In the novel's postface, Rufin explains his intentions in writing the book. In line with Alexis de Tocqueville's much earlier warnings about democracy in America, Rufin highlights the dangerous effects of American globalization and imperialism. Although a secondary thread of the plot, environmental policies are one of the ways in which government in the novel exercises absolute control over citizens.

Described as an "eco-thriller," a spy novel, and an adventure novel, *Le Parfum d'Adam* develops as its main plot line the idea of environmentalism as a dangerous ideology. It brings readers back to a present-day reality with events taking place in the USA, France, Switzerland, Austria, Brazil, and South Africa.[74] International relations play a crucial role in the plot as two agents with a private American investigation firm work to stop an international radical ecological group whose goal is to reduce the human population through the spread of a deadly new strain of cholera in the favelas of Rio di Janeiro. As Rufin explains in the novel's postface, the novel is built on his reflections about what would happen if the debate about Earth's carrying capacity were combined with certain attitudes toward humanitarian aid that he has encountered in his work, illustrated by people casually suggesting that the West should not intervene in famines, wars, and epidemics in developing countries, since these are "natural" ways to reduce the human population. Weaving together a critique of radical ecology, globalization, and relations between the North and the Global South, Rufin's novel presents an important challenge to ecological politics.

The trouble with "nature"

In some ways, Rufin's critique of environmentalism in *Globalia* echoes Latour's rejection of the call to "preserve nature," not because we do not need a planet to live on, but because this call glosses over the real work of the politics of nature. In the global united states of Globalia, protecting nature is taken to an extreme. As official government discourse, environmental laws are part of Globalia's brainwashing efforts to convince citizens of the need for certain security measures. Globalians may enjoy nature, but only in designated areas – not because they might destroy nature beyond these boundaries, but because they must remain within Globalia's protective glass bubbles. In addition, Globalians are not allowed to eat meat, and are required to celebrate different species of animals on designated festival days. Environmentalism and animal rights become another way to control citizens and to keep them distracted from ever really questioning the rules of the "perfect" democracy in which they live.

Rufin's novel illustrates what happens when environmentalism and animal ethics are institutionalized without any real change in terms of ecological politics. Because of the totalitarian system depicted in the novel, fewer and fewer things are made public, and fewer and fewer entities are invited to compose a common world. Although Globalia is supposedly a democracy, no one votes, and the government is only a screen for a powerful oligarchy. Globalians have no idea that the economy relies on heavily polluting industries that lie beyond the glass bubbles, in the areas called the non-zones.[75] While they accept the law of vegetarianism, they care very little for animals. Rufin is obviously parodying strains of environmental and animal ethics as they have developed in the anglophone world. But he is also highlighting an important issue in the way environmental policies in the West affect developing countries, the case in point being when companies move their factories to poorer areas in the South to avoid stricter environmental laws in the North. So what may seem at first to be a facile parody of American environmentalism in Rufin's novel also raises deeper questions about policies that compound the problem of poor living conditions in other countries.[76]

Parodying environmentalism is not the only way in which Rufin raises the issue of how nature is made to matter. In Globalia, nature is "preserved" and carefully managed in parks, with bird music piped in and pine needles strewn on paths to create a sense of "pristine" nature. This raises the question of how "untouched" nature really is in national parks: are wilderness spaces not the result of years of careful scientific management? As for the nature outside of Globalia, it has seemingly been left to its own devices. But these areas, called the "non-zones," are in no way a form of prehuman wilderness. The novel first describes them as a place hostile to any life, an apocalyptic landscape after a catastrophic event: "Le sol boueux apparaissait comme un interminable tapis rouge. Par endroits des bouquets d'arbres secs formaient comme des bourres grises ... Les rochers, eux, étaient fendus net par le gel qui, la nuit, étendait son baume cruel sur les brûlures de la journée."[77] This initial representation of nature is countered by the descriptions of abandoned factories overgrown with vegetation. The main character, Baïkal, notes as he further explores the non-zones: "Toute rupture était abolie entre ces ruines et la nature, au point qu'elles paraissent en faire partie."[78] The nature/culture division is broken down in the non-zones, which teem with diverse forms of life growing in and around former vestiges of capitalist civilization. These landscapes stand in direct contrast to the "preserved" nature of Globalia's parks, which is meant to represent a controlled wilderness ideal.[79]

Experiencing the hardships of the physical world outside of the controlled climates of Globalia is part of Baïkal's voyage of self-discovery. By feeling hunger, cold, and physical discomfort, he begins to identify with the people living in the non-zones and reject Globalia's discourse of these places as dangerous, wild, and uncivilized.[80] According to Christian Moraru, the "evasionist message" that Rufin conveys in the novel is far from original.[81] And yet the portrayal of nature-culture in the non-zones complicates a too-easy reading of the novel as a finding-oneself-in-nature narrative. In fact, Baïkal never truly escapes Globalia's control, as he becomes a pawn in a much larger game that seeks to weed out revolutionaries in the non-zones. Unbeknownst to him, he carries out his role perfectly, with the rising group of dissenters whose leader he becomes – the *Déchus* – predictably quashed at the end of the novel.

Taking up another familiar trope in the dystopian narrative, Rufin explores literature's potential for stirring up dissent within the totalitarian system. The choice of revolutionary text, Henry David Thoreau's *Walden*, affords Rufin another opportunity to rework a well-known narrative of escaping into nature. In Globalia, very few people read, not because books are illegal, but because the market has been flooded with terrible books. The members of the Walden Association are the exception. Once they are accepted into the association, members have access to books of many different genres, largely from the pre-Globalian era, all stocked in warehouses. Not surprisingly, reading these books leads the members to question Globalia's official political discourse of freedom, as they discover what the founder's association calls "la réalité sous les rêves de Globalia" and "une vérité d'un autre ordre."[82] It is this group that manages to obtain the documents necessary for Baïkal and his group to attack Globalia. Even if Baïkal fails miserably in the end, the novel underlines the role of literary texts and the circulation of counter ideas in fostering revolutionary sentiment.

Central to the American environmental movement, Thoreau's *Walden* has led many readers to reject consumer capitalism and search for an alternative way of life. In Rufin's novel, the book is not read as a nonfiction account of living in nature, nor does it inspire its readers to live a simpler life in the woods. It is instead understood as a book of fiction, the description of a completely fantastical world, "un conte à la limite de l'absurde, plein de fraîcheur et de poésie."[83] In other words, it is not the "truth" value of the book but its imaginative power that plants seeds of revolt and resistance in the minds of its Globalian readers. Even though the Walden Association is eradicated at the end of the novel, *Walden* retains its power because it inspires readers to continue to search for happiness, not in wilderness or nature, but in a world of old technologies, new growth, and nature-cultures.[84] No longer about the need to reconnect with nature, Thoreau's *Walden* is instead about literature's power to inspire the imagination.

Rufin's novel critiques the American environmental imagination on various fronts. Idealized wilderness is portrayed as a cultural construction, literally in Globalia's carefully managed "parks" and symbolically in the reading of *Walden* as a purely imaginative place. However, this does not mean denying the reality of a physical world. The novel emphasizes the materiality of planet Earth, the difficult living conditions of a majority of the human population, and the dependence of humans on this planet. In addition, the novel raises the deeper question of social and economic inequalities in today's global world. Nature matters, not because it has inherent value or needs our protection but because its materiality is bound up in the well-being of human beings around the world.[85]

Le Parfum d'Adam takes these issues and critiques even farther, targeting radical ecology as a dangerous ideology. The novel opens with Juliette, a young disillusioned French woman, breaking into a lab in Poland, freeing the animals kept there, and spray-painting the walls with the words "Front Libération Animale" as a cover for stealing a small test tube that contains a new strain of cholera. Not knowing the contents of the tube, Juliette nevertheless realizes the importance of what she has taken. The story follows her as she forces herself into the inner circle of an American radical ecological group that goes by the name "the New Predators." Her initiation into the group illustrates the shift from a moderate or shallow environmentalism – participating in Greenpeace protests against the construction of nuclear power plants in France – to a much more radical ecological politics.[86]

As part of Juliette's initiation, she is brought to live in the Colorado desert, in a mountain cave with the leader of the New Predators, Ted Harrow, who introduces Juliette to the nature of the American West. Her first reaction is that of a typical European faced with the sublime: "Cette nature écrasante lui parut … ne laisser qu'une place infime, insignifiante au spectateur humain. Écrasée par cette beauté, il était clair pour Juliette que la nature vivait d'une existence propre et ne devait rien à l'homme sinon sa destruction."[87] The beauty of the wilderness and unmodified nature overwhelms Juliette. After a few weeks, she begins to assimilate Harrow's view of nature as good and beautiful only when it carries no traces of the human.[88] The love of untouched nature leads her to accept the group's radical belief that the number of humans on earth needs to be reduced.

In contemporary environmental debates about Earth's carrying capacity, the issue of overpopulation has often been the elephant in the room. Paul Ehrlich laid this issue out in his 1968 book *The Population Bomb*, and the Club of Rome brought increased international attention to the matter in its 1972 report *The Limits to Growth*. In Rufin's novel, overpopulation is presented as the key ecological issue. The New Predators develop a theory that nature's capacity for equilibrium has come undone because humanity's advances in the areas of medicine and technology have reduced mortality rates and increased life expectancy. But instead of being critical of such technology (which has given rise to energy-intensive lifestyles in the West), the New Predators target developing countries in which birth rates remain high. The group decides to re-establish "nature's" equilibrium by becoming "nature's" predators and radically reducing the human population in developing countries.

The novel's fictional account of a radical ecological group that combines a love of pristine nature with a deep hatred of the global South and the poor more generally may appear exaggerated or inflated. In the postface to *Le Parfum d'Adam*, Rufin explains that he wanted to make French readers more aware of the radical strains of deep ecology while also critiquing the opposition to humanitarian aid that he had encountered as a representative for *Médecins Sans Frontières*. He bases some of his narrative on real events related to ecoterrorist attempts in the USA and Britain.[89] The shadow of Luc Ferry looms large over Rufin's postface as he identifies anti-humanist elements in the writing of thinkers as diverse as Singer, Regan, Carson, Leopold, Naess, Sessions, Devall, Jonas, Ehrenfeld, and Lovelock. Associating all of these thinkers with deep ecology (*écologie radicale*), Rufin perpetuates Ferry's misreading of what are in reality very different eco-political positions. Even if Rufin claims that his book is "un livre d'aventure" and not "un cours magistral,"[90] he includes barely disguised references to groups like Earth First! (One Earth! in the novel) and Greenpeace (Greenworld in the novel), and to books by Edward Abbey and Aldo Leopold. Rufin's novel runs the risk of reducing environmentalism to a single ideological position and furthering Ferry's anti-Americanism.[91]

It is worth noting the other ways in which Rufin fictionalizes elements of Ferry's philosophy or, more generally, a French universal humanism. At the end of the novel, the young Frenchwoman, Juliette, comes to the realization that all humans have inherent worth and that she is part of the much larger family of humanity. After helping the American agents foil the New Predators's plan to release a new strain of cholera into the waterways of the Rio favelas, Juliette decides to remain in Rio and teach writing, math, and history to children in the favelas. Echoes of Ferry's humanism can be heard in the final passages of the novel when Juliette asserts that humanity can be saved "en renforçant sa part humaine."[92] The characteristics of this "human side" are alluded to in Juliette's description of her newfound capacity to identify and empathize with others. Similarly, Ferry asserts that altruism can emerge only when humans distance themselves from a state of nature associated with competition and survival.[93]

But Rufin's novel goes farther than Ferry's philosophy in terms of acknowledging the root causes of the destruction of nature. Whereas Ferry continues to assert that "man *can* and *must* modify nature,"[94] Juliette critiques the changes wrought by the arrival of European colonizers in South America. From her vantage point above the bustling port of Rio, she traces the history of ecological destruction and colonization and concludes that property rights are at the root of the problem. In short, she develops a social justice perspective that situates claims about nature in a larger human historical context.

(Im)possible global collectives

While the critique of environmentalism is an essential element of Rufin's literary project in both novels, so is his critique of the ways in which we have been composing a collective in the global world. In the postface to *Globalia,* he explains his goal of drawing attention to "la rencontre entre les civilisations et les malentendus, les espoirs, les violences qui en procèdent."[95] The noun *malentendus* means those who are misunderstood, but is also etymologically related to the idea of not being heard clearly or correctly. This brings to mind Latour's concept of the increasing number of voices that must be heard if we want to move toward a common world. In both *Globalia* and *Le Parfum,* the *malentendus* are those in the global South, the poor, the underfed, the sick, and the dying. As Rufin explains, massive development in the North has produced a large group of suffering others. And yet instead of taking responsibility for these injustices, developed countries have started blaming developing countries for the state of the planet: "De la lutte contre la pauvreté, nous sommes en train de passer à la guerre contre les pauvres."[96] In *Globalia,* these people are found in the non-zones, where they have no political voice and no hope of being spoken for. In *Le Parfum,* they are found in the very real favelas of Rio di Janeiro, where crime, poverty, and disease prevail. In short, Rufin portrays social and economic inequalities as endemic to our contemporary, globalized world.

In the protected, secure zones of Globalia, the political collective is pure illusion. The people are lost in a sea of publicity, overconsumption, and virtual reality. They are brainwashed to believe that they live in the best of all possible worlds, or more precisely, that they live in the only world possible. Within Globalia, democracy is a sham. Never seen assembled together, the thirty or so members of the founding states of Globalia control the economy, the "elected" government, the armed forces, and the media. The truth behind the system is that the founding members themselves no longer have any power either; capitalism takes on the proportions of a self-breeding, self-sustaining machine in this future dystopia. Globalians are free, but only to be in total agreement with each other. Whereas Latour outlines a carefully restructured democracy that represents a larger number of voices, Rufin's novel emphasizes democracy's excesses and offers no real alternative political system.

In terms of forming a *common world*, the novel highlights the dangers of such a world when it is driven by economic globalization. Here, the French distinction between *globalisation* – a "système-monde," a "fait social total" – and *mondialisation* – the extension of international relations among different nation states on a global scale – is useful. Globalia truly aims for *globalisation* in the sense of a single political and economic system covering the planet. World maps are illegal because they would give people a sense of the geographical limits of Globalia when they are supposed to believe that there is nothing outside of it. At the same time, the reader quickly learns that the image of Globalia as global is false. Its control lies largely in the Northern Hemisphere, with the non-zones being more dominant in the Southern Hemisphere. This emphasizes the novel's point about the power relations between North and South in today's neoliberal market economy.

Globalia arbitrarily attacks the poor, devastated regions in the non-zones and then provides them with "humanitarian" aid. This "force humanitaire globale" creates a relationship of dependency that keeps the non-zones in Globalia's powerful grip. The novel's critique of this relationship can be mapped onto debates about the types of "aid" provided by First World countries to developing countries. The novel clearly exposes the deep contradictions at the heart of these relations when the West provides, first, guns for conflicts in unstable zones, and then medical help to deal with the devastation. As a former *médecin sans frontières*, Rufin is keenly aware of such contradictions.[97]

Even though the non-zones are characterized by violence, crime, and death, they represent an interesting alternative for imagining a common world. Made up of an extremely heterogeneous group of people, the non-zones are home to great physical diversity: "Le plus frappant … était la grande variété des types physiques: on voyait toutes les pigmentations, du noir foncé au blanc très pâle, toutes les pilosités … et toutes les morphologies."[98] With no ruling authority, the people come together to form different tribes, but, interestingly, these are not based on appearance or religion or race. When Globalia was founded, it forced mass migrations, with people fleeing to the South from all directions, mixing together in surprising ways, often combining various languages and cultures.[99] Tribes were composed on the basis of community rather than similarity. These loose collectives grew out of "l'immense brassage historique des peuples des non-zones."[100] Even if these collectives remain under the control of Globalia, the novel portrays the non-zones as the only place where it is still possible to experience happiness – "l'arme la plus puissante dont disposent les êtres humains."[101]

Because of its critique of economic globalization and American imperialism, Rufin's novel *Globalia* has been called "la bible des altermondialistes."[102] In France, *altermondialisme* has been associated with events as diverse as José Bové's attack on McDonald's in the name of local farming practices to strikes against the *plan Juppé* to reform retirement packages.[103] But it also includes strong opposition to the First World's treatment of developing countries. In *Le Parfum d'Adam*, Rufin leaves no doubt as to the neoliberal, globalizing economic forces of which he is so critical. The funding for the radical ecological group in the novel comes from the head of a multinational company. Moreover, the novel includes references to the contradictions at the heart of world politics – for example, the American government's participation in South African apartheid politics in the 1980s. International relations are critiqued as a complex web of economic and political power with the rights of actual citizens being reduced or ignored in the process. The poor and the weak end up being the victims of international politics. Once again, democracy does not appear to hold any sway in the face of economic, capitalist globalization.

As I have noted, Rufin's decision to take up deep ecology reflects a certain attitude in France that associates radical environmental politics with anti-humanism. But Rufin is also deeply concerned with the social and economic inequalities of a globalized world. In the book's postface, Rufin asserts that *Le Parfum d'Adam* is more about these inequalities than it is about deep ecology: "Fidèle aux thèmes de tous mes autres romans, il était moins question pour moi de détailler la pensée écologique que de réfléchir sur le regard que nous portons sur le tiers-monde et la pauvreté."[104] Whether readers take away from the novel the critique of globalization or the critique of radical ecology depends in part upon what leaves the strongest impression on them: the postface, or the novel's ending.

The novel's ending clearly articulates the need to rethink relationships between the North and the South. Critical of capitalism's destruction of nature and human communities, Juliette questions how humans in modern society appropriate the land, setting up barriers and staking more and more claim to the earth. While capitalism may seem like a successful economic system in the West, it is dependent on that which it exploits, rejects, and contaminates, and so is also "une gigantesque machine à produire de la pauvreté, du malheur, de la destruction."[105] Juliette adds that she can no longer sit by while modern society ignores the destruction it has wreaked on developing countries. In the end, Rufin comes back to the question of humanitarian aid that takes the form not of food containers or monetary donations, but of education. This reveals the novel's larger didactic framework as it aims to teach the reader that humanism works for the equality of all human beings.

It is worth briefly pausing to examine the problems and potential of Rufin's use of fiction to convey a political message. As literary critics, how do we respond to what appears at times to be a heavy-handed didacticism? For some, Rufin's novels fall into the trap of "romans à thèse" despite the fact that he himself claims to avoid such a genre by "staging" his ideas rather than "transposing" them into fiction.[106] The "thesis novel" has not, however, always been viewed negatively; the phrase has been used to describe texts such as Voltaire's *Candide* and Camus's *L'Étranger*. According to Susan Suleiman, the "roman à these" has three main defining traits: "un système de valeurs in-ambigu, dualiste," "une règle d'action addressée au lecteur" and "un intertexte doctrinal."[107] In the case of Rufin's two novels, the non-fictional, philosophical intertext on which the story's system of values and rules of action are built is universal humanism. Rather than dismiss Rufin's attempts to bring his ideas into the world of fiction, why not give serious consideration to the "roman à thèse" as a form for mixing the genres of essay and the novel? My point is not to reduce literature to a political message, but to take seriously experiments in fiction – such as *autofiction*, climate change fiction, science fiction – that blur the line between literary production on the one hand and contemporary social debate on the other.

Renewing a (French) universal humanism

At the same time, Rufin's novels exceed the boundaries of the literary project that the author lays out for them in his postfaces. One of the differences between fiction and non-fiction writing is that the reader has the freedom to build a story world in a multitude of ways. Having focussed largely on plot lines and character development, I turn my attention to particular descriptive passages in Rufin's novels. Reading these in light of Latour's insistence on the political role of non-humans opens up a less author-directed interpretation of the novels. There are curious and compelling examples of the agency of objects that appear not front-and-centre in the novels, but rather on the margins of the human action and drama. They present an interesting contrast to Rufin's insistence on universal humanism as the only foundation for building a politics of human value and worth.

In the protected zones of Globalia, non-humans are constructed, regulated, and controlled in the same way as humans are. Environmental protection laws keep Globalians from harming animals or plants. According to Latour, this is, however, not how non-humans obtain a voice within a parliament of things. Giving animals or plants rights simply reduces them to pre-conceived identities, imposing on them an idea of the human. There is no room for object agency in the totalitarian state of Globalia. It is in the non-zones that a different relationship to organic and inorganic life starts to take shape. Old industrial machinery, for example, is given a second life, detached from its initial use-value, with car doors being used as walls and windows and old trucks being converted into henhouses.[108]

No longer reduced to one single function, these "ancient creatures of industry"[109] play a key role in forming the collectives in the non-zones. Intertwined with the vitality of the physical world, their composition and decomposition are part of the social fabric; their enduring nature assures them a place not as technology, but as matter that can be used in a multitude of ways. The natural, vegetal, and industrial all form part of the world as humans know it in the non-zones. In this world, many of the binary oppositions of the modern Constitution break down: nature and culture, object and subject, history and story. Even if the novel does not develop these ideas, it makes room for an ecological politics that requires as much critical attention as the negative portrayal of environmentalism.

In *Le Parfum*, it is the cholera virus and the role of science that echo some of the ideas of Latour's political ecology. The opening scene describes the science lab as "un mélange d'instruments compliqués et d'intimités humaines."[110] The high-tech lab equipment and the framed family photos sit side-by-side, reminding the reader of science's embeddedness in the social fabric. This is further emphasized when Paul, one of the private investigators, arrives at the *Institut Pasteur* in Paris, where scientists conduct research on various viruses. The institute keeps strains of the virus, conserving "la mémoire du choléra" even if this no longer a "trendy" or well-funded branch of genetics and biology.[111] For Serres, the scientific practice of keeping strains of deadly virus alive is an example of the natural contract: humans decide to enter into an agreement with the natural world so as to coexist harmoniously.[112] Latour would say that such viruses have become part of the democratic processes in a common world. They illustrate the multiple attachments and responsibilities that bind our future to that of the physical world.

But the novel also emphasizes the social inequalities that scientific advancements end up deepening. The narrator reminds the reader that cholera is also "la face cachée de l'aventure humaine."[113] While developed countries have the infrastructure needed to stop the spread of the virus, many developing regions do not. Cholera reminds us of the "victims" who have been sacrificed on the road to progress: "Le choléra, c'est la conscience de nos échecs, le témoin de nos faiblesses, le symbole de la terre à laquelle nous ne cessons d'appartenir, même quand notre esprit croit pouvoir s'envoler vers le ciel des idées, du progrès, de l'immortalité."[114] As the West develops vaccines and negotiates with the non-human world, thousands of humans have died, excluded from the collective taking shape on the other side of the world.[115]

Even if the novels include descriptions of negotiations between humans and the non-human world in a dystopic future and a contemporary present, they are firmly rooted in the belief that humans are inherently different from the rest of the living world. Revisiting the question of whether an ecological politics is possible, Rufin responds:

> Le discours écologiste est défendable à condition de le contrebalancer par l'humanisme. Non, l'homme n'est pas comparable aux animaux. L'espèce humaine a quelque chose que les autres n'ont pas. Elle doit donc être l'objet d'un intérêt spécifique. Si on ne donne pas une part sacrée à l'être humain, tout devient possible et légitime.[116]

The thesis of human exceptionalism is clearly upheld in both novels in the opposition between a "base" animal nature and a human capacity to experience love, happiness, and freedom. Rufin's humanism is in this sense doubly traditional: in addition to the belief in a universal humanity, it holds fast to a Cartesian dualism that places humans over animals, reason over emotion, and freedom over instinct.

In *Globalia*, humans have lost their freedom – whether this be in the protected zones, where people have given up their capacity to think for themselves, their desires dictated by consumer capitalism, or in the non-zones, where human activities are reduced to trying to meet basic needs like food and water. No matter the setting, violence simmers just below the surface because of this loss of freedom. In the secured zones, consumers turn against themselves, unable to find happiness even while buying more and more products.[117] In the non-zones, the tribes pillage, raid, and plunder, with leaders rising to the top by way of greed and violence. The traits of human empathy and happiness are barely visible in either the secured zones or the non-zones. And yet it is in the hostile non-zone territory that Baïkal discovers freedom from the Globalian totalitarian state and an escape from the vicious cycle of consumer capitalism. This creates a problematic narrative of the dissatisfied Globalian (in other words, rich Northerner) finding happiness in the non-zones (in other words, the South).[118] At the end of the novel, Baïkal's joyful assertion to his girlfriend, Kate, that they are "plus libres que libres" reinforces the message about human freedom, love, and happiness as the ultimate goals of a truly human life available only to the "exiled" Globalians.[119]

Le Parfum d'Adam takes up the human/animal binary opposition even more explicitly. The New Predators's view of humans as animals is presented as extremely dangerous because it leads them to dismiss certain humans as largely expendable. To correct such a view, Paul explains that humans are inherently different from other animals and that it is this human side that will save humanity. It is not surprising, then, that the novel represents animality negatively. Running through the brush, trying to escape her pursuers, the second American agent, Kerry, is driven by "l'instinct de survie," her mind emptied of "tout souvenir, toute humanité."[120] This primal state of fear is described as "un sursaut du corps sur l'esprit."[121] For Rufin and Ferry, humans only become human by tearing themselves away from this animal state. According to Ferry, it is this "tearing away" that makes universalism possible: "It is because he is capable of taking his distances not only from the cycle of his biological life but also from his particular language, nation, and culture that man can enter into communication with others. His capacity for universality is a direct function of this distancing."[122] At the heart of Ferry's humanism is a categorical, dualist logic: either humans are not part of nature and are capable of arts, culture, intelligence, beauty, etc., or they remain part of nature and are reduced to animal survival.[123]

For Latour, this is an example of the logic of the modern Constitution that reduces many possible different positions with and in the world to a set of binary relationships. In opposition to "either/or" logic, Latour illustrates a "both/and" thinking, according to which we are becoming more and more attached to the world as our habitats extend around the globe. Latour is not doing away with the human ideals of empathy, love, and happiness, but instead asking what attachments are part of these ideals, who is involved, who decides for or against whom, and on what basis inclusion and exclusion are made. This means we need to take into account more and more entities and avoid categorizing pre-emptively the meaning of terms like "human" and "animal." While Rufin returns to a traditional universal humanism, Latour calls for a redistributed humanism that takes none of its concepts, such as empathy, solidarity, justice, or rights, for granted.[124]

While claiming to be universal, Rufin's humanism takes up a specific French intellectual tradition that dates at least as far back as Rousseau's notion of perfectibility through to Ferry's attack on animal rights and environmentalism. The same tension can be found in Ferry's book as in Rufin's novels between universal principles and a particular socio-historical context. At the end of *Le Parfum*, Juliette becomes the spokesperson for a universal humanity. After spending a night in the Rio favelas, she discovers that even the harshest conditions cannot destroy a sense of human solidarity: "Dans l'humidité puante de cette cabane … Juliette se sentait appartenir à une famille, celle-ci et au-delà d'elle, la famille humaine."[125] The fact that Juliette is French does not escape the reader's attention. Moreover, the narrative of a white French woman coming to a realization about the inherent worth of all humans among the poorest of the poor in the Rio favelas raises the same questions as Baïkal's escape to the non-zones in Globalia. On the one hand, the novels can be read as a critique of consumer capitalism and Western culture and a return to universal values of human love and freedom. On the other, they narrate a one-sided story of discovery in which the Other remains a victim of the forces of global capitalism. The reader is left wondering how universal humanism is viewed by those not representing Western perspectives in the novels. Even if Rufin's aim is to use fiction to reveal the increasing social inequalities caused by neoliberal globalization, he paints a problematic picture of the North speaking for the global South. In the end, his novels reveal the dangers of not making politics truly ecological in Latour's sense of asking who is speaking for whom, in what capacity, and at what expense of exclusion.

Conclusion: Capitalism's ill affects/effects

Ecological politics, then, have a doubly difficult role: first, they need to pay more attention to non-humans; second, they need to pay more attention to humans excluded from the common world. Rather than see these two roles in opposition – either we focus more on humans, or we focus more on non-humans – it is possible to imagine a common world in which both are present to a greater extent than they are today. This will mean more intense discussion and disputes, more negotiation and disagreements, but it will also lead to a more common world. Even if it may seem idealist or utopian, I prefer Latour's call for a political ecology to Rufin's return to a universal humanism. Rather than once again argue for human solidarity and human freedom, Latour opens the door to a world view that asks what we mean when we speak of solidarity (which objects, beings, non-humans, and humans?) and freedom (what other forms of agency are available to humans and non-humans?). His political ecology does not see poverty as endemic, but instead as one effect among others of the practices of our current economic system that could be different. Democratic processes are necessary to composing a common world, but capitalism is not.

At a lecture given at the Royal Academy in Copenhagen, Latour tackled the subject of capitalism, critiquing not its effects, but rather its affects: a sense of helplessness on the part of victims, an attitude of total triumph on the part of the rich, and finally, a sense of fate, as if no other economic system existed aside from capitalism's free-market "laws."[126] Latour responded that we have constructed economy as an automated system over which we have no control, when we should be concentrating on ecology as a system with which we are constantly negotiating. Latour's point is that by coming back to ecological issues, we can counter capitalism's hold over our imagination. He does not mean a return to nature, but a turn to the mixed nature-culture to which we are bound by so many attachments. By focussing more closely on the processes by which we compose a common world, we can begin to see capitalism for what it is, not a monolithic whole, but one economic system among others. For Latour, then, ecological politics are a way to counter the affects of capitalism. By giving voice to a common world, they reveal a path toward deeper systemic change than simply "greening" current "economic" practices.

This brings me to the role of literature in imagining future worlds. In *Globalia*, Rufin describes a future dystopia that emphasizes capitalism's hold on all things, including politics. As he states in the novel's postface: "S'agissant du futur, un roman peut tout au plus contribuer à ce que le lecteur conserve une defiance légitime."[127] Although it clearly underscores the dangerous tendencies of global, neoliberal capitalism already present in today's society, the novel does not offer any viable alternatives. In the non-zones, a system of bartering and exchange takes place, but this system ends up reproducing the same social inequalities as the all-consuming capitalism in the secured zones. In *Le Parfum*, Rufin proposes a society similar to our own, in which global surveillance systems are necessary to control (eco)terrorist groups like the New Predators. The novel proposes education as one possible path for reducing social inequality, but does not offer any ideas for an alternative economic system. While both novels warn the reader of the excesses of capitalism and globalization, they also underline the immense difficulty of imagining any other reality.

Ecological politics are not just a way of theorizing relationships between humans and nonhumans, of bringing more voices into the *polis*, of instituting a new parliament of things. They are also a way of imagining a way out of capitalism. In Rufin's novels, capitalism acts as a convenient antagonist, but the reader is left to imagine alternative economic systems. Interestingly, Latour himself recognizes the need for more stories that can help us move from economics to ecology.[128] In light of the Anthropocene, he speaks of a geostory, not because it tells of a return to the earth, but because it provides us with the images, metaphors, and vocabulary necessary to describe an agential world that had been reduced to inanimate matter (at least in the Western world, where the main world view is rooted in the modern Constitution). I have highlighted some of the passages in Rufin's novels in which language reveals the animacy of non-humans and the agency of things. These examples do not constitute a geostory, but they can be used to construct an ecological politics that is both theoretical and imaginative. Moreover, they illustrate a way of reading against the grain of the text and opening the story up to perspectives other than those endorsed by the author. Even though Rufin clearly has a message about universal humanism to convey to his readers, the literary text cannot be reduced to the author's intentions. The novels create room for ecological readings that identify other ways of viewing and experiencing the world, that bring an awareness of political issues to the text rather than reducing the text to a single political message.

4 Ecological Ends: Schaeffer and Houellebecq

Fin de parcours possible

À quoi bon s'agiter? J'aurai vécu quand même,
Et j'aurai observé les nuages et les gens
J'ai peu participé, j'ai tout connu quand même
Surtout l'après-midi, il y a eu des moments.
La configuration des meubles de jardin
Je l'ai très bien connue, à défaut d'innocence ;
La grande distribution et les parcours urbains,
Et l'immobile ennui des séjours de vacances.
J'aurai vécu ici, en cette fin de siècle,
Et mon parcours n'a pas toujours été pénible
(Le soleil sur la peau et les brûlures de l'être) ;
Je veux me reposer dans les herbes impassibles.
Comme elles je suis vieux et très contemporain,
Le printemps me remplit d'insectes et d'illusions
J'aurai vécu comme elles, torturé et serein,
Les dernières années de la civilisation.

– Michel Houellebecq, *Non réconcilié. Anthologie personnelle 1991–2013*, 53[1]

Although Michel Houellebecq is less well known for his poetry than for his novels, I begin this chapter with one of his poems because it captures so well the *fin-de-siècle* malaise and weariness that runs through his work. It also describes an ending that contrasts with the kind of apocalyptic imagination often associated with the environmental crisis. Instead of an explosion of violence, death, and destruction, Houellebecq's poem describes a slow fading away of curiously juxtaposed moments: lazy afternoons and garden furniture with urban commutes and boring holidays, sun-warmed skin and grass with a sense of burning and torment. While it is true that apocalyptic rhetoric has been used to mobilize the public around environmental issues,[2] it has also been associated with failed predictions and attempts at mobilization. Ecocritics are divided on the usefulness of the apocalypse as a rhetorical tool for environmental discourse. Buell contends that the apocalypse remains "the most powerful master metaphor" of the environmental imagination, whereas Garrard questions its political efficacy.[3] Given the overabundance of apocalyptic imagery and tropes in contemporary popular culture, it is worth considering less-sensational ecological endings that are plural, involve multiple temporalities, and remain circumscribed in time and place.

In French intellectual circles, there has been a particularly strong reaction against environmental apocalypticism. In his book *Le Fanatisme de l'Apocalypse* (2011), Pascal Bruckner associates the environmental movement's narrative of a civilization gone wrong with previous religious accounts of the Fall. He questions the state's increasing attempts to institutionalize environmental policies and control individual citizens' behaviour. Like Ferry, he does not completely reject the reality of a less-livable habitat, but he calls for a democratic ecology, one that is for reason and against raging, for growth and against restrictions.[4] Even if Bruckner does not go so far as Ferry in his critique of environmental philosophy, he questions the motives of discourses that predict the end of the human species and/or call for an end to consumer capitalism. In his epilogue, Bruckner asserts his faith in human innovation (particularly science and technology), ending on a strong humanist note: "L'humanité ne s'émancipera que par le haut."[5] It is easy to dismiss Bruckner's defence of the status quo; he nevertheless identifies the problematic tone of environmental narratives – one of guilt, despair, joylessness, pessimism – and, ultimately, the construction of a deeply divisive politics – us versus them, the good versus the bad.

In *Les Écofictions. Mythologies de la fin du monde* (2012), Christian Chelebourg examines over two hundred contemporary novels and films that portray ecological disasters as part of end-of-the-world scenarios. For Chelebourg, such fictions need to be critiqued because of the important influence they have on the ways in which environmental issues are discussed and imagined more broadly today. He argues that the role of literary studies is to reveal "le sens des imaginaires dont la circulation façonne les mentalités."[6] In his discussion of a wide variety of eco-disaster scenarios (epidemics, pollution, tsunamis, etc.), Chelebourg provides a useful model for analysing the symbols, tropes, and narrative templates of the apocalyptic imagination. He nevertheless avoids taking a position on ecological issues and offers no explanation for the overabundance of eco-fictions.[7] He thus introduces ecocritical subjects to a French readership without engaging in their politics.[8]

In this chapter, I propose to adopt a more explicitly political approach to ask how literary theory and speculative fiction can help us move beyond anthropocentrism without appealing to the apocalyptic imagination. I have chosen to pair Jean-Marie Schaeffer's theoretical, literary, and philosophical work with Michel Houellebecq's fictional worlds because they both articulate an ecological end to humans as exceptional beings having some distinct trait that separates them from the rest of the living world. "Ecological end" means not an end to ecology or an end to nature or an end to the planet, but rather an end to nature/culture dualism and a rethinking of humans as physical creatures, as biological organisms. Both Schaeffer and Houellebecq appeal to the sciences – cognitive science and biology respectively – to develop a notion of the human as matter. They thus counter the position of French thinkers like Ferry for whom philosophy, art, culture, and literature are pure endeavours of the mind, modes of transcending needs of the body to attain higher knowledge about universal humanity. By opening up literary studies (Schaeffer) and literature (Houellebecq) to the sciences, they put an end to long-standing disciplinary divisions.

One of the risks of moving toward a more material understanding of the human is biological reductionism. While Schaeffer carefully articulates a non-dualistic view of the nature/culture continuum, Houellebecq's novels illustrate a problematic determinism according to which humans and animals are bound – as biological and evolutionary creatures – to the "laws of nature." Examining more closely the stakes of ecological ends – the stakes of putting an end to humanism founded on notions of mind, spirit, and reason – will require revisiting the concept of nature but also of the animal. As seen in the previous chapter, humanism constructs humanity against an "animal" nature defined in terms of survival and reproduction. What, then, does the animal become when the human/animal binary opposition has been rejected, when a posthumanist perspective begins to emerge?

It is true that ecocriticism has had difficulty integrating the "animal question" or Animal Studies more broadly because its focus has been on environmental issues. The two fields have developed largely independently, with very few crossovers, a division that reproduces the much older schism between animal rights/ethics and environmentalism. (One need only think of the practices of culling in order to control animal populations for the health of an ecosystem.) Within French literary studies, however, the "animal question" has given rise to a more sustained critical approach than ecocriticism. Moreover, there has not been the same division between environmental questions and animal ethics.[9] With a solid philosophical foundation in the work of thinkers such as Jacques Derrida, Élisabeth de Fontenay, and Dominique Lestel, French Animal Studies offer a way of analysing texts from a decentred human perspective.[10] The field thus opens the door for French *écocritique* to read texts politically. This does not mean prioritizing animal concerns over environmental concerns, but rather working to deconstruct notions of the animal and the environment (or nature).

Posthumanism offers one such bridge for bringing together ecocriticism and animal studies. Thus far, the latter has been more closely aligned with posthumanist thinking than the former.[11] According to Buell, however, "ecocritics ... have a stake in generating the models for so-called posthumanist identity."[12] Given the amount of literature available on posthumanism (especially in the anglophone world), I offer only a rapid sketch of its main characteristics. First, it is necessary to differentiate between transhumanism and posthumanism. A continuation of the humanist project, transhumanism places its faith in science and technology to create a new and improved version of humans in the future (Ray Kurzweil is often cited as a strong supporter of this view). Posthumanism, on the other hand, is extremely critical of the discourse of progress and the dualist thinking that underlies the (trans)humanist project. Second, it is necessary to differentiate between two branches within posthumanism: 1) one focuses on the human/machine binary opposition as a way of thinking about our relationship to technology (Katherine Hayles's *How We Became Posthuman* [1999] is often cited in this regard); and 2) the other undoes the human/animal binary opposition in order to rethink our ethical responsibility toward animals (see, for example, Cary Wolfe's *What is Posthumanism?* [2009]).[13] Whereas posthumanism and transhumanism stand in stark opposition to each other, the two branches of posthumanism are rooted in a similar philosophical and ethical stance.

In this chapter, I will reference these varying perspectives in order to compare and contrast the ways in which Schaeffer and Houellebecq attempt to put an end to human exceptionalism. Schaeffer most clearly adopts a posthumanist stance, undoing the animal/human binary opposition by defining humans as creatures within the living world. While his thinking about ecological ends does not include the creation of imaginary future worlds, Schaeffer is nonetheless calling for a deep paradigm shift that acts as a useful point of comparison to Houellebecq's novels. Imagining humans as animals is at the heart of Houellebecq's project in *The Elementary Particles* and *The Possibility of an Island* (and, I would add, at the heart of his literary project overall). While both novels portray animality reductively (i.e., humans' so-called "animal" characteristics), the second novel revisits the question of what it means to be human in the context of experiencing the natural and living world. In this way, Schaeffer and Houellebecq explore the possibilities and problems not only of the posthuman condition but also of posthumanist attempts to articulate this condition.

Theory

Portrait: Jean-Marie Schaeffer

Unlike Félix Guattari, Bruno Latour, and Michel Serres, Jean-Marie Schaeffer is not well-known outside of French academic and intellectual circles. A philosopher and a literary critic, his work touches on a variety of subjects related to art, aesthetics, and theories of reception. His reflections go beyond, however, the boundaries of the humanities to embrace issues in the social sciences and the sciences more generally (Schaeffer describes his research as an example of *SHS*, that is *sciences humaines et sociales*). According to Schaeffer, the sciences are mapping out understandings of the human as part of larger biological and ecological systems that literary critics and philosophers need to take into account in their analysis of cultural texts. He asserts that literary studies need to work from a much more "integrationist" concept of the human – in other words, from a concept of the human as it is being outlined in ethology, anthropology, evolutionary psychology, and cognitive science.

In her book *A Biocultural Approach to Literary Theory and Interpretation* (2012), Nancy Easterlin defines the main objectives of research that seeks to close the gaps between the human, social, and natural sciences. As Easterlin explains, a biocultural approach does not mean adopting a "scientific methodology" or a "specified set of analytic concepts" or "a common groundwork for explanation."[14] According to Easterlin, each literary text must be considered individually in order to determine what discoveries about humans from the social and natural sciences might be most useful for analysing that particular text. In her overview of biocultural approaches, Easterlin includes ecocriticism, but she points out that ecocriticism has not gone far enough in (re)thinking the human.[15] While ecocritical studies have been attentive to findings in the biological and ecological sciences,[16] they have remained silent with respect to work being done in the cognitive sciences, evolutionary psychology, and comparative anthropology. For Easterlin, these sciences bring the human back into focus from a much less anthropocentric perspective, and so should be essential to literary studies more generally.

In many respects, Schaeffer's work represents a biocultural approach. Like Easterlin, Schaeffer considers work being done in the hard sciences, but also in the area of the philosophy of language and the mind, as a way of asserting the cognitive, social, and aesthetic value of literature. But where Easterlin emphasizes the analysis of individual texts, Schaeffer advocates more generally for a theory of fiction that takes into account recent scientific findings. Without subscribing to Schaeffer's general theory of literature, I will follow both Schaeffer and Easterlin's lead in situating the human condition within the larger context of a changing world of information, knowledge, and science. This does not mean once again placing human needs over and above those of the physical world; it means taking into account and becoming responsible for more and more connections between humans and non-humans.

I will examine three of Schaeffer's texts – *Pourquoi la fiction?* (1999), *La Fin de l'exception humaine* (2007), and *Petite écologie des études littéraires* (2011) – that are most relevant to the subject of redefining the human. These texts lay the foundation for questions about the human species and the role of storytelling that I will come back to in my analysis of Houellebecq. In his first book, *Pourquoi la fiction?*, Schaeffer extends the theory of fiction to new forms of storytelling such as video games, avatars, and virtual reality more generally. In the second book, *La Fin de l'exception humaine*, he adopts a more philosophical perspective to critique Cartesian dualism and the thesis of human exceptionalism. In the third book, *Petite écologie des etudes littéraires*, Schaeffer revisits the question of the "crisis" of literary studies. He rejects the lament that the humanities is a dying discipline and asserts the value of literary studies in understanding our present human condition. The three texts reveal an interesting and useful tension in Schaeffer's thinking about what it means to be human: on the one hand, Schaeffer looks to redefine the human as part of the living world; on the other, he continues to uphold the idea of human difference in terms of our capacity to imagine alternative realities and create new story worlds.

From literature to fiction

Appearing in English translation in 2010, Schaeffer's *Why Fiction*? addresses the misconception that literature is coming to an end because of the rising popularity of television, films, and video games.[17] Using the term "fiction" to refer more generally to mimetic activities and arts, Schaeffer argues that fiction has not fundamentally changed during the digital revolution; it continues to play a "central role in human culture."[18] Critiquing the notion of "great literature" as "better" than video games or films, Schaeffer asks instead how all of these forms of fiction demonstrate the "doing-as-if" capacity in humans. His aim is to develop a general theory of fiction that is built on an evolutionary and psychological understanding of the capacity to imitate and imagine.

To build this argument, Schaeffer comes back to early theories of mimesis as found in Plato and Aristotle. For Schaeffer, the contemporary debate between the value of written fiction versus virtual reality simply echoes a much earlier debate about "making" and "making as if" found in Plato's works. In response to Plato's critique of "making as if," Schaeffer points to the fact that such a capacity is essential to children's psychological development. The capacity to make up stories and play make-believe is part of what Schaeffer calls "the psychologically and culturally stable state of fiction."[19] To understand the multiple (and often contradictory) meanings of the word *mimesis*, Schaeffer turns away from literary theory and toward the study of mimetic activities in other disciplines such as ethology, psychology, and artificial intelligence. Schaeffer looks at the "psychic and cognitive" acts of mimesis that include feint, resemblance, imitation, representation, and simulation. He underlines the fact that mimetic representation is a means of knowing the world.[20] He then takes up the question of whether these conclusions about learning through imitation and cognitive simulation can be applied to fictional representations.[21] To determine whether immersion in an imaginary world can have a cognitive function, he asks more directly: What is fiction?[22]

To answer this question, Schaeffer considers the case of a book that many read as a non-fictional biography of a historical person when in fact the person in question never existed – Wolfgang Hildesheimer's

Marbot (1981).[23] This example of a text read as fact rather than fiction is a way for Schaeffer to outline the necessary conditions of fiction's success as fiction. One of these conditions is the shared ludic feint, meaning the author, the reader, the paratext, and the social context all contribute to the successful creation of an imaginary world. Schaeffer calls this the "phylogenesis of fiction" or the socially shared conditions of fiction.[24] He then goes on to discuss the "ontogenesis of fiction," that is, the more general psychological and cognitive conditions of fiction that first emerge in children's make-believe games ("imaginative self-stimulation").[25] Immersion in an imaginary world is another necessary condition of fiction's success; this does not imply, explains Schaeffer, "a cut between the world of mimetic stimuli and the repertory of mental representations that are issued by our past interactions with actual reality."[26] On the contrary, the two are bound together in what Schaeffer calls a "feedback loop" in which fiction can give rise to real emotions and affects.[27] Finally, Schaeffer points out that it is less useful to compare fiction to factual reality than it is to understand how fiction "operates *in* reality, that is, in our lives."[28]

While this discussion of Schaeffer's theory of fiction may at first appear to lead away from ecocriticism, it speaks directly to an issue at the heart of literary representation as outlined by Buell in *The Environmental Imagination*. For Buell, mimesis means closing the gap between word and world in order to assert the value of non-fiction environmental literature. Schaeffer's theory of fiction offers a very different way for thinking about this relationship because it places fiction in a material world from the start: as a cognitive operator that is part of a human being's mental capacities. Moreover, Schaeffer's insistence on the need for fictional representations nicely counters Buell's emphasis on non-fiction nature writing (or what Schaeffer would consider factual representations and not fictional ones). In the end, Schaeffer acknowledges more broadly the primary function of the imagination as "the faculty of mental modelling" in our development as human beings and so offers an alternative framework for rethinking literature in and of the physical world.

Schaeffer's emphasis on the capacity of the human imagination and the centrality of fiction in our interactions with the real world does, however, raise some questions from a posthumanist perspective. Schaeffer is outlining a uniquely human capacity in his theory of fiction: "Fictional competence seems not to be a cultural convention but a universal psychological given, a basic modality of human intentionality."[29]

Even if fictional forms – plays, films, installations, paintings, cartoons, photography – vary widely and imply many different "vectors and postures of immersion,"[30] they are rooted in common psychological capacities that are shared by all humans.[31] Even if Schaeffer starts moving toward a less human-centred understanding of literature, he does not fully dismiss the notion of humans as inherently different from other living beings. This illustrates to some extent the limits of his ecological ends, at least in this text.

The movement both beyond and within humanism is characteristic of another biocultural approach that began to emerge in the anglophone world in the 1990s. It is worth briefly outlining this approach because of its similarities and differences with Schaeffer's theory of fiction. First introduced by Joseph Carroll, literary Darwinism integrates findings from evolutionary psychology in order to define the function of literature and storytelling in humans. Literary Darwinists examine literary texts in terms of the ways in which they represent human nature. As Joseph Carroll asserts, "Any effort to build a new framework for literary study would have to start there, with an evolved and adapted human nature, a human body and brain, giving due heed to biologically grounded motives, passions, and forms of cognition."[32] This echoes in part Schaeffer's call to better understand human cognition and capacity for imagination from a scientific perspective.

The similarities between literary Darwinism and Schaeffer's theory of fiction end here, however. Even though Schaeffer speaks of a distinctly human capacity for creating imaginary worlds, he notes that both animals and humans are capable of imitation, feint, and game playing. Literary Darwinism, on the other hand, emphasizes a moment of rupture when human beings broke from their animal nature because they were capable of storytelling.[33] This may be because literary Darwinists root their understanding of literature and storytelling in evolutionary theory and, more broadly, in a narrative of human progress. Even if Schaeffer does cite evolutionary psychology, he draws more on knowledge about human development and on findings in animal ethology that illustrate the narrowing gap between humans and animals.

I will come back to both literary Darwinism and Schaeffer's theory of fiction in my discussion of Houellebecq's novels, but for now, it is worth noting that both seek to redefine the human in terms of a capacity to create imaginary worlds and tell stories. Schaeffer in particular begins the move beyond the humanist project that posited culture as the "best that has been said and thought in the world," to quote Matthew

Arnold's well-known phrase. Fiction becomes instead the capacity of a biological being, part of the fabric of a material world. What Schaeffer's theory of fiction does not, however, imagine are possible future worlds: What will fiction look like if we evolve into something else, less biological and more artificial? Will we continue to tell stories? What conditions might make storytelling obsolete or, on the contrary, even more necessary to survival? Even if Schaeffer reflects on the changing forms of fiction, especially in terms of video games and virtual reality, it is in Houellebecq's novels that some of these hypothetical situations are given fictional form. Schaeffer looks instead more carefully at the issue of human exceptionalism, taking a decisive step away from the humanist project and toward posthumanism.

Animality and the living world

In *La Fin de l'exception humaine*, published eight years after *Pourquoi la fiction?*,[34] Schaeffer examines the philosophical problem of human exceptionalism, drawing once again on work in the cognitive sciences, evolutionary psychology, and comparative anthropology to argue for a more integrated concept of human nature.[35] He critiques dualism and reminds the reader that the notion of the human as necessarily anti-natural is a construct of Western philosophy. Avoiding biological determinism, Schaeffer offers a way out of the humanist/anti-humanist impasse so prevalent in Ferry's 1992 book. He carefully considers the long tradition of French humanist thought, looking in particular at Descartes's concept of the *cogito* and Merleau-Ponty's phenomenology.[36] One of the keys to Schaeffer's paradigm shift to a non-anthropocentric view of the human is the concept of animality, not as the worst of all characteristics in humans (as the concept has long been constructed), but as that which describes humans as creatures, part of the living world.

While debate in the anglophone world has for a long time evolved around the notion of animal rights, Animal Studies in France has focussed more on the concept of *animalité*. An early example of this appears in a 1979 issue of the journal *Critique* in which philosophers rethink *animalité* not as some pre-human, pre-modern, negative or regressive state, but rather as a set of differences deserving of merit in their own right.[37] For Florence Burgat, this attempt to rethink *animalité* from a philosophical perspective is fundamentally different from zoological or ethological approaches to human-animal relations.[38] As for Dominique Lestel, he does not make this distinction between philosophy and ethology, highlighting instead the need to rethink *animalité* not only in terms of human-animal hybrid communities, but also in terms of evolving human-machine-animal relationships.[39] In addition, Lestel underlines the fact that the animal question requires both a critical engagement with the notion of the human and a more complex and nuanced understanding of the living world: "L'animalité ne constitue pas seulement une notion renvoyant aux relations de l'homme à l'animal, elle se réfère aussi aux relations de l'animal à la machine et oscille sans cesse entre la question du statut du vivant et celle du statut de l'humain."[40] It is this notion of the living world or what he calls *le vivant* that is at the heart of Schaeffer's attempt to move beyond humanist principles.[41]

To outline this idea, Schaeffer summarizes four main principles of evolutionary theory: 1) all of life on earth is subject to evolutionary change; 2) natural selection is only one of the causes of evolution; 3) evolution is non-teleological; 4) no living beings, including humans, have a universal, unchanging nature. Building on these principles, Schaeffer redefines biological naturalism not as a naturalization of social phenomena, nor as the reduction of mental events to neurological ones, but as an undoing of the nature/culture opposition. He explains sociality as evolutive and relational, embedded in an organic system of constraints and events. This means that not only humans have developed multiple forms of sociality, but some non-human animals have as well. Because social phenomena are embedded in evolutionary life, they must be studied from a variety of perspectives within the natural sciences, the social sciences, and the human sciences.[42]

To explain biological naturalism further, Schaeffer turns to the concept of cultures and asserts the merits of a comparative perspective. It is not a question of characterizing animal cultures as "closer to nature" than human cultures, but of studying cultures as specific types of acquisition, transmission, and diffusion of information from one group to another.[43] It is not until the final chapter, after securely rooting the concept of the human in an evolutionary view of the living world (*le vivant*), that Schaeffer addresses the problem of consciousness. While highly critical of Descartes's notion of the *cogito*, Schaeffer avoids a purely physicalist description of mental phenomena. Pointing out that we still do not know enough about consciousness, he describes what he calls the "plurifunctionality of representations," or the ways in which different groups create different world views. Schaeffer notes that scientific, empirical knowledge is the way in which the West has come to know the world, but that this is only one possible way of knowing. To conclude, he underlines the "exorbitant price" that the Western world view has exacted from others, citing the number of animals kept in atrocious conditions on factory farms. In the end, he tentatively calls for a less-speciesist attitude toward non-human animals.[44]

For ecocritics, Schaeffer's critique of humanism may seem to have little to offer in terms of an environmentalist ethics. But Schaeffer's approach overlaps in many ways with that of ecocriticism. Both call for more consideration of recent scientific findings in humanities disciplines. But where ecocriticism looks to the environmental sciences that deal with climate change and pollution, Schaeffer looks to the social sciences like anthropology and evolutionary psychology to redefine the human. He illustrates that it is possible to bring the human back into literary studies without reinstating anthropocentrism or traditional humanism. Moreover, his notion of the living world does not distinguish between animals and environment,[45] and so offers a post-nature, posthumanist position from which to ask what conditions are necessary for life in general to survive on Earth in the future.

Literary studies as ecological niche

In *Petite écologie des études littéraires: Pourquoi et comment étudier la littérature?* (2011), Schaeffer shifts his attention to the crisis within the humanities, and, more specifically, within literary studies. He first notes that in France, this crisis has at times been conflated with a crisis of literature, as contemporary texts are deemed "unreadable" or "indigestible" by critics. According to Schaeffer, this so-called crisis of literature is in fact a crisis of Literature with a capital "L" as literary scholars lament the end of the Golden Age of French literature. Coming back to some of the arguments made in *Pourquoi la fiction?* Schaeffer asserts that fiction in the form of films, graphic novels, video games, etc. is doing extraordinarily well. He then turns his attention to what he calls an "ecology of literary studies" in the hopes of better highlighting the continued philosophical and epistemological value of literary studies.[46]

Schaeffer's use of the term *écologie* in the title *Petite écologie des études littéraires* first brings to mind ecocriticism's appeal to ecology as a world view and a science on which to build a literary theory. But a quick reading of the first chapter reveals that this is not how Schaeffer is using the term; he is instead using the word "ecology" as a metaphor to describe the habits and practices of those working in the humanities and the sciences. He begins by identifying two groups of scholars: scientists who work internationally, building on previous concepts and theories, to become a voice of authority; and humanities scholars and social scientists who work in small, often conflicting groups, developing theories specific to their political interests, and much less capable of crossing national boundaries.[47] For Schaeffer, the ecological niche of humanities and social science scholars remains rooted in cultural and socio-historical differences.

In the next section of the book, Schaeffer turns his attention to these differences, citing the schism between Anglo-American analytic philosophy and continental European philosophy throughout much of the twentieth century. Critical of these divisions, Schaeffer advises literary scholars to adopt a comparative approach.[48] More interested in unity than in diversity, he calls for a common theory of literature across social, cultural, and historical differences: "un programme, ouvert du point de vue méthodologique et acceptant des 'procédures de preuve' reconnues par tous les chercheurs oeuvrant dans le même champ."[49] While I have been arguing for a comparative approach more attentive to differences, Schaeffer endorses a comparatist approach in line with earlier thinkers like René Wellek who develop "overarching models and methods that account for the wide variety of literary forms and genres across cultures, for the circulation of texts beyond their regions and languages of origin."[50]

At the same time, Schaeffer recognizes the specificities of literary studies in France. The distinction between *enseignant-chercheur* (teacher-researcher) and *chercheur* (researcher) in France is very different from the North American model, in which professors are both teachers and researchers in university institutions. According to Schaeffer, the task of the *enseignant-chercheur* is to convey and critique literary and cultural values through the study and teaching of individual texts, while the task of the *chercheur* is to build a shared scientific tradition around the acts of fiction and reading. In addition, he distinguishes between an evaluative approach that critiques the literary canon from the perspective of feminism, postcolonialism, posthumanism, and cultural studies, and a descriptive approach that works to define the nature of literary practices universally. While he appreciates the evaluative approach, Schaeffer presents himself as a *chercheur* whose task it is to outline a general theory of literature based on new philosophies of the mind and language. This is what he spends the rest of the book doing.

Schaeffer's book points to the tension between acknowledging the constraints and conditions of doing literary studies in France and developing a theory of literature that goes beyond such conditions. This tension is at the heart of the culture of literary studies in France today. Evaluative approaches like animal studies and ecocriticism continue to be seen as secondary to descriptive approaches whose aim is to transcend the politics of difference. Yet Schaeffer's own work on a general theory of literature cannot escape its cultural and intellectual context. The fact that Schaeffer can dedicate so much time to writing and theorizing is due in part to his position as *chercheur* at CNRS, the French National Centre for Research in the Sciences. This government institution pays scholars to work on research projects, so that they do not need to teach, nor do they need to be affiliated with a university. These are the sociopolitical conditions of the kind of theory of literature that Schaeffer aims to build. Being aware of this larger cultural ecology is an essential element of the kind of ecocritical approach for which I am advocating here, one that takes into account the institutional, political, and intellectual contexts in which literary theories emerge and circulate.

Rather than oppose, as Schaeffer does, "traditions étrangères" (or literary approaches that are imported from elsewhere) and "traditions indigènes" (or literary approaches that are "native" to national soils), I prefer to use Haraway's expression of "situated knowledges" to locate literary theories, critiques of the human, and political readings in specific times and places.[51] This means focussing on cultural particularities, but also on the ways in which literary texts complicate such understandings of difference and challenge notions of national and cultural identity. While I find Schaeffer's work extremely useful for building a French *écocritique* that rejects humanism without rejecting the human, I am wary of a general theory of literature founded on a supposed universal, scientific understanding of the living world. As Haraway asserts, "the god trick is forbidden."[52] But so is absolute relativism. There are not, on the one hand, politically motivated readings of literary texts, and on the other, an apolitical universal theory of literature. Rather, there are multiple "views from somewhere" that promise "ongoing finite embodiment" and "living within limits and contradictions."[53] In the end, Schaeffer's theory about the human as embedded in the living world suffers from its own lack of embeddedness.[54] One way of re-engaging with "views from somewhere" is coming back to individual literary texts. Indeed, this is the practice prescribed by Easterlin in her book on biocultural approaches to literature. Turning to Houellebecq's fictional universe will offer such an opportunity for delving into the limits and contradictions of living in today's contemporary society from a situated and (painfully) embodied point of view.

Fiction

Portrait: Michel Houellebecq

Despite having published only a few novels – *Extension du domaine de la lutte* (1994), *Les Particules élémentaires* (1998), *Plateforme* (2001), *La Possibilité d'une île* (2005), *La Carte et le territoire* (2010), *Soumission* (2015) – Houellebecq is an internationally known author. Of all the novelists considered in this book, he is by far the most translated, discussed, and debated. This may be because, as Carole Sweeney explains, the reception of Houellebecq's novels has as much to do with the author as with the books themselves, as he has succeeded in creating for himself a recognizable media persona by way of a series of scandals.[55] Because Houellebecq incorporates autobiographical elements and polemical statements into all his novels, it is difficult to read his fiction without constructing this author persona. While I will try to avoid the spectre of the author, it will at times be necessary to make connections between Houellebecq's interviews and essays and his narrators' remarks and attitudes.

Characterized as a "literature of despair,"[56] Houellebecq's novels seem to encapsulate perfectly the notion of ecological ends as the loss of hope about the future of the human species.[57] Sweeney convincingly argues that Houellebecq's fiction reflects the angst of a generation that feels there is no possible alternative to current global consumer capitalism, and no way out of the environmental mess we have gotten ourselves into in the Western world. From this perspective, Houellebecq's fiction seems to illustrate the end of imagining, period. There is no outside from which we can conceive of a world other than the post-industrial, consumer capitalist world in which we live. While I agree in part with Sweeney's argument, I will illustrate that there is a future for ecological ends in Houellebecq's work, however paradoxical this sounds. Fiction and poetry represent a possible island from which to imagine alternative worlds and scenarios, alternative relationships between humans and the non-human world. While eschewing the possibility of living in harmony with nature, Houellebecq's fiction searches for a place, an *oikos*, where imagining and writing take place alongside the climate of crisis in which we live.[58]

I will not be covering all of Houellebecq's interviews, essays, poetry, and articles in this chapter. I will not even be discussing all of his novels. Since the aim of my analysis is to understand how Houellebecq illustrates the end(s) of human exceptionalism, I will focus on the two novels in which he experiments with speculative fiction (or "romans d'anticipation" in French). All of Houellebecq's novels have an *air de famille* about them in their dark portrayal of contemporary society, their "flat" prose, their use of multiple genres. But *Les Particules élémentaires* (1998), translated into English as *The Elementary Particles*,[59] and *La Possibilité d'une île* (2005), translated into English as *The Possibility of an Island*,[60] are the only two that portray the end of the human species in future worlds.[61] The first novel, *The Elementary Particles*, outlines the end of the human species and celebrates the birth of a new posthuman species, but only describes in the barest details a future utopia at the beginning and the end of the novel. The second novel, *The Possibility of an Island*, also narrates the possible end of the human species, but introduces an intermediate species between corrupt humanity and a perfect posthumanity, so that the passage from one species to another is not as simple nor as quick as envisaged in the earlier novel.

Both novels imagine future worlds, yet avoid apocalypse. There is no fire and brimstone in Houellebecq's novels. There are references to sea levels rising, but the natural world is, in fact, doing quite well. By adopting a deadpan, flat style – quite the opposite of the alarmist tones of environmentalist catastrophism – Houellebecq makes "the end" more "an end," both in the sense of one possible goal and one possible finality among others. In this way, his novels offer a stage for thinking about ecological ends in terms of multiple ends or endings, but also in terms of much longer temporalities that stretch beyond human history: What happens to nature when humans disappear from the planet? What value do humans have when viewed from a posthuman future? And what role does literature play when there are no more humans on Earth? Reading the novels together, I will illustrate that none of the "ends" considered here – the end(s) of nature, the end(s) of the human, and the end(s) of literature – are absolute. Houellebecq leaves the reader with an ambiguous, contradictory view of (im)possible future worlds.

The end(s) of nature: Material landscapes and embodiment

Since its inception, ecocriticism has struggled with the notion of Nature with a capital "N" as that which exists outside of human influence, human activity, and human culture. In *Ecology without Nature* (2009), Morton highlights these struggles and proposes to develop an ecological thought that does away with the notion of an idealized, untouched

Nature.[62] This does not mean that Morton denies the existence of the material, physical world, but rather that he is not holding this world up as some separate sphere to be revered and protected. For Morton, a world without Nature represents a world in which we pay careful attention to the icky, sticky, smelly, unlikeable bits of our bodies and environments, in which we embrace our strange, cyborg, biotech creations as part of environmental care and ethics, and in which we examine our difficult position within global consumer capitalism instead of constantly trying to find a way out.

Morton's critique of Nature represents a useful starting point for analysing the ideological work that nature and the natural are made to do in *The Elementary Particles* and *The Possibility of an Island.* More traditional ecocritical approaches would no doubt reject Houellebecq's novels on the grounds that there is little in these novels that aligns with a call for a less-destructive relationship with planet Earth. They may be shocked by the anti-environmentalist rants that surface here and there in the books. But a closer look reveals that the idea of nature in the novels gives rise to paradoxes and dilemmas that are no less characteristic of the ways we discuss, represent, and imagine nature in the Western world when, for example, we idealize Nature as untouched yet want to experience this Nature for ourselves (thus making it less "untouched"), or when we continue to accept unquestioningly the pastoral settings on milk cartons, knowing full well that this does not come close to the conditions on factory farms.

At the heart of Houellebecq's representation of nature is a messy pile of contradictions. In *The Possibility of an Island,* the narrator Daniel25 critiques environmentalism's call to save nature as a barely disguised plot to put an end to the human species. And yet this end is exactly what Houellebecq imagines in both *The Elementary Particles* and *The Possibility of an Island.* Houellebecq himself holds a degree in agronomy with a specialization in "mise en valeur du milieu naturel et écologie,"[63] yet he portrays nature simplistically in terms of the evolutionary "laws" of the survival of the fittest.[64] Far from the sentimental poet hoping one day to reconnect with harmonious nature, Houellebecq is the *poète maudit* who curses society and nature. And yet both Houellebecq's fiction and his poetry include descriptions of landscapes that are rooted in the pastoral ideal of gentle, sloping green hills in the countryside.[65] In addition, Houellebecq's narrators are often the exception to the rule in the deterministic universe of the text as they refuse to comply with their species' "drive" to reproduce. Such contradictions are what make

Houellebecq's fiction such a perplexing and fascinating object of study for an ecocritical reading.

In *The Elementary Particles,* Houellebecq portrays today's consumer society as reducing humans to a state in which every human is out for himself, trying to mate with the greatest number of other beings or just trying to survive in a predator-eat-prey world. Humans are incapable of rising above this state because civil society, in the form of family and politics, has broken down. Driven by the laws of "nature," humans suffer terribly; they are deprived of love, joy, and happiness for the majority of their lives. This is why Michel, the scientist in *The Elementary Particles,* is so intent on creating a new species: "Nature was a repulsive cesspit. All in all, nature deserved to be wiped out in a holocaust – and man's mission on earth was probably to do just that."[66] Nature is not the fragile ecosystems of the Amazon rain forest or the Arctic north; it is nature "red in tooth and claw," to borrow a well-known line from Alfred, Lord Tennyson (1809–92).

Leaving his job as a molecular biologist in a large research centre, Michel sets out to find a way to create a new species that is no longer subject to natural selection and sexual reproduction. Although he will not be around to see this post-sexual, post-natural revolution, he is recognized as the key figure in bringing about a new era in which a new species lives without suffering and pain. Laurence Dahan-Gaida calls this new world "méta-naturelle," that is, beyond nature.[67] Plants and animals seem to have disappeared. While physical elements are described – the new species speak of "living in the light" "by the water's edge,"[68] – this landscape appears to be largely symbolic, not located anywhere on Earth. This future world is a utopia both in the sense of a perfect place and in the etymological sense of nowhere (*u*- meaning "not" and *topos* "place"). This reinforces the reader's impression that a posthuman, post-natural future can only happen once nature – understood as the "structures, processes and causal powers that are constantly operative within the physical world"[69] – truly comes to an end.

Houellebecq's *The Possibility of an Island* both extends and critiques the idea of a possible end to nature in a future world. The posthuman species in this novel do not live in utopia (in either sense of the word); they inhabit Earth after a series of natural disasters and global wars. While there are drastically modified landscapes, such as the large grey zone (a type of ashy substance) covering most of Spain and a deep crevice running through Europe from North to South, nature is still alive and well. This thriving natural world stands in stark contrast to the neo-humans who live alone in a state of stasis in a sterile environment, awaiting the creation of the Future Ones. These two worlds – the natural world and the neohuman world – remain entirely separate until the book's epilogue, which recounts the adventures of the twenty-fifth-generation clone, Daniel25, after he leaves his gated residence and heads out with his dog Fox (also a clone) into the surrounding forests. In other words, it is after the "official" end of the novel that the story of a possible posthuman nature takes place.

This sets the epilogue apart from the rest of the novel. Houellebecq points out the importance of the book's epilogue during an interview with *The Paris Review*:

> I personally like the last part of *The Possibility of an Island*. I don't think it resembles anything I've done before, but no reviewer has mentioned it. It's hard to explain but I have the feeling that there's something very, very beautiful in that last part. He [Daniel25] opens the door, and it's another world. When I wrote that passage I wasn't thinking much about the story, I was completely intoxicated by the beauty of my own words.[70]

While most of Houellebecq's novels adopt a conventional form, the (lengthy) epilogue at the end of *The Possibility of an Island* represents a break from convention. Rather than comment on the main story, Houellebecq uses the epilogue to introduce "another world," but a world that is highly familiar to the reader, a world of natural landscapes on planet Earth. Playing with para-textual matter, Houellebecq undoes the idea of the story as bound by the text. In addition, language is used differently in the epilogue. Whether the words are actually more beautiful is not immediately clear to the reader, but the long descriptions of the natural world diverge from the short shrift that such landscapes are usually given in Houellebecq's story worlds. The setting becomes the catalyst for telling another possible story.

Contrary to the symbolic, posthuman landscape elliptically described in *The Elementary Particles*, Daniel25 recounts in great detail in *The Possibility of an Island*'s epilogue the natural landscapes of a regenerated planet: dense forests, ponds in which streams bubble up, dense prairies, cliffs of bluish basalt, a marshy zone, mountain ranges, plateaus, limestone peaks, tall trees, and short grasses. He notes the passage of the seasons, with autumn leading into the first signs of winter. For the first time ever, Daniel25 experiences happiness, traversing these diverse regions with his dog Fox. He speaks of his desire "to travel with

Fox across the prairies and mountains, to experience the awakenings, the baths in a freezing river, the minutes spent drying in the sun, the evenings spent around the fire in the starlight."[71] Given Daniel1's (the clone's original, human ancestor) cynical comments about natural beauty in the rest of the novel, the reader expects Daniel25's descriptions to be laced with irony and sarcasm. And yet the comments about the "living world's capacity for adaptation" and the "speed at which it reconstituted new equilibriums on top of the ruins of a destroyed world"[72] remain free of Houellebecq's narrators' usual contempt. The novel imagines a posthuman future for planet Earth as living and flourishing.

It would be hasty to propose that Houellebecq is writing a return-to-nature narrative. The epilogue also includes passages that recount nature in all its "cruelty"; for example, when Fox hunts a rabbit, breaks its neck, and begins to devour its internal organs, Daniel25 remarks: "Thus was the natural world." Cruel "nature" rears its ugly head once again when a group of so-called savages kills Fox, thus putting a definitive end to his genetic line. Harmonious existence in nature is (im)possible for neohumans, just as it was for humans. However, this does not mean an end to nature and material matter more generally. Essential to Daniel25's encounter of the world is the discovery of his own body. During his crossing of the Great Grey Zone, he experiences extreme physical suffering for the first time, almost dying from a lack of water and mineral salts (the neohumans are an autotrophic species, they no longer have an animal's digestive system, and live off water, sun, and salt). Upon finally arriving at the seashore, he savours the "nutritive, benevolent wave" of water washing over his body. Whereas in *The Elementary Particles* Houellebecq writes physical reality and corporeal experience out of a future posthuman world, in *The Possibility of an Island*, he writes them back in.

But the novel ends by bringing the reader back to a landscape of light and water, a "universe" that is "close to the archetypal image of eternity."[73] After experiencing the concrete presence of the physical world, Daniel25 will spend the rest of his days in an unchanging, elemental world of earth, air, fire, and water. His final words are: "My body belonged to me for only a brief lapse of time; I would never reach the goal I had been set. The future was empty; it was the mountain. My dreams were populated with emotional presences. I was, I was no longer. Life was real."[74] Whereas Daniel25's former sterile neohuman environment was void of affect, his thoughts and dreams are now populated with "emotional presences." He will continue to remember walking through the woods and prairies, next to streams and lakes, with his dog Fox, and so continue to render homage to life as lived in a physically diverse environment.

In her article "Houellebecq et le monde: contre ou au milieu?" Maud Granger Remy concludes that Houellebecq's novels illustrate the impossibility of escaping the world: "L'entrelacement construit ainsi un circuit fermé et sans échappatoire. Et *La Possibilité d'une île* fit précisément cette impossibilité. Quand la participation au monde devient impossible, l'humanité ne le devient-elle pas aussi ?"[75] For Granger Remy, Houellebecq's novel portrays a double failure: the failure to participate in the world, and the failure to escape from it. But another way of reading the epilogue of *The Possibility of an Island* is in terms of what is made possible rather than what remains impossible. First, Daniel25 discovers the physical reality of a flourishing natural world, even if this nature is still perceived as cruel and violent. Second, Daniel25 has known a wide array of emotions, from happiness to sorrow, from joy to revenge, from love to anger. The use of the word "real" in the final line of the novel is telling – "Life was real." Only during his adventures in the natural world does Daniel25 experience life as reality, and experience himself as a living organism exposed to the conditions of changing environments.

In the end, Houellebecq has not solved the problem of the "possibility of an island" as a place that feeds our hopes for and imagination of something better. Daniel25's final landscape is much like that of the posthuman species described in *The Elementary Particles*: one of light and water, unchanging days, an eternal summer. But there is a crucial difference in how these settings are portrayed: in the first novel, this landscape represents utopia, while in the second, it is a background against which Daniel25's non-life fades away. Rather than endorsing an imaginary utopia and an end to nature, the second novel can be read as a warning against such futures, with the narrator repeatedly reminding the reader in the opening pages, "Fear what I say."[76] If, as Schaeffer asserts, fiction is a mode of imagining the world "as-if," Houellebecq's novels point to the dangers of imagining a possible end to nature. In the end, they do not give up on nature as a physical and material landscape, nor on the body as an essential site of lived experience.

The end(s) of the human: Animality and the posthuman

Like Schaeffer's literary theory, Houellebecq's fictional universe portrays humans as creatures embedded in the living world. But where Schaeffer emphasizes the processes of human development, Houellebecq adopts a pessimistic view of the living world as bound up in a constant struggle against death. He imagines the end of a human life not as celebratory, but as a return to another sort of materiality. Descriptions of the decomposing body as a habitat for other organisms adopt a clinical, scientific realism: "The now-decomposed cadaver becomes a host to *Acaridae*, which absorb the last traces of residual moisture. Desiccated and mummified, the corpse still harbors parasites, the larvae of beetles, *Aglossa cuprealis* and *Tineola biselliella* maggots, which complete the cycle."[77] This perspective on the end(s) of the human creates a sense of determinism and illustrates the dark side of defining humans as a biological species. For Houellebecq, humans are "animals," but in the sense that they display cruel and violent behaviour, driven by the "law" of species reproduction. The only solution is to put an end to the human species and to imagine the creation of a posthuman species.

As already mentioned, Houellebecq's novels have been the focus of intense debate because of their starkly pessimistic view of Western contemporary society's rampant consumer capitalism, eroding family values, and increasing individualism. According to Sweeney, Houellebecq's novels illustrate the impossibility of humanity, leaving the reader with little hope for the future. But there is a second voice in Houellebecq's writing, one that is less pessimistic, less cynical, and that is difficult to categorize because it continues to assert the possibility of a society founded on love and happiness.[78] The contradictions that arise because of these two opposing voices drive Houellebecq's literary project: "À titre personnel, il me semble que la seule voie est de continuer à exprimer, sans compromis, les contradictions qui me déchirent; tout en sachant que ces contradictions s'avéreront, très vraisemblablement, représentatives de mon époque."[79] Literary critics have been particularly attentive to the contradictory nature of Houellebecq's portrayal of women, religion, science, and technology. But the contradictions inherent in his description of the human animal have only come up in a handful of articles and books.[80]

When critics first consider the representation of the (human) animal in Houellebecq's novels, they note that "'animal' consonne avec 'mal.'"[81] In *The Elementary Particles*, the biologist Michel remembers episodes of a TV documentary, *La Vie des animaux*, in which animals lie in wait and then attack each other in bloody battles. Savagery is in these animals' very nature, he concludes.[82] But at the same time, Michel identifies less-negative traits in animals. Thinking back to a different episode of *La Vie des animaux* in which a female calamari fiercely protects her eggs,

Michel notes: "Amid the vile filth, the ceaseless carnage which was the lot of animals, the only glimmer of devotion and altruism was the protective maternal instinct, which had gradually evolved into mother love."[83] Looking for the genetic origins of love and altruism (in order to recreate them through cloning), Michel also attributes "higher-order" behaviours, such as consciousness, to non-human animals.

> Self-consciousness, which is absent in nematodes, was clearly observable in inferior lizards like *Lacerta agilis*, implying the presence of both a central nervous system and something more. What that something was remained completely mysterious. Consciousness did not seem to depend on any single factor, whether anatomical, biochemical or cellular.[84]

Michel's description of animals as inherently cruel, but also capable of maternal love and consciousness, closes the gap between humans and animals.

This is also true of the description of human behaviour in the novel. Even though Michel has managed to remove himself from the world of (male) competition and (unsatisfactory) sexual relations, his half-brother Bruno is a complicit victim from childhood on. In boarding school, he experiences being the "weaker animal" who suffers "acts of gratuitous cruelty" at the hands of the "alpha males." This view of human society as organized hierarchically is rooted in a simplified and outdated understanding of the theory of evolution. As Morrey points out:

> The view of evolution presented by Houellebecq is an ideologically loaded one ... The kind of evolution discussed by Houellebecq remains thoroughly rooted in its nineteenth-century origins of statistical mechanics, Malthusian population theory and Victorian sexual morality ... throughout the novel, the stress is on predation, cruelty and ruthless sexual selection as the truth of life.[85]

Like other living creatures, humans are bound to the "laws" of the survival of the fittest, their lives "determined" by the principles of evolution.

Portraying humans in this way is one way of striking a blow at the Enlightenment ideals of human emancipation, freedom, and progress. But as Schaeffer points out, negatively portraying animality does not in the end get one beyond the problem of human exceptionalism:

> Il s'agit d'amputer l'homme des traits dont le dualisme se sert pour affirmer la thèse de la rupture ontique. Mais ceci signifie en réalité que leur conception de l'homme est prisonnière de la conception dualiste de l'animalité, et que donc, au lieu de se déprendre de la Thèse, ils ne font que réduire un de ses pôles à l'autre.[86]

Reducing humans to the worst of all animals simply eludes the problem of dualism. By subscribing to the notion of animals as lesser beings, Houellebecq deforms the image of both animals and humans. In this way, his biological naturalism stands in direct opposition to that of Schaeffer, who holds that to move beyond humanism, it is necessary to rethink evolution as non-teleological and as based on principles other than natural selection. Because Houellebecq's novels adhere to a reductive and deterministic view of evolution, there is little room for a less-negative notion of animality.[87]

In *The Possibility of an Island,* humans are portrayed similarly by the various narrators in the novel: Daniel1, the contemporary human telling his story, and Daniel24 and Daniel25, the neohuman clones commenting on Daniel1's story (and, more generally, the end of humanity) two thousand years later. But this cruel, animal nature takes on even greater proportions in a new species that emerges after many violent wars and devastating ecological disasters. While these conditions have all but eliminated humans, this extremely cruel species has managed to survive. Once again, a reductive evolutionary explanation is given for the behaviour of the members of this species: "It was natural that it would be the most brutal and cruel individuals, having a higher potential for aggressiveness, who survived in greater number a succession of lengthy conflicts, and transmitted their character to their descendants."[88] Communicating with grunts and gestures, the savages are meant to epitomize a sub-human species. Yet their gratuitous violence makes them more violent than any human or animal species: "No feast among the savages could be imagined without violence, the spilling of blood, and the spectacle of torture; the invention of complicated and atrocious tortures seemed to be the only area in which they had preserved something of the ingeniousness of the ancient humans; that was the limit of their civilization."[89]

The descriptions of the new species in the novel – both the savages and the neohumans – reveal the paradoxes inherent in trying to define what is human and what is not. For example, Daniel24 describes the savages as "slightly more intelligent than monkeys" but also "more dangerous."[90] Moreover, the savages have certain traits, such as standing upright and using fire to prepare their food, that have been identified as human. Species thinking, even in this reductive form, reveals the cracks in humanism's previous attempts to establish a set of fixed characteristics unique to humans. This is also true of the descriptions of the neohumans. On the one hand, Daniel24 and Daniel25 are a different species from humans in the sense that they have a different genetic makeup and are produced through cloning. On the other hand, they are described as having a similar physiognomy to that of the savages. Upon being "offered" a young female savage for his "pleasure," Daniel25 remarks that his sexual apparatus is exactly the same as humans and so he could in theory copulate with a female savage. This raises the question of how different the savages and the neohumans actually are. What would the hybrid offspring of such a coupling be like? If they were fertile, biologists would consider neohumans and savages as members of the same species.

These questions point to the need to situate Houellebecq's description of the end of the human species in a larger philosophical framework. One of the clearest expressions of posthumanism can be found in the work of Rosi Braidotti: "The posthuman condition introduces a qualitative shift in our thinking about what exactly is the basic unit of reference for our species, our polity and our relationship to the other inhabitants of this planet."[91] The savages are posthuman in the chronological sense of coming after the human species, but they are also posthuman in the philosophical sense of calling into question which traits are human and which are not. The neohumans are also posthuman in the temporal sense. But there is an important distinction between the two novels. *The Elementary Particles* embraces a transhumanist view rather than a posthumanist strategy for moving beyond the human. Science and technology are celebrated in the creation of a new and improved species to replace the old, imperfect human species.[92] There is an absolute rupture between the species that leaves little room for questioning the traits associated with human nature (the lack of description of the new posthuman species in the novel means that it is difficult to say what their traits are at all).

In *The Possibility of an Island*, an intermediary species is imagined between the humans and the Future Ones. Calling these beings "neohumans" and placing them in a dystopian setting is one way of raising doubts about the transhumanist project. Although they are posthuman in the sense of coming after humans, the neohumans are not clearly "improved." Even if neohumans experience almost no emotions and are reproduced through cloning, there is no absolute rupture between them and the human species. They share characteristics with humans and with the savages, which raises the issue of what exactly constitutes "human" traits. In this case, posthuman does not mean the end of the human species, but rather a rethinking of the possible human traces left in future evolved species.

These differences between a transhumanist and a posthumanist perspective also appear on the formal level in Houellebecq's two novels. In *The Elementary Particles*, a member of the posthuman species narrates the story of Michel and Bruno from a future time period, looking back to the past. Recounting the events that led up to the end of humankind, this narrator occasionally uses the first-person pronoun "we" in the prologue and the epilogue. This imbues the novel with the spirit of these new beings, their critical perspective on the human species. By adopting an omniscient point of view, the novel closes down other possible readings of the past, even as it recounts a hypothetical future. In this way, it contributes to the imagining of one single end with no other possible solutions. The reader is bound to this transhumanist vision of a utopia that is brought about thanks to science and technology, bioengineering, and genetic modification.

In contrast, *The Possibility of an Island* is divided into chapters narrated by Daniel1, the contemporary human, and by Daniel24 and Daniel25, the future clones of Daniel1. Abandoning the omniscient perspective and using first-person point of view, the novel does not offer a closed story about the end of the human species. Each of the three narrators, Daniel1, Daniel24, and Daniel25, describes his views of the reality in which he lives, and no overarching narrative of the trajectory of human history is given. This opens up the possibility of imagining other endings, other events, other directions than the ones described in *The Elementary Paricles*. Adopting the limits of the first-person point of view, the second novel portrays the future not from some impossible, God-like perspective, but instead from individual perspectives that reveal the contradictions and ambiguities of such endings.

While I have underlined the differences between Schaeffer's careful rethinking of the notion of animality, the living world, and the complex principles of a non-teleological evolution, and Houellebecq's cruel and deterministic notion of the human (animals), it is unfair to reduce his novels to this one trait. Much more could be said about a less-pessimistic voice in Houellebecq's novels that holds out for a glimmer of hope and love.[93] Houellebecq is not ready to embrace the posthuman future outlined in *The Elementary Particles* quite yet. Daniel25 leaves his gated residence in order to experience life as described in the life story of his human ancestor Daniel1. Although his experiences of suffering, happiness, and pain are his own, they bridge the gap between neohumans and humans. The novel raises the question of whether there is not something worth saving in terms of the human species. What exactly that "thing" will be is the subject of the next section.

The end(s) of literature: Life stories and story worlds

The problematic end(s) of literature have been announced more than once in the history of literary studies. In the French context, the most recent example is that of literary critics who point out a number of reasons why literature has come to an end: 1) the "poor" quality of contemporary French novels; 2) the diminishing number of readers; and 3) the flooding of an already saturated publishing market.[94] But as Schaeffer points out in *Why Fiction?*, these pronouncements about the "end of literature" are more about a certain idea of literature. Schaeffer calls for literary critics to develop a theory of fiction that is applicable to a much larger collection of cultural texts, such as video games, film, and digital storytelling. Imagining life two thousand years in the future, Houellebecq's novels offer a setting for developing this larger perspective: What role will storytelling and make-believe play two thousand years in the future? If there are no longer humans on this planet, will there still be literature and fiction? Will a posthuman species take up these practices as part of their own psychological and social development?

As I noted in the section on Schaeffer's work, literary Darwinists make a strong claim about literature and storytelling in general. As Jonathan Gottschall asserts, "We live in Neverland because we can't not live in Neverland. Neverland is our nature. We are the storytelling animal."[95] Such assertions are rooted in the hypothesis that humans developed storytelling as a way of remembering events from the past and projecting possible events into the future. In other words, humans became human in part because they began to tell stories.[96] While this explanation of the function of storytelling relates largely to our evolutionary past, we can ask what the role of storytelling will be in the future. Gottschall explores briefly what is happening in the age of reality TV, RPGs (role-playing games), interactive stories, MMORPGs (massively multiplayer online role-playing games) – in other words, in an era moving toward more and more virtual forms of fiction and make-believe. His conclusion is that we will continue to tell stories even if media and environments change radically.

Writing, narrating, and storytelling are all important to the characters in *The Elementary Particles* and *The Possibility of an Island*, yet the novels make important distinctions between the function and nature of such activities in the contemporary human world and the future world of a new species. In *The Elementary Particles,* Bruno is the "man of letters," writing poetry and stories, teaching literature, and publishing articles, in opposition to his half-brother Michel, who is the "man of science." While Bruno, the literature professor, tries to lose himself in the search for sexual satisfaction, Michel, the biologist, withdraws and disengages from society. In the end, it is Michel's vision of the world that endures as he discovers the scientific knowledge needed to clone and perfect the human species. Despite this transhumanist view, the novel reveals that literature and art are also necessary to the creation of a new species. Interestingly, Michel is unable to "solve" the mystery of creating life artificially until he encounters the Book of Kells, an illuminated manuscript that is the work of seventh-century monks. According to the narrator, "his long study of the book allowed him – in a series of intuitions which in retrospect seem miraculous – to overcome the complexities of calculating energy stability in biological macromolecules."[97] Michel also writes poetry, further undoing the notion of two distinct cultures, literary and scientific. Upon discovering that his closest female childhood friend is in a coma, Michel expresses his love and suffering in a poem about the need to put an end "to all our pain."[98]

Poetry emerges as a higher form of expression in the novel. To describe their utopian world, the new posthuman species use only verse: "We live today under a new world order, / The web which weaves together all things envelops our bodies, / Bathes our limbs, / In a halo of joy."[99] According to Houellebecq, "la poésie est le moyen le plus naturel de traduire l'intuition pure d'un instant. Il y a vraiment un noyau d'intuition pure, qui peut être directement traduit en images ou en mots."[100] Poems are used at key points in both novels as a way of expressing another world, one experienced more deeply but less chronologically. The status of storytelling prose remains ambiguous in a future perfect world. While using prose to recount the lives of Michel and Bruno, the Future Ones eschew telling their own story. In this way, the novel suggests that storytelling may come to an end if a future species moves on to more poetic forms of expression in their (utopian) realities.

According to Gottschall, all humans have a life story to tell, even if they do not write or publish books. He explains: "A life story is a 'personal myth' about who we are deep down – where we come from, how we got this way, and what it all means. Our life stories are who we are. They are our identity."[101] The concept of a life story or *récit de vie* is given literal form in *The Possibility of an Island*.[102] All the human ancestors of neohuman clones have life stories: the scientist, the military man, Vincent the prophet, Daniel's girlfriend Esther, etc. These humans write their life story even if they have no literary ambitions because they are told that cloning on its own will not suffice for transferring identity and personality from one clone to the next. Daniel1's life story dominates the novel (it constitutes more than two-thirds of the novel's total length), even though Daniel1 is not a notable, successful, self-made (hu)man. As Delphine Grass notes, "the weakest characters" in Houellebecq's novels "make the strongest lyricists for emotional survival."[103] This contradiction is key to understanding the role of life stories in the novel.

Neohumans are commentators who read and reread their human ancestors' life stories. Whether it is because of the sterile environments in which they live or the lack of contact with other neohumans or their state of absolute indifference, the neohumans do not tell their own stories. The first clone, Daniel24, uses cryptic codes and bits of verse to allude to his life, but these hardly constitute a life story. They could represent a kind of proto-poetic form, but they are clearly just fragments (whereas the poems in *The Elementary Particles* are more stylistically and formally developed). Daniel25 explains that the practices of reflecting on and then writing about one's human ancestor's life story represent two of the three pillars of the neohuman "faith" along with the "rigorous duplication of the genetic code."[104] In other words, life stories are part of the indoctrination of the neohuman species. As Daniel1 explains, his life story will convince its readers to embrace the scientific revolution that will terminate the human species: "My life story, once distributed and commented on, was going to put an end to mankind as we knew it."[105] Two thousand years later, Daniel25 corroborates the power of this story: "The life story of Daniel1 is often considered by commentators to be central and canonical ... he often seems to be the only one to have taken a small step back, and to have really understood the importance of what was happening before his eyes."[106] Such belief in the power of a story is part of the paradox of

Houellebecq's fiction: either the author suffers from a severe case of egocentrism and is asserting that his own novels will bring about the end of the human species, or he is writing to warn the reader to resist the power of a story that calls for such an end. In either case, Houellebecq is illustrating that science alone, or what Sweeney calls "über-rationalist methodologies," "positivism of the scientific solution," and a "rationalized world view,"[107] is not enough to convince humanity to follow the path to extinction. Storytelling is what brings about this end, and what makes imagining the future possible.

This brings me back to the problem of literature in a future world. The neohumans' immersion in a virtual reality with no real contact with other individuals leads to the end of storytelling. According to Christian Moraru, Houellebecq's neohumans live in a "dedifferentiated world that smudges the vital demarcations between … self and other, private and public, interior and exterior, egological and ecological, culture and nature."[108] These social and material conditions make it impossible to tell life stories. Though Houellebecq emphasizes the power of literature, he outlines the possibility that storytelling is not an innate, biological, unchanging, universal trait, as literary Darwinists argue. He instead presents it as a capacity that changes in accordance with natural and cultural evolution.[109] If we lose contact with a real, physical world and live in complete isolation and total stasis, we may no longer tell stories. This would be the ultimate dystopia for an author like Houellebecq.

Such a condition is not, however, permanent. Daniel25 has no story to tell until he leaves his gated neohuman residence. The novel's epilogue narrates his life story as he discovers "life" as "real." According to Moraru, Daniel25 decides to leave because of the "existential *malaise*" he feels after finishing the life story of Daniel1: "*The Possibility of an Island* points … to a little more heartening scenario, with the human as the 'rest' (see the French *reste, différence*) still in play – still vibrant, unique, 'differential.'"[110] While I agree with Moraru's conclusion that the novel's epilogue illustrates the continuity between humans and neohumans, I prefer to place the emphasis on the capacity to tell stories. Experiencing the natural world and discovering his body as a feeling and emotional creature, Daniel25 begins to tell his own story. The world may have "betrayed" him in the sense that he did not find utopia; but he has had the chance to tell his own story, no longer just a reader of and commentator on his human ancestor's story.

In classical times, the expression *homo literatus* meant either a man marked with a letter – for example, a slave who was branded with his master's initials – or a learned, well-educated man.[111] Houellebecq's characters hardly fit either of these descriptions. They refuse to subscribe to the culture of consumer capitalism (which has become the "master" of many) and they often mock the cultivation of erudition and knowledge in educational institutions. They do, however, fit with the broader notion of *homo literatus* as a producer of life stories. In *The Possibility of an Island,* the seed of *homo literatus* lay dormant for two thousand years, with clone after clone simply reading and commenting on Daniel1's life story. And yet something sparks in Daniel25 so that he too becomes *homo literatus,* telling his own story about exploring the natural world with his dog Fox.[112] This suggests that Houellebecq has not given up on literature and its role in contemporary society. Even a life story that is written and read in a specific ideological context – to convince humans and then neohumans after them to accept the path toward the Future Ones – can have unexpectedly subversive consequences.

According to Ruth Cruikshank, "Houellebecq evinces faith in the capacity for literature to make sense of this situation, and, what is more, claims that it is still possible to adopt a challenging stance to precipitate a critical turning point."[113] To conclude that Houellebecq sees literature as a solution to contemporary society's problems would, however, be wrong. His novels do not soothe the reader; instead, they use a very different strategy. Rita Schober speaks of "un activisme négatif de l'attaque" that gives rise to reflection and response.[114] Taking a more pessimistic perspective, Granger Remy underlines the role of literature as human legacy, a material trace of the end of humankind in Houellebecq's work: "Le romanesque se conçoit ainsi chez Houellebecq comme une activité essentiellement testamentaire, qui doit rendre compte de ce qui reste, ce 'résidu' de l'humain. Après la fin des temps, il nous restera encore la littérature."[115] What these different interpretations illustrate is the ambiguity in Houellebecq's work around the possible function of literature in today's society. On the one hand, there appears to be a humanist belief in literature as essential to the human condition and to the human experience. On the other, there is a posthumanist belief that it is time to move beyond the human and so, to some extent, to move beyond literature as well. In the end, both novels clearly illustrate the contradictory function of *homo literatus*.

Conclusion: Posthumanist (re)turns

Even though Schaeffer and Houellebecq work from very different perspectives, they both end up underlining the power of literature and stories. Without raising humans up once again as a superior species, they bring to light one of the paradoxes within posthumanism itself: How far can such a perspective go in critiquing the humanist project? Does this mean decentring literature, philosophy, and history as well? Can we arrive at some form of posthumanities? Schaeffer's careful engagement with biological naturalism points to one possible path toward a more integrated approach to the human in literature and philosophy. As for Houellebecq, his novels decentre the human but also, problematically, reduce life to a set of determined laws. In their own ways, they reveal a productive tension between a posthumanist view of humans as part of the natural world and a humanist rethinking of the role of literature and stories in the larger context of humans as species.

In terms of future ecological ends, Schaeffer reflects on the present changes in the ways we tell stories, while Houellebecq anticipates a possible world in which stories are no longer told. With Facebook, Twitter, and Instagram, we appear to be documenting our lives more and more. We may not be losing the capacity to tell stories, but we are becoming more and more immersed in them. As Schaeffer notes, one of the potential problems with digital fiction is that we remain transfixed, unable to come back to the material world. In Houellebecq's novels, the possibility of living in an immaterial world is first presented as a utopia, but then the worst of all dystopias. The experience of material reality becomes a key component in being able to tell one's own story. If we increasingly spend our time in virtual realities, what will become of our bodies? If we are unable to tell our stories, what will become of humanity? Literature allows us to imagine different worlds in which such eventualities come to pass. They then require us to formulate a politics of reading in response to rapidly changing material and virtual realities.

Conclusion: Further Ecological Readings

As the previous chapter clearly illustrates, discussing ecological ends does not mean putting an end to reading ecologically. There are many future directions for French *écocritique*. Before considering a few of them, it is useful to come back to the term "ends" in the sense of "objectives" or "goals": Why read literary texts ecologically at all? While many ecocritics respond to this question by insisting on the urgency of the environmental crisis, such a response has the disadvantage of downplaying the possible literary reasons for reading texts ecologically. The goal of ecological reading is not to reduce the literary text to a single, political message, but instead to attend to its multiple discursive and thematic threads, sometimes contradictory, certainly always nuanced. Reading theory and fiction together, French *écocritique* works to construct a new set of concepts that do not rely solely on either theory or fiction. An ecological reading does not impose theory on fiction as if there existed a set of general, abstract ecological principles that could be applied to the literary text's themes and form. For example, the notion of ecological subjectivity cannot be found in Guattari's writings, and yet it can begin to take form when the reader reflects on ecosophical thought in light of Darrieussecq's novels. Similarly, the idea of ecological ends is a product of reading Schaeffer's literary theory and Houellebecq's fiction together, but the concept cannot be found in either of their writings, and neither Schaeffer or Houellebecq aligns himself with ecological thought. Theory and fiction become sounding boards for new eco-concepts, illustrating both their limitations and their potential.

Another goal of the French *écocritique* I outline in this book has been to construct an understanding of the ecological that challenges Ferry's category of anti-humanism and more generally his humanism/

anti-humanism binary. While critical of the humanistic self, my ecocritical approach includes the human without resurrecting the universal (white, male) human subject. It does so by emphasizing processes of subjectivity, examining the modes of embodiment, opening politics up to the agency of non-humans, and accepting science as a way of making forms of life matter, as a way of "rendering" certain material processes and not others.[1] My ecological readings align in many respects with posthumanism's efforts to construct new subject positions. Braidotti aims, for example, to "define the posthuman subject within an eco-philosophy of multiple belongings, as a relational subject constituted in and by multiplicity, ... a subject that works across differences and is also internally differentiated, but still grounded and accountable."[2] In the wake of poststructuralism's continuous deconstruction of the subject, posthumanism proposes relational subjectivity, differentiated subjects, and new forms of trans-species solidarity.

Despite these similarities, I am not advocating for a French *écocritique* that perfectly aligns with posthumanist thinking. There are still possible links between ecological thought and humanism that need to be acknowledged. Humanism is, after all, not a monolithic block. As Kate Soper remarks, it is important to consider which strain of humanist thought is being critiqued if one hopes to propose something new: A more contemporary "technical fix" humanism that continues to place its faith in science and technology? A Renaissance humanism that believes in the self-emancipation of humans (often in the form of the Vitruvian man) in their capacity to determine their own nature?[3] As I have emphasized throughout this book, anti-humanism is not the only way of challenging and rethinking the long tradition of humanism. There are other available positions within, next to, and beyond humanism that can be reconciled with ecological thought.[4]

Ecological humanism

According to Whiteside, French *écologie politique* has been humanist from the start, but in a sense very different from the oft-decried anglophone sense of the term. Decoupling humanism and anthropocentrism, Whiteside explains that "humanism becomes ecological when it opens itself to reflecting on how nature and humanity are mutually reflecting."[5] He offers convincing examples, such as Latour's redistributed humanism, which accords agency to non-humans, and Serres's philosophy, which draws on Montaigne's sceptical humanism. More generally, Whiteside describes ecological humanism as "question[ing] facile assumptions about 'human' nature and thereby … ton[ing] down the hubris of Cartesian humanism."[6] French *écologie politique* adopts a positive, non-centred humanism, asserts Whiteside, whereas North American environmentalism is known for its outright rejection of all things humanist. While I agree that ecological humanism does appear more prevalent in French intellectual circles, it is not exclusive to it.

In *Pioneers of Ecological Humanism* (2012), Brian Morris identifies Lewis Mumford, René Dubos, and Murray Bookchin as three key thinkers of ecological humanism.[7] All Americans (René Dubos was born in France, but lived most of his life in the USA), these thinkers were critical of anthropocentrism and Cartesian dualism, but also strove to understand humans as social and biological creatures. In terms of Enlightenment ideals, all three upheld the values of freedom, social justice, and cosmopolitanism.[8] There is, however, one important difference between the ecological humanism outlined by Morris and the one described by Whiteside. All three thinkers in Morris's book supported the conservation of wilderness areas, with Bookchin going so far as to embrace biocentrism. Their ecological humanism may have been non-anthropocentric, but it was not non-centred like the French *écologie politique* analysed by Whiteside.

In the field of ecocriticism, one of the few scholars to consider the links between ecocriticism and humanism is Serenella Iovino.[9] An Italian philosopher and a leading figure of Italian ecocriticism, Iovino is attentive to the staying power of humanistic thought in the European context. Working to bring the human into ecocritical studies, she asks: "Can ecocriticism indeed be a 'discourse on the human'? And how might the idea of Otherness (an Otherness more radical than the socially constructed one) play a role in this 'discourse on the human,' an implicit – and yet essential – concept in ecological culture?"[10] In her affirmative response to these questions, Iovino proposes "a concept and practice of the human proceeding from its irreducible otherness *in itself*."[11] Non-anthropocentric humanism recognizes difference, but refuses hierarchical structures. From this perspective, "literature becomes … a non-monologuing way of saying and seeing the otherness, and a sort of sensuous code of the world."[12] Although Iovino has since moved on to a material feminist perspective,[13] her attempt to redefine humanism from an ecological perspective points to an important alternative thought trajectory for ecocritical studies.

To what extent does French *écocritique* represent the ideas of ecological humanism? While I have identified the intersections with posthumanism, it is worth revisiting the link with different strains of humanist thought. Drawing on Serres and Latour, my analysis has necessarily been indebted to the ecological humanism outlined by Whiteside, a humanism that works against Cartesian dualism and toward an understanding of nature and the human as co-constituting. For both Latour and Serres, it is necessary to construct a common world, and so the notion of humanity remains central to their ecological thought. Serres holds out great hope for the coming together of the humanities and the sciences as they work to arrive at "un humanisme décentré, pour la première fois authentiquement universel."[14] Latour, too, asserts the role of the sciences in writing our common geostory (Serres uses the expression *le grand récit*) and continues to endorse the idea of making the universal. While my ecological readings have followed Latour's and Serres's non-anthropocentric thinking about the human, they have avoided calls for a universal humanity.

This may in part be due to Guattari's place in the French *écocritique* I outline in this book. As Whiteside points out, Guattari stretches "the strands of noncentred ecologism past the breaking point."[15] His ecosophy does not seek to theorize nature and the human as co-constituting; instead, it breaks ecological thought into three overlapping, co-dependent spheres – mental, social, and environmental. Analysing the processes of subjectification and desubjectification, Guattari radically rejects the stability and rationality of the human subject.[16] His thinking is thoroughly relational, which is why it seems closer to a material posthumanism than to an ecological humanism. And yet Guattari speaks of a "collective human awareness" in the face of the ecological crisis.[17] He emphasizes the global scope of environmental issues, but questions "structural 'Universals' of subjectivity."[18] His thinking thus offers a useful counterpoint to calls for a universal ecological response or a "global environmental imagination" (see, for example, Buell's work here). As I have outlined it in this book, French *écocritique* follows Guattari's call for "multi-componential ... machinic multiplicity,"[19] and "singularising and heterogenetic becomings."[20]

Schaeffer's project reveals other ways of contending with humanist thinking more specifically in the area of literary studies and literary theory. First, Schaeffer clearly rejects the main tenets of humanist thought: nature/culture dualism, the thesis of human exceptionalism, and non-biologically defined traits such as thought and mind (in particular the Cartesian notion of the *cogito*). Second, his theory of fiction opposes much of literary theory's underlying humanism by calling into question the long-standing distinction between "low" and "high" art, and by embedding mimesis and representation in cognitive psychology's explanations of human development. Art does not exist on a higher, immaterial realm; it is a social practice, among other things. At the same time, Schaeffer's faith in the sciences echoes a humanist belief in objective truth and a capacity to explain all things human, ranging from literature to music, from video games to film. Even if Schaeffer avoids biological reductionism, he constructs a notion of the "human" as a homogeneous species that tends to flatten difference and singularity.[21] There are then multiple positions for bringing the human into a French *écocritique*, some of which follow familiar humanist lines, whereas others require the adoption of new posthumanist perspectives.

Literature's (post)humanist roles

Without mythologizing Ferry's influence as a French intellectual, I want to come back to the way his thinking epitomizes a type of secular, liberal humanism. At multiple points in his book, Ferry defends a French way of thinking (about nature, reason, human rights, etc.) against German and/or American traditions (romanticism, anti-humanism, wilderness and/or wild, etc.).[22] But he then asserts that this French way of thinking represents a universal humanism and rejects an "ideology of difference" because difference means division and hierarchy, and inevitably leads to regionalist or nationalist sentiment.[23] In other words, Ferry himself underscores cultural differences, but he then makes the move toward the universal that I find so problematic: he adopts one perspective that is supposedly free of such nationalisms and erects it as universal truth. Similarly, he takes liberalism as such a truth, asserting the right of every individual to claim the "infinite processes" of "progress."[24] While the Universal Declaration of Human Rights has institutionalized the basic rights of the individual, it does not include the right to "progress." And so again, Ferry's humanism reveals the cracks in universalist thinking.

While it is easy to dismiss Ferry's all-too-familiar faith in human progress, the book's epilogue outlines a less-easily contested faith in the universal power of art. Why end a book attacking radical ecological movements by discussing great works of art? Far from proposing a new theory of aesthetics, Ferry is placing art within the civilizing processes of universal humanism: "And it is in this expansion of horizons [in art], which is impossible without the articulation of elements which some would like to separate out for ideological reasons, that true greatness resides."[25] Ferry's rhetorical flourishes at the end of his text give full expression to the categorical thinking at the heart of his thought. Either the reader is for humanity (culture, progress, art, the intellect, etc.) or for barbary (destruction, savagery, cruelty, violence, division, etc.). Ferry's polemics obscure the fact that he is promoting a commonly held conception of the arts as expressing human greatness, as the highest achievements of humankind – in short, as one of the pillars of liberal humanism.

In *A Brief History of Thought* (2010 [2006]), Ferry writes a short introduction to philosophy for a general (younger) audience. Many of his points echo the kinds of general, abstract truths about humanism that can be found in the rest of his work – philosophy's capacity to teach us how to learn to live, know ourselves, transcend difference, and arrive at a universal acceptance of others. Ferry revisits the question of literature in the humanist project in a way that is worth summarizing briefly in light of ecocriticism's call for less emphasis on national differences.[26] According to Ferry, literature has the capacity to possess "a universal human meaning, which ... is able to affect all readers."[27] He cites at length V.S. Naipaul's 2001 Nobel Prize for literature acceptance speech to illustrate that a text is capable of transcending its socio-historical particularities.[28] The fact that Ferry chooses a postcolonial author signals to some extent the changing landscape of literary studies as it adopts a broad World Literature view.[29] But Ferry then goes on to cite Plato, Homer, Molière, Shakespeare, Bach, and Chopin as examples of art that expose us to "enlarged thought," and so once again promotes a classically humanist, canonical list of male authors.[30] My point in summarizing Ferry's explanation of literature's role in the humanist project is not simply to dismiss it; rather, I am using his explanation to reveal the difficulties of making arguments about the universal value of specific literary texts.[31]

Acknowledging these difficulties does not mean limiting a literary text's significance to its socio-historical context, as if a Greek tragedy like *Antigone* could no longer have any meaning for an iPhone-touting seventeen-year-old today. To counter both universalist and relativist views of literature, I will briefly come back to the literary texts included in this study. Working on contemporary literature, I do not have the benefit of a long historical perspective to determine a text's "universal appeal." I do not know whether the novels I have chosen will stand the test of time. Darrieussecq and Houellebecq have been translated into many different languages and appeal to a wide readership, but Rufin and Lafon have not. But this is not, I am arguing, what makes the texts "worthy" of study or not. It is instead "what a text … can do, what it has done, how it has impacted upon one's self and others."[32] In my case, this has been a question of asking what the texts can do to construct a set of general ecological concepts.

Sometimes it is the incompatibilities between theory and fiction that prove the most productive. For example, Guattari's thinking does not allow for so stable a subject as Darrieussecq's recurring female subjectivities. And yet Darrieussecq is not appealing to a universal, essentialized notion of womanhood; she embeds female subjectivity in the gendering processes of the French language. In this way, her fiction challenges the notion of a general concept of ecological subjectivity. A tension also arises in the chapter on ecological dwelling between Lafon's careful portrait of a specific rural setting in south-central France and Serres's global model for a symbiotic relation between humanity and planet Earth. This tension dissipates once the connection to sensory experience is made, as both Lafon and Serres illustrate that ecological dwelling requires bodies making space together. The French language represents an *oikos* for both Lafon and Serres, and so becomes one of ways in which they live and convey a sense of embodiment.

Even if Latour critiques environmentalism and Rufin radical ecology, they do so from polar-opposite perspectives: the anthropologist-sociologist calls for a major overhaul of modern thought, and the former doctor-diplomat for a renewed universalism of human rights and equality. These important differences allow me to articulate an ecological politics in terms of varying cultural influences in France rather than as some global platform for changing the world. Similarly, Schaeffer and Houellebecq have very different reasons for describing humans as a biological species in the living world. And yet they both include in their decentring of the human an emphasis on the capacity to tell stories, to recount tales, and to invent fictional worlds. The chapter on ecological ends is a way of coming full circle, asking what social, material, and political roles literature is made and will be made to play in the present and the future.

Stripped down to a set of generalities or abstractions, the four concepts lose much of their interest. Ecological subjectivity and dwelling draw attention to how life is experienced as corporeal and material reality, while ecological politics and ends highlight the structures, institutions, and patterns that give form to these lives. While they still hold some value for thinking ecologically, these concepts become much more interesting when they come into contact with the literary texts. First, the stability and rationality of the human subject is broken down by swirling narrative voices; second, the rootedness of dwelling is undone by porous bodies and evolving socioeconomic conditions; third, the inclusion of non-humans in politics comes into conflict with questions of social equality; and finally, the centrality of humans is called into question by reconceptualizing animality and imagining a future world without them. Theory and fiction are embedded in the evolving *oikos* of cultures, languages, and literatures.

Rather than aspire to literature's (humanist) universal value, ecological readings foster (posthumanist) encounters with a literary text's specificities. In place of an objective truth that exists outside of the text somewhere, "what comes to the fore," Braidotti explains, is "the creative capacity that consists in being able to remember and to endure the affective charges of texts as events."[33] Affective encounters are posited on the presence of a reader, an embodied reader who has been marked in terms of gender, class, and race. In my encounters with the literary texts studied in this book, I have become increasingly aware of this embodiment. How has my own corporeality remembered Darrieussecq's female subjectivities as porous sites of interaction with the material world and Lafon's sensing, smelling, perceiving bodies as sites of ecological dwelling? How has it worked to forget Houellebecq's reductive portraits of female characters as sexual objects and Rufin's politely conservative representations of female traits?[34] More generally, how has it been a part of my theorization of ecological readings and a French *écocritique*?

Embodiment is not, however, a passage to the universal body. As feminist work has shown, the female body cannot serve as a reference point for a common identity because such a body erases marked differences and only exists in the abstract.[35] So how much more so for the "human body" taken as a general given. Situatedness requires identifying the particular relations and the role of place (geographical, social, etc.) that make one meaning or a kind of knowledge possible. While similarities across difference are possible, solidarity is a temporary configuration. A particular collective of humans and non-humans come together around a common political cause (necessarily including some and excluding others), but this does not create a set of permanent bonds.[36] A politics of location raises important questions about the specific conditions that underlie claims about adopting a global perspective even when issues like climate change are being discussed.

Situating French *écocritique*

In their article "Globalizing French *écologie politique*," Denis Chartier and Estienne Rodary describe some of the potential problems of insisting on difference and diversity in terms of intellectual traditions and linguistic communities.[37] First, they describe the phenomenon of "knowledge brokerage" in which French scholars become "experts" in concepts and theories from the English-speaking world, the novelty of which overshadows contributions being made in similar fields in France.[38] Second, they outline the problem of "internalizing a provincialist position" in the case of English scholars "discovering" French thinkers and then "exoticizing" such ways of thinking instead of truly engaging with diversity and difference.[39] Third, they describe the problem of essentializing French difference in order to make "France (and French academe) stand out more."[40] To counter these problems, Chartier and Rodary speak of moving beyond "national and scientific boundaries" and of globalizing political ecology.[41] Yet they conclude their article by coming back to Haraway's notion of "situated knowledges" and by insisting on the need to "focus on the language question."[42] Paying more attention to language is, they assert, "very much an ecological and political stance."[43] Chartier and Rodary's article foregrounds the issues I have been addressing in this book while also serving as a reminder of the pitfalls into which a specifically French *écocritique* can fall.

As a scholar of contemporary French literature, I have chosen to write a book in English about French *écocritique* rather than a book in French about anglophone ecocriticism. This means I am not playing the role of "knowledge broker" who tries to "sell" her expertise in an anglophone field to French literary scholars.[44] While I am introducing less-well-known French ecological approaches and perspectives to an anglophone audience, I avoid exoticizing these approaches by acknowledging the ways in which the concepts I consider are already part of cross-cultural dialogue. Rather than "essentialize difference," I contextualize it by paying careful attention to the "language problem." In my ecological readings, I attend to the ways in which language inflects the meaning of the text and inflects understandings of what constitutes culture. In addition, I am careful to distinguish between nation and culture, underlining the fact that culture occurs at many different levels, from the regional to the transnational, from the local to the global, and that it cannot be reduced to geopolitical borders. Working from a literary perspective, I am much less interested in defending a "national heritage perspective" than I am in the way culture is subverted and inverted, regenerated and renewed through literature and language.

What is missing from my outline of a French *écocritique* is the kind of global view advocated by Chartier and Rodary. For these two geographers, it is necessary for French *écologie politique* to "overcom[e] methodological nationalism" and to "develop a theoretical approach" for understanding such differences.[45] I prefer to resist the increasing pressure to adopt a global perspective in light of the advent of the Anthropocene or the urgency of climate change. Doing literary studies in a language other than English facilitates this position of resistance. It makes me very conscious of the problem of creating a common language for global environmentalism.[46] The French *écocritique* I am developing in this book remains rooted in the specificities of the texts and concepts I have chosen. It is also bound to some extent to French as a language, which is why I have retained the French word *écocritique* throughout my text rather than using the English "French ecocriticism" (Chartier and Rodary adopt a similar strategy to describe a French *écologie politique*).

It is clearly not my intention to construct impermeable cultural and linguistic barriers. Much of this book explains and contextualizes the ways in which nature and ecology are theorized and represented in the French texts I have chosen. I cite English translations of French originals when they are available. My aim is both to facilitate and complicate cross-cultural dialogue. This is also true of my publications in French that present ecocriticism as a viable approach to reading texts, but always within a specific cultural and linguistic context. If I have chosen to write this book in English, it is to create more cross-cultural negotiations around the problem of planetarity (in keeping with comparatists like Spivak): What do we gain or lose by insisting on the tensions that are characteristic of cultural specificities? What do we gain or lose by embracing the call for a "sustainable universal" or a "global environmentalism"?

Insisting on language as a defining characteristic for a French *écocritique* has created certain restrictions that need to be acknowledged and troubled. Choosing only authors published in France, I have to some extent contributed to a problematic monocultural view of the French language. Obviously, French is not spoken solely in France. Living in Montréal, Quebec, I am keenly aware of the ways in which French has evolved differently around the world. If I have not included francophone authors from outside of France in this book, it is not because of a certain bias toward the French spoken in France (even this is far from being homogeneous), but because I am interested in the "French" effect in the sense of France as a geographical, political, cultural, and linguistic reality. Another reason I have limited my ecological readings to literature published in France is because this is the area in which I have invested the most time researching and studying. But this does not mean that ecological readings of other francophone texts are not just as important.

I want to come back to the political work that the term *écocritique* can be made to do. In an English text like the one I am writing, I have used a French word in italics in order to draw attention to the ways in which the meanings of concepts are tied to the effects of culture and history. When writing articles about ecocriticism in French, I use the word *écocritique* to create a sense of unfamiliarity (the term is still relatively uncommon), and so remind the reader of the careful comparative approach that is needed to work cross-culturally. In the end, this book's aim is not to make ecocriticism more global or even international, but to ensure that *écocritique* carries the traces of the cultural and intellectual contexts in which it can and has been deployed.

In light of the need to recognize French as a diverse collection of languages, a possible future direction for *écocritique* would be to work comparatively with colleagues developing other francophone ecocritical approaches. For example, Étienne-Marie Lassi's edited collection *Aspects écocritiques de l'imaginaire africain* (2013) is aligned more with post-colonial studies than with French *écologie politique*. As Lassi explains, ecocritical studies of African literature pay careful attention to the ways in which environmentalism has served as a vector for further oppression.[47] In this case, colonial pasts are a stronger connector than language. As for the development of ecocriticism in Quebec, scholars have pointed to the confluences not only with North American literary models but also with intellectual traditions of French *écologie politique*.[48] Consideration of the cultural, historical, and linguistic differences of these other *écocritiques* troubles the idea of a single French *écocritique*. But is opening up to plural *écocritiques* enough to avoid the centre-periphery structure that continues to plague the notion of *francophone* (often used to reference the use of French outside of France)?[49]

Another way to continue pluralizing a French *écocritique* is to configure new concepts and constellations for reading ecologically. For example, I take up Animal Studies in the chapter on ecological ends, but the concept of ecological animals may help to create a perspective combining ecocriticism and zoopoetics. Bringing together the ethological, anthropological philosophy of Vinciane Despret and the novels of Joy Sorman could be one way of constructing the concept of ecological animals. In her illustrated collection *Bêtes et hommes* (2007), Despret outlines the many ways in which animals surprise us and have a hold on us (to take up both etymological meanings of the French verb *surprendre*).[50] Her description of animal-human relationships highlights the many ways in which the affects and effects of these relationships go far beyond simple cohabitation. Despret's work could be brought into dialogue with Sorman's novels, which raise the ethical issue of animal-human relations.[51] This pairing could lead to a rereading of both Schaeffer and Houellebecq in order to create additional connective threads between the concept of ecological ends and ecological animals.

While working on this book, I have become increasingly aware of the need to interrogate a French *écocritique* built solely on theories developed by men. It is true that I have cited female scholars such as Haraway, but the bulk of my theoretical attention has been directed toward Guattari, Latour, Schaeffer, and Serres. What new directions would a French *écocritique* take if it began integrating the work of female philosophers such as Corine Pelluchon and Émilie Hache? Taking up the animal question, Pelluchon constructs an ethics of vulnerability[52] that extends far beyond Schaeffer's passing comments about the suffering inflicted on factory farm animals at the end of *La Fin de l'exception humaine*. Without identifying as a feminist, she has been articulating a philosophy of political bodies around the practices of eating and feeding and insisting on the *corporéité* of the subject (both human and animal).[53] A former student of Latour, Hache brings together animal welfare and environmental concerns under the umbrella of a broadly constructed pragmatic ecology.[54] She expressly aligns herself with ecofeminism in order to articulate ecological practices that include gender politics. Reading the work of these philosophers, I have felt compelled to ask how a feminist epistemology and politics of location can inform a French *écocritique*.[55]

Emerging from these questions is a French *écocritique* open to other points of comparison. Colonial pasts, gender issues, and species concerns can serve as organizing principles for new ecological concepts. At the same time, I do not want to lose sight of what I have been calling the "French effect" or what could be called more generally the "language effect." While ecocriticism has become more and more attentive to the politics of gender, class, and race, it has often viewed language differences as getting in the way of building a common vocabulary around environmental issues. This book asserts the importance of speaking the politics of language and theorizing culturally informed *écocritiques*. If we accept that language affects the ways in which we organize and understand the world,[56] knowing multiple languages affords the opportunity to know multiple natures.

Notes

Introduction

1 Ferry, *The New Ecological Order* 15–16.
2 See, for example, Bruno Latour's critique of Ferry's reductionist analysis of Serres in "Arrachement ou attachement à la nature?" 21–5; and Kerry Whiteside's similar comments in *Divided Natures* 116–17.
3 Catherine Larrère has done much to further the study of environmental philosophy in France. See, for example, *Les Philosophies de l'environnement*, and her co-authored books with Raphaël Larrère, *Du bon usage de la nature* and *Penser et agir avec la nature*.
4 As I will explain later, this marginalization has also had an effect on the emergence of other environmental disciplines in France; environmental history and environmental literary theory have both only recently appeared on the scene.
5 The way in which Ferry attacks Serres is a telling example of the former's anti-Americanism. In the preface to the English translation *The New Ecological Order*, Ferry characterizes Serres's book *Le Contrat naturel* as part of an "authentic American-style crusade against anthropocentrism" adding in parentheses that "(Serres has been teaching in California)" (xxiv). Ferry wields the binary oppositions of French versus American, us versus them, humanism versus anti-humanism at various key points in his book.
6 All quoted in Garrard, *Ecocriticism* 3–5.
7 I am not using quotes around the word "nature," but I do want to underline the heavy philosophical and ideological lifting that this term has been made to do in the past (see, for example, Neil Evernden's *The Social Creation of Nature* and Val Plumwood's *Feminism and the Mastery of Nature*). As the rest of my analysis will show in this book, I understand nature as a physical

reality that is experienced by way of bodies that are always and necessarily limited in time and space, bounded by cultural and historical parameters.

8 Schoentjes; Suberchicot.

9 Phillips xi.

10 Trans.: "landscape representations," "postmodern landscapes, interface landscapes … landscapes where occurrences of exchange, contact, and contamination of places prevail" (Kalaora 162). All translations are my own unless stated otherwise.

11 Bramwell 40.

12 Vercier and Viart.

13 Trans.: "A mirror that one carries while walking down the road."

14 In France in particular, there has been a tendency to dismiss literature published in the last forty years as having little literary value. See, for example, Jourde; Maingueneau; Todorov.

15 Darrieussecq's *Bref séjour* was translated into English as *A Brief Stay with the Living*, whereas *Le Pays* has not yet been translated. I will quote from the English translation for the first novel.

16 None of Lafon's novels has yet been translated into English, but her work is garnering more and more critical attention in France. About Lafon's novel *Les Pays*, literary critic Pierre Assouline writes on his blog "La République des lettres" that the prose is remarkable because of its precision and its sharp sense of observation. Assouline also situates Lafon's work in a line of well-known French writers such as Pierre Michon and Richard Millet who set their stories in *la province* (Assouline).

17 Latour, *Politics of Nature*.

18 Neither of these novels has been translated. Rufin's novels are bestsellers in France, appealing to a wide public, yet they have attracted very little scholarly attention. By including Rufin in this study, I am arguing for an ecocritical approach that remains attentive to the important effect of popular culture on the general public's environmental imagination.

19 Schaeffer.

20 Houellebecq is the best-known French contemporary author of the four I have chosen. All of his novels have been translated into English. *Les Particules élémentaires* has two English titles: *Atomised*, translated by Frank Wynne, came out in Britain in 2001; *The Elementary Particles*, also translated by Wynne, came out in the USA in 2001. *The Possibility of an Island*, translated by Gavin Bowd, was available the same year as the French original (2005). Houellebecq's novel *La Carte et le territoire* (2010) won the most prestigious French literary prize, the *Prix Goncourt*.

21 Trans.: "Fringed with sleep and dreams," "immersed in madness and beauty," "concrete, flowing, solid, fragile, sharp and blurred, holding fast or slipping" (Michel Serres, *Hermès V. Le Passage du Nord-Ouest* 161).
22 See, for example, *Tristes tropiques*, a more personal text in which Lévi-Strauss critiques the destruction of the Amazon rainforest and that he wrote during one of his trips to Brazil.
23 Trans.: "The world before life, life before humans, and respect of other beings before love of self" (Lévi-Strauss, *Mythologiques 3. L'Origine des manières de table* 422).
24 Andermatt Conley 47. See also my book *La Nature et l'écologie chez Lévi-Strauss, Serres et Tournier*.
25 Whiteside 3, emphasis in original. For another positive reading of French attitudes towards nature and environment, see Bess's *The Light-Green Society*.
26 Trans.: "This debate has primarily affected the English language community, especially in the USA … France has, until now, stayed out of it" (Larrère, *Les Philosophies de l'environnement* 5).
27 Catherine Larrère, "Éthiques de l'environnement."
28 Locher and Quenet.
29 See the entry for "environment," *Oxford English Dictionary*, online.
30 The term can be traced back to the Old French *environemenz* meaning a contour or circuit. See "Environnement," *Centre National de Ressources Textuelles et Lexicales*, online.
31 Trans.: "Forget about the word *environment*, commonly used in these matters. It assumes that we humans sit at the centre of a system of things that gravitate around us, navels of the universe, masters and possessors of nature" (Serres, *Le Contrat naturel* 60).
32 The term *environnementalisme* is identified as coming from English rather than from the original French word *environnement*. While it was previously categorized as an Anglicism (with the French *écologisme* being recommended), it is now accepted as part of common parlance. This etymological history illustrates the many ways in which languages come into contact, borrow from each other, and yet still evolve differently within their specific sociocultural contexts.
33 Célestin, DalMolin, Dambre, and Golsan 317.
34 And it continues to be the object of study. In her careful analysis of the French nation-state, Monica Prasad argues that centralization and the welfare state have given rise to a pragmatic neoliberalism in France that differs quite markedly from American neoliberalism. Prasad does not

go so far as to speak of French exceptionalism, but she does enumerate a number of important sociopolitical and economic differences.

35 Morrison.

36 Lévy.

37 Ford 186.

38 Ford does not discuss the Canadian model of national parks in her comparative analysis. For an interesting study of three very different national park models, see G. Blanc.

39 Trans.: "Restorative, nationalist, profitable" (J. Viard 98).

40 Trans.: "It is necessary to plunge into the inmost religious depths of the organization of our cultures to understand why some have favoured natural monuments and others human monuments" (J. Viard 12).

41 Abu-Lughod.

42 Fox 474.

43 Breidenbach and Nyíri.

44 Breidenbach and Nyíri 344.

45 The thinkers included in my study have also moved back and forth between French and anglophone worlds, publishing in French but being translated into English, and teaching in both French and North American institutions. Latour and Serres are particularly representative of the ways in which ideas circulate in global contexts, while Guattari and Schaeffer are better known in a European context. Characterizing these thinkers as representative of some form of "French" culture would be extremely reductive.

46 Spivak, *Death of a Discipline* 26.

47 Spivak, *Death of a Discipline* 19.

48 Heise, "The Hitchhiker's Guide to Ecocriticism" 513.

49 Heise, *Sense of Place and Sense of Planet* 60.

50 Buell, "Ecocriticism: Some Emerging Trends" 107. The online Babel project of the *Environment & Society Portal* is doing just this by asking thinkers and scholars from different areas around the world what wilderness means in their language.

51 See, for example, Patrick Murphy's work, which is in English, but has been crossing many cultural and linguistic boundaries since the late 1990s – see *Farther Afield in the Study of Nature-Oriented Literature*, and more recently, *Transversal Ecocritical Praxis*. For ecocritical work in major European languages, see Iovino's *Ecologia Litteraria*; Goodbody's *Nature, Technology, and Cultural Change in Twentieth-Century German Literature;* Rojas Pérez's *La Ecocrítica hoy;* and my own work ("Penser l'imagination environnementale française sous le signe de la différence"; "Vers une écocritique

française"; "État des lieux de la pensée écocritique française"; "Translating Ecocriticism").

52 This is, however, the position that Buell takes in his first text on ecocriticism, *The Environmental Imagination,* in which he argues for a common, global awareness of ecological problems over and against national and cultural differences; see in particular the section "Environmental Response and Cultural Difference," 14–22.

53 Spivak, *An Aesthetic Education in the Era of Globalization*.

54 In many respects, even the idea that such a thing as "French" theory exists highlights the point I am trying to make. The construction of French theory as French is clearly the product of a complex set of translations (French texts into English), exchanges (French thinkers going to the USA to teach), and transformations (Foucault's philosophy taken up by feminist and gender studies). Its "Frenchness" has more to do with a certain perception of what is "French" outside of France (because of the original language in which the texts were written and the writing style of the thinkers in question) than with the French intellectual climate of the time.

55 Cusset's use of the English "French theory" in the title to his French book further illustrates the distance he is taking with respect to this literary and cultural movement.

56 In terms of the reception of queer theory in France, see Gunther, "*Alors,* Are We Queer Yet?"; and Boyle's more in-depth "Post-Queer (Un)Made in France?"

57 See Simon's careful comparative analysis of the rise of Animal Studies in North America in contrast to its development as "la question animale" in France. She makes the point that the CNRS has set categories for research projects, and if a scholar's profile does not fit in one of these boxes, it is extremely difficult to obtain funding ("Animality and Contemporary French Literary Studies").

58 Jaccomard.

59 Trans.: "Preoccupations lodged at the heart of American cultural history" (Pughe and Granger 2).

60 The attitude towards American nature writing can sometimes take a condescending tone. For example, Larrère describes this genre as "le récit de ce-que-j'ai-vu-dans-la-forêt" ("Éthiques de l'environnement" 80) [Trans.: "the story of what I saw in the forest"].

61 See, for example, Thornber, or Iovino's *Ecocriticism and Italy*. In rebuttal to the emergence of cultural ecocriticisms, see Bergthaller.

62 Trans.: "A true landscape turn" (Bergé 87).

63 See Bouloumié and Trivisani-Moreau, as well as Coyault-Dublanchet.

64 Trans.: "That image of the world, inseparable from an image of the self that a writer composes and imposes using dispersed but recurring characteristics in his work" (Collot, *Les Enjeux du paysage* 8).

65 Trans.: "Landscape presents itself … as a recourse, or rather a model for reinventing a more harmonious relationship between the cosmos and anthropos … as a terrain of action where a new modernity can be built, one that is capable of reconciling scientific and technological progress with the respect of humans and the environment" (Collot and Bergé 12).

66 See also Kalaora's work on the notion of the environment in France: "L'environnement est du côté de la réflexivité, de l'épistémologie, des sciences plutôt que de celui de la responsabilité, de la civilité, du devoir et de l'éthique" [Trans.: "Environment is on the side of reflexivity, epistemology, and the sciences rather than on the side of responsibility, civility, obligation, and ethics"] (Kalaora 114).

67 As Prieto notes in his review of Westphal's book, there is no engagement or even mention of environmental politics (Prieto).

68 It is true that Westphal is a Belgian scholar working in the area of comparative studies, which means he has more room to move toward such an approach. Yet even in his more recent book, *Le Monde plausible*, Westphal avoids engaging with postcolonial literary studies even while raising an issue at its very heart: the undoing of centre-periphery views of the world.

69 Collot, *Pour une géographie littéraire*.

70 Bouvet and Posthumus.

71 White.

72 A special 2006 issue of *L'Esprit créateur* devoted to *éco-littérature* begins the work of examining French literary texts from an ecocritical perspective but without considering how such a perspective might account for French cultural difference. See Desblache.

73 Ecopoetics is not, however, unique to the French literary landscape. British literary scholar Jonathan Bate first adopts this word in his seminal work *The Song of the Earth*. Blanc, Chartier, and Pughe acknowledge the origins of the term, but distance themselves with respect to Bate's aesthetic theory, which tries to reduce the gap between word and world. In North America, there is also a group of scholars and poets working to develop an ecopoetics from a creative writing perspective – see Hume.

74 Trans.: "The work of writing" (Schoentjes 16).

75 Trans.: "A term better-suited to French specificity is one that places less emphasis on [political] engagement and more emphasis on the strictly

literary component" (Schoentjes 24). Later in his analysis, Schoentjes notes that the animal question has nevertheless given rise to more politically engaged readings of French literary texts (78).

76 I am thinking of the publication of Serres's *Le Contrat naturel*, but another key text is Catherine and Raphaël Larrère's *Du bon usage de la nature*.

77 See also Louisa Mackenzie's brilliant readings that bring together early modern French literature and Latour's politics of nature ("Guillaume Rondelet's Sea-Monsters and Bruno Latour's Modern Constitution"; "It's a Queer Thing: Early Modern French Ecocriticism").

78 It is this larger cultural context that is missing from Suberchicot's work in *Littérature et environnement. Pour une écocritique comparée*. Working with three national literatures – American, Chinese, and French – Suberchicot analyses various examples of "environmental literature." While I applaud his call for a comparative ecocriticism, Suberchicot looks principally for similarities across different national literatures, leaving less room for the specificities of the cultural contexts under consideration.

79 Cassin, "Introduction," *Vocabulaire européen des philosophies* xvii–xx.

80 Cassin, "Introduction," *Dictionary of Untranslatables* xvii–xx.

81 Cassin, "Introduction," *Dictionary of Untranslatables* xvii.

82 Cassin, "Introduction," *Dictionary of Untranslatables* xix, my emphasis.

83 Badiou.

84 Badiou 351, emphasis in text.

85 Badiou 349.

86 Badiou 351.

87 Badiou 354.

1 Ecological Subjectivity: Guattari and Darrieussecq

1 Trans.: "Before being scientific, organizational, political, industrial, the stakes of ecology are ethical and aesthetic. They are ethical because they require a relationship to alterity and finitude that follows from their collective modalities: human, animal, vegetal, cosmic, machinic … Neither endangered natural species nor declining cultural species … will be saved if potentialities of life previously unheard-of on the planet are not engendered. So, no nostalgic return to an irreversible past swept away by humanity-machine symbiosis, but instead a collective involvement in the production of a new subjectivity, a new sociality and a new 'nature'" (Guattari, "La grand-peur écologique," in *Qu'est-ce que l'écosphie?* 517–18).

2 Trans.: "The subject was methodically expulsed from multiple, heterogeneous matters of expression. It is now time to re-examine machinic productions of the image, signs, artificial intelligence, etc. as new matter for subjectivity" (Guattari, "Vers une écosophie," in *Qu'est-ce que l'écosophie?* 69–70).
3 Trans.: "A kernel of uncertainty" (Guattari, "Pour une refondation des pratiques sociales," in *Qu'est-ce que l'écosophie?* 507–8).
4 Buell, *The Environmental Imagination* 7–8.
5 Love.
6 Naess, "Self Realization."
7 Van Wyck 2.
8 Morton 118.
9 Whiteside 8.
10 Whiteside 68.
11 Darrieussecq, "Entretien. Je suis devenue psychanalyste."
12 See, for example, Albrecht's work on solastalgia, the psychic distress caused by changes in the environment such as global warming, persistent drought, and open-pit mining; for a less-clinical analysis, see Dodds.
13 As Matts points out, ecocriticism has been much more comfortable adopting perspectives that draw on eco-psychology.
14 Matts 32.
15 In her analysis of ecological naturalism, Lorraine Code writes about an "embodied, materially situated subjectivity for which locatedness and interdependence are integral to the possibility of knowledge and action" (Code 128). This is very similar to the notion of ecological subjectivity that I will be outlining in this chapter.
16 Herzogenrath.
17 One exception to this general assertion about Guattari's work is John Tinnell, who asserts: "Guattari's ecosophical perspective promises to re-motivate the ecological turn in the humanities towards radical transformations in the production of subjectivity and concepts that carry with them the potential to sustain a more transversalised conception of identity" (Tinnell 37).
18 Nadaud 15.
19 Trans.: "It is a matter of conceptualizing practices of social intervention, including political [and] governmental, that are coherent with grass-roots social practices, with dissensual, cultural, analytical, individual and collective practices, [and] also aesthetic, and developing a politics and means, *dispositifs*, that allow for this dissensual character" (Guattari, "Félix Guattari: qu'est ce que l'écosophie?").

20 Guattari, "La Grand-peur écologique (1989)" 517–18.
21 This debate came to a head in S.K. Robisch's article "The Woodshed: A Response to "Ecocriticism and Ecophobia." For a follow-up response to Robisch's attack on theory as empty "ideological positioning," see my article with Louisa Mackenzie, "Reading Latour Outside."
22 Andermatt Conley 4.
23 There are exceptions to ecocriticism's initial allergic reaction to post-modernism and poststructuralism. In "The (Im)possibility of Ecocriticism," Dominique Head holds that postmodernism can aid ecocriticism in restructuring the subject after poststructuralism's deconstruction of the subject. In "The Land and Language of Desire: Where Deep Ecology and Poststructuralism Meet," SueEllen Campbell attempts to bridge the gap between theory – "that sees everything as textuality, as networks of signifying systems of some kind" – and ecology – "that insists we pay attention … to the way the rest of the world – the nonhuman part – exists apart from us and our languages" (Campbell 133).
24 Aliocha Wald Lasowski traces the filiation between Sartre and Guattari less in terms of existential subject-object relations and more in terms of an anti-psychiatry sentiment in France.
25 Andermatt Conley 88.
26 Guattari, "Vertige de l'immanence," in *Qu'est-ce que l'écosophie?* 307.
27 Guattari, *The Three Ecologies* 44. I will use the abbreviation *TE* to cite the text.
28 Guattari, *TE* 50.
29 Guattari, *Chaosmosis* 119–20.
30 Trans.: "A political-ethical choice for diversity, creative dissensus, responsibility with respect to difference and alterity" (Guattari, "Pratiques écosophiques et restauration de la cité subjective," in *Qu'est-ce que l'écosophie?* 33).
31 Guattari, "Pratiques écosophiques et restauration de la cité subjective," in *Qu'est-ce que l'écosophie?* 32.
32 Naess, *Ecology, Community and Lifestyle.*
33 Guattari, *TE* 34.
34 Guattari, *TE* 44.
35 It may be helpful to point out that Guattari was strongly influenced by Gregory Bateson's *Steps to an Ecology of Mind* (1972). For Bateson, mental processes and more generally ideas are not reduced to the human mind in the strict sense. The nature of play in animals, the human-environment relationship, the structure of language, among others, are all ideas that outlast and outlive any one individual. The circulation of these ideas makes up what Bateson calls an ecology of mind.

36 Guattari, *TE* 54.
37 Guattari, *TE* 43.
38 Guattari, *TE* 42, emphasis in original.
39 Guattari, *TE* 49.
40 Guattari, *TE* 67–8.
41 Guattari, *TE* 52.
42 Guattari, *TE* 52.
43 Guattari, *TE* 64.
44 Guattari, *TE* 64.
45 Guattari, *TE* 67.
46 Guattari passed away in 1992, the same year he was nominated as one of the candidates for *les Verts* in the region of Île-de-France.
47 Trans.: "Commitment to this perspective is not just a question of ideas and communication, but equally, and maybe primarily, a renewing of [political] practices" (Guattari, "Vers une nouvelle démocratie écologique" 1).
48 "Motion F."
49 Asp and Jacqué 53.
50 Asp and Jacqué 67.
51 Benjamin, qtd. in Guattari, *TE* 67; ellipses in original.
52 Benjamin, qtd. in Guattari, *TE* 67.
53 Guattari, *Chaosmosis* 1.
54 Genosko 103.
55 Guattari, *Chaosmosis* 22.
56 Guattari, *Chaosmosis* 9.
57 Guattari, *Chaosmosis* 105–6.
58 Guattari, "La Passion des machines," in *Qu'est-ce que l'écosophie?* 252.
59 Guattari, *Chaosmosis* 112.
60 Genosko 105.
61 Guattari, *Chaosmosis* 132.
62 Guattari, *Chaosmosis* 35.
63 Guattari, *Chaosmosis* 112.
64 Guattari, *Chaosmosis* 118.
65 Guattari, *Chaosmosis* 118.
66 Tinnell 41.
67 Guattari, *Chaosmosis* 16.
68 Guattari, *TE* 46.
69 Guattari, *Chaosmosis* 93.
70 See, for example, Darrieussecq's interviews with Thomas Pierre and Jean-Pierre Bourcier.

71 Darrieussecq discusses the issue of language worlds in a presentation about her recent translation from Latin to French of Ovid's *Metamorphosis* ("Marie Darrieussecq parle d'Ovide et du latin" *YouTube*).

72 See Darrieussecq's article "Je est unE autre ou pour qui elle se prend."

73 Audrey Lasserre critiques the ways in which literary historians in France created the myth of a purely French literature.

74 The event of the young boy's drowning in *Brief Stay* is echoed in the disappearance of Marie Rivière's brother when he was still an infant in *Le Pays*. These fictional events can be seen as related to the biographical fact that Marie Darrieussecq's older brother died when she was quite young. Yet fiction does not mirror fact; fictional writing cannot be reduced to a writer's psychological trauma. Darrieussecq asserts on multiple occasions that she draws on the processes of desubjectification to write her novels – that is, she empties herself of a single subject position in order to allow the sentences to emerge on their own. (I will come back to the subject of writing processes later in my analysis.)

75 Rodgers, "Aux limites du moi, des mots et du monde."

76 Chadderton, *Marie Darrieussecq's Textual Worlds*.

77 Guattari, *TE* 67.

78 While the original French text includes no identifying characteristics for these four narrative voices, indicating with a single asterisk the change from one voice to another, the English translation begins with the "cast of voices" and also identifies each passage with the narrating character's name. In other words, anglophone readers are provided with keys to understanding the novel's narrative experimentation. French readers, on the other hand, must work to identify the character traits of each narrative voice. Unfortunately, the English translation works counter to Darrieussecq's literary project to some extent. As she explains, she writes not to please her readers but to make them work to see the world differently: "Or je demande à mon lecteur un effort, une intelligence: je n'écris pas pour le distraire ni pour lui plaire mais pour l'inviter à regarder le monde d'une autre façon, et pas forcément d'une façon commode" [Trans.: "I ask my readers to make an effort, to use their intelligence: I don't write to distract or please them, but rather I invite them to see the world in a different way, a less convenient way. My books are demanding, and I hope to leave a lasting impression"] ("Les mots du vide"). I will cite from the English translation in my analysis, but want to underscore that the French original offers a more polyphonic experience of interconnected narrative voices.

79 Chadderton, "Rendering Memory in the Work of Marie Darrieussecq" 4.

80 Kemp, "Darrieussecq's Mind" 429.
81 Darrieussecq, *Brief Stay* 44.
82 Darrieussecq, *Brief Stay* 154.
83 Darrieussecq, *Brief Stay* 133.
84 Darrieussecq, *Brief Stay* 27.
85 Darrieussecq, *Brief Stay* 33.
86 Darrieussecq, *Brief Stay* 41.
87 Deitering.
88 Darrieussecq, *Brief Stay* 1.
89 Darrieussecq, *Brief Stay* 145.
90 Darrieussecq, *Brief Stay* 138.
91 Darrieussecq, *Brief Stay* 146.
92 Bess 28.
93 See Bess 76–104.
94 See Bess 104–14.
95 Guattari, *TE* 29.
96 Guattari, *TE* 34.
97 Global warming also appears as a spectre in Darrieussecq's novel a couple of times. See Anne's comments: "Outside, people are talking. The weather's not what it used to be ... The planet is heating up" (*Brief Stay* 130–1).
98 Darrieussecq, *Brief Stay* 138.
99 Darrieussecq, *Brief Stay* 115.
100 Heise, *Sense of Place, Sense of Planet* 28–49.
101 Heise, *Sense of Place, Sense of Planet* 61.
102 Darrieussecq, *Brief Stay* 80.
103 Darrieussecq, *Brief Stay* 45.
104 Darrieussecq, *Brief Stay* 57.
105 Trans.: "The key to the problem seems to be finding a neutral terrain – literal or figurative – to construct an identity that is completely free of geographical belonging" (Kemp, "Homeland" 166).
106 Rodgers, "Marie Darrieussecq: écrivaine de l'entre-deux" 105–17.
107 Darrieussecq, *Brief Stay* 97.
108 Guattari, *Chaosmosis* 118.
109 Darrieussecq, *Brief Stay* 32.
110 Darrieussecq, *Brief Stay* 45.
111 See Heise's analysis of this problematic global image of the Blue Marble (*Sense of Place, Sense of Planet* 22–4).
112 Darrieussecq, *Brief Stay* 75.
113 Darrieussecq, *Brief Stay* 73.

114 This title is particularly hard to translate because Darrieussecq is not following the rules of article agreement for the noun "other," which is masculine in French. She is thus highlighting the problem of the masculinization of the feminine in French. One possible translation might be "I am a (female) other, or who does she think she is" (Darrieussecq, "Je est unE autre").

115 Trans.: "I have the recurring sense of needing to impose on my female body the language of men … or to impose this female body on French, that language of men" (Darrieussecq, "Je est unE autre" 116).

116 Trans.: "A world of women" (Darrieussecq, "Je est unE autre" 120–1).

117 Alaimo and Hekman 4.

118 Trans.: "The world is also made up of electrons, microbes, waves, planets … and soon, no doubt, clones, GMOs, new sounds, new smells … etc. … I am part of the ongoing movement of discoverers. I want to open the eyes that are underneath the readers' eyes, the ears underneath their ears, the skin underneath their skin" (Darrieussecq, "Entretien réalisé par Becky Miller et Martha Holmes").

119 Darrieussecq, *Le Pays*.

120 Darrieussecq explains that the word "Yuoangui" was a "generic word" that she invented when writing *Naissance des fantômes* to mean a place where the immigrants and outcasts of the world live (interview with Jeanne Gaudet, "'Des livres sur la liberté': conversation avec Marie Darrieussecq" 112).

121 Entitled *Moments critiques dans l'autobiographie contemporaine. Ironie tragique et autofiction chez Georges Perec, Michel Leiris, Serge Doubrovsky et Hervé Guibert*, Darrieussecq's doctoral thesis points to her early interest in *autofiction*.

122 Darrieussecq's last name means "a dry riverbed," while the last name of the main character in this novel means "river." Moreover, Darrieussecq does not hide the fact that she wrote *Le Pays* in the spirit of *autofiction*: "À part sans doute *Le Pays*, je n'ai jamais écrit d'autofiction" [Trans.: "Aside from *Le Pays*, I have never written any *autofiction*"] ("Je est unE autre" 112).

123 Even though the Basque country is called *le pays Basque* in France, it is not an independent country. Covering parts of Spain and France, the Basque country unites people with a common language, cultural traditions, and history. By according independence to Yuoangui, the novel imagines a scenario in which the (problematic) relationship between country and nation can be explored.

124 As Gill Rye notes, the cities in the novel correspond closely to those in the Basque country – B. Nord (Bayonne), B. Sud (Bilbao), B. sur mer (Biarritz) (Rye 35).
125 During an interview with a local Basque newspaper, Darrieussecq explained that her goal was to write a novel about the plight of "small countries" in general: "Chacun a un petit pays de référence. *Le Pays* est un texte qui fait référence à tous les petits pays. Dans mon roman, il s'agit d'un pays imaginaire, le 'Pays Yuoangui.' Il fait référence à l'expérience qu'ont beaucoup de gens qui ont été élevés dans plusieurs langues" [Trans.: "Everyone has a small country of reference. *Le Pays* is a book that refers to all small countries. My novel is about an imaginary country, the 'Yuoangui country.' It speaks about the experience that people who have been raised with many languages have"] (Darrieussecq, interview with Thomas Pierre, *Euskonews*).
126 Rodgers also underlines this play between reality and fiction in the novel: "Elle [Darrieussecq] transgresse constamment les limites entre la réalité et la fiction. Darrieussecq joue avec les similitudes entre sa réalité biographique et celle de sa protagoniste" [Trans.: "She constantly transgresses the boundaries between reality and fiction. Darrieussecq plays with the similarities between her biographical reality and that of her protagonist"] (Rodgers, "Aux limites du moi" 412–13).
127 Jean Ricardou brought these two expressions together in his book *Pour une théorie du nouveau roman*.
128 Trans.: "I was running, unaware of what was going on. I was running, *thump, thump, thump, thump,* feeling, at my speed. It was rising up my legs, my knees were warming up, the muscle joints were filling up. I had started running when I arrived here. Unaware of what was going on. I would slip on my shoes, and hup! I went running. I had the feeling of doing something. Like when smoking or writing: time passes. One can physically feel it flowing. One feels the flow" (Darrieussecq, *Le Pays* 11).
129 Guattari, *TE* 38.
130 Guattari, *TE* 38.
131 Trans.: "Absorbed in, absorbing the landscape, as part of thinking" (Darrieussecq, *Le Pays* 14).
132 Guattari, *TE* 37.
133 Trans.: "What moved forward on the road were spheres playing one 'round the other, an equilibrium of drops and bounces, a series of jumps. Not me not another no one. Air, landscape, running. I/me was thinking of nothing and piercing this nothingness were sentences, faster and faster" (Darrieussecq, *Le Pays* 15).

134 Kemp, "Darrieussecq's Mind" 429.
135 Guattari, *TE* 53.
136 Trans.: "Your molecules mix with the sky and water, solitude spreads out. Words and things move apart, thinking no longer follows, signs become unmoored; and the self gapes open full of salt water" (Darrieussecq, *Le Pays* 84).
137 Trans.: "I liked the globe on my desk and I liked the promontory overlooking the sea because I often needed to experience sideration as a point of origin for writing" (Darrieussecq, *Le Pays* 187–8).
138 *Wiktionary*, accessed 14 May 2016.
139 Trans.: "To speak of the world, it is necessary to be in a reverie that is close to a kind of ecstasy in language, where one leaves one's private self" (Darrieussecq, interview with Jean-Marc Terrasse, "Comment j'écris" 261).
140 Guattari understands this paradox as essential to the practice of writing a story more generally: "Pour pouvoir faire du récit, raconter le monde, sa vie, il faut partir d'un point qui est innommable, inracontable, qui est le point même de rupture de sens et le point de non-récit absolu, de non-discursivité absolue. Et cela, c'est quelque chose qui n'est pas non plus abandonné à une subjectivité transcendante, indifférenciée, c'est quelque chose qui se travaille. C'est cela, l'art" [Trans.: "To be able to construct a narrative or tell of the world, one's life, it is necessary to start from an unnameable, untellable point, that is, the point of ruptured meaning itself, the point of absolute non-narrative, absolute non-discursivity. And this is not a question of abandoning oneself to a transcendent, undifferentiated subjectivity; it is something that works on itself. That's what art is"] ("Félix Guattari et l'art contemporain," in *Qu'est-ce que l'écosophie?* 162–3).
141 Trans.: "I wanted a landscape for Tiot … I wanted to offer a country/land to Tiot" (Darrieussecq, *Le Pays* 44).
142 Trans.: "A cliché and a nostalgia" (Darrieussecq, *Le Pays* 65).
143 Trans.: "Beauty, fresh air, sea" (Darrieussecq, *Le Pays* 43).
144 Trans.: "The country is federated by the landscape seen from the Corniche" (Darrieussecq, *Le Pays* 80).
145 Trans.: "She had come back to the country, but despite her attempts to measure it, wearing out soles and tires on its crust and sands, everything escaped her. The country was not the one of memories. Everything was similar and everything was different, the times could not be juxtaposed, the landscapes left gaps" (Darrieussecq, *Le Pays* 76).
146 Trans.: "Practiced landscape" and "remembered landscape" (Droz and Miéville-Ott, 11, 12–13).

147 Nabhan 87–101.
148 Trans.: "What to do/how to get on with this country" (Darrieussecq, *Le Pays* 48).
149 Trans.: "Write: 'I was there,' she did not really know what that meant. It was necessary to experiment, place the subject in a place, study the common places of people and countries. It started like that, landscapes and questions" (Darrieussecq, *Le Pays* 85).
150 Guattari, *TE* 64.
151 Darrieussecq, *Le Pays* 124.
152 Trans.: "Walid's and her favourite conversation was about where to live. What city can replace the world, since it's not possible to inhabit the entire world? Representative of the most well-off Earthlings – passport, money, health, time – they never tired of making their well-thought-out lists of cities" (Darrieussecq, *Le Pays* 213).
153 During one of her landscape experiences, Marie makes a trip to the top of Mount Glyph, a geographical landmark in Yuoangui. She is, however, unable to concentrate on the view below and instead makes comparisons to different places around the world: "Océan à l'ouest, forêt au Nord, montagnes à l'est et Sud jaune. Une très petite Chine. Une grande île Lofoten" [Trans.: "Ocean to the west, forest to the north, mountains to the east and a yellow South. A very small China. A very large Lofoten island"] (Darrieussecq, *Le Pays* 49).
154 Guattari, *TE* 27.
155 Guattari 35.
156 Trans.: "The *we* came to me spontaneously, some sort of local solidarity, when I evoked our funeral traditions" (Darrieussecq, *Le Pays* 179).
157 Trans.: "The universe, the world, Europe, the country, a car, a body, a uterus, and little rotating bubbles make up a nice concentricity" (Darrieussecq, *Le Pays* 119).
158 Trans.: "I am full of numerous fauna. I am a landscape full of animals, I am an amniotic land" (Darrieussecq, *Le Pays* 119).
159 Trans.: "I was hearing the old language without thinking about it. I was drinking in the language. I was swimming in it" (Darrieussecq, *Le Pays* 245).
160 Trans.: "Phantoms do not roam about in limbo. They only exist at the moment of encounter … They exist for us" (Darrieussecq, *Le Pays* 248).
161 Trans.: "The defense of a homeland," "a very utopian book that imagines a planet of small countries" (Darrieussecq, interview with Thomas Pierre, *Euskonews*).
162 Guattari, *TE* 51.

163 Trans.: "Lodged in this body," "consented to bring together in this flesh (and no other) the body that has allowed her to appear" (Darrieussecq, *Le Pays* 247–8).
164 Guattari, *TE* 68.
165 Richard.
166 Trans.: "A common, livable world," "a vitalist, creative, sometimes exuberant, perspective," and "the globality of the living world" (Blanc and Lolive 359–60).

2 Ecological Dwelling: Serres and Lafon

1 "Animal on the move, he [homo sapiens] stops and builds a vegetal structure; like a bird in a nest, like a nest in the branches. Upright, animal-vegetal, he builds arborescent houses like himself. That's it for his local habitat or renter's place. And now for the global habitat, the terrestrial globe. The Earth does not quite have the form of a sphere. A ball moving in orbit, like a moving animal, it turns on itself around a north-south axis, vertical like a plant. Swollen at the equator, flattened at the poles, a rotating tree, an orbiting animal. Animal-vegetal, homo sapiens lives on a vegetal-animal globe. A small chimera lives on a large chimera; a large amphibian welcomes us small amphibians" (Serres, *Habiter* 170).
2 Stock.
3 This notion of dwelling contrasts in many ways with Martin Heidegger's thinking in his essay "Building Thinking Dwelling," in which he elaborates the idea of a kind of being in place that is unique to humans: "To be a human being means to be on the earth as a mortal. It means to dwell" (349). He goes on to describe dwelling as a state of being that precedes building, making, and doing. Without denying the influence of Heidegger's thinking on ecocriticism, I am using the term dwelling to include human and non-human ways of inhabiting the land.
4 Bate 109.
5 In contrast to Bate, Garrard refuses to separate Heidegger's politics (his association with the Nazi party in Germany) from his poetics (his call to leave things be). Garrard is adamant about developing an "ecocriticism without Heidegger" (Garrard, "Heidegger Nazism Ecocriticism").
6 Garrard, *Ecocriticism* 108.
7 Garrard, *Ecocriticism* 135.
8 Le Goff 11.
9 I am using the French word *paysan* because there is no real equivalent in the English language; it means farmer, peasant, and villager. As part of its

etymological root, the word contains the idea of *pays* as in a connection to the land and the country, connotations that are lost in the English words "peasant" and "farmer."

10 The final chapter of Le Goff's book is entitled "Les Derniers Survivants."
11 Mathieu.
12 Trans.: "Representations of the countryside as a homogenous place like those referring to different terms such as 'the remote rural,' 'the deserted rural,' even 'the living countryside,' are out of touch with the complex reality of economic differentiation in rural places" (Mathieu 18).
13 Trans.: "A plural belonging to places lived variably in time and space" (Mathieu 11).
14 Latour, "The Enlightenment Without the Critique."
15 Paulson, "Writing that Matters."
16 Sydney Levy uses the expression "ecology of knowledge" to describe the ways in which Serres's concepts and operators function like organisms in an ecosystem – that is, they are all interconnected to each other, with meaning emerging from their relations (Levy 3–5).
17 For a more in-depth analysis of Serres's philosophy from his early structuralist years to his thinking about networks, see my book *La Nature et l'écologie chez Lévi-Strauss, Serres et Tournier*. For an initial study of the ecocritical potential of Serres's more recent texts, see my article "Translating Ecocriticism."
18 Posthumus, "Translating Ecocriticism" 97.
19 Serres, *Éclaircissements* 245.
20 Serres, *Éclaircissements* 245.
21 In his analysis of Serres's writing style, William Paulson notes that part of the reason Serres may not have attracted as wide a following as other French theorists and philosophers is because he is writing to a readership that does not yet exist, one that is well-read but not bound to a specific discipline, one that has experienced the real (rock climbing, earthquakes, sailing, etc.) and the literary (Tintin, fairy tales, Jules Verne, etc.) (Paulson, "Michel Serres's Utopia of Language"). While I agree that Serres's books require a persistent reader, I'm not sure the reader has to have all the experiences that Serres describes to be able to follow his interdisciplinary and wide-ranging philosophical wanderings. If Serres has been less "popular," it may because his writing does not fit with "French theory" or with "Continental philosophy" and does not target one specific kind of reader.
22 Serres, *Genesis* 2.
23 Serres, *Éclaircissements* 112; Serres, *Incandescent* 275.

24 See William Paulson's articles "Writing that Matters" and "Michel Serres's Utopia of Language."
25 Serres, *Détachement* 15–21.
26 Trans.: "I sow letters and I plant words, I sow signs from lines" (Serres, *Détachement* 47–8).
27 Serres, *The Five Senses* 227.
28 Serres pairs *paysan* and *paysage* in a way that gives value to the farmer's creation of landscape, whereas art historian Alain Roger denigrates the farmer's lack of "aesthetic appreciation": "On n'en constate pas moins un réel déficit esthétique dans la perception de leur propre pays, qui demeure, pour l'essentiel, le lieu de labeur et de la rentabilité" [Trans.: "One notes a real aesthetic deficit in their [the farmers'] perception of the land, that remains essentially a place of labour and profitability"] (Roger 26). According to Serres, it was the *paysan* who created the patterns, borders, edges, and openings of landscapes (*The Five Senses* 237).
29 Serres, *The Five Senses* 240.
30 Serres, *The Five Senses* 248.
31 It is clear that the natural contract is central to Serres's eco-thought. He explicitly revisits this concept on three different occasions: 1) *Le Retour au Contrat naturel*, a conference given at the BNF in Paris in 1998 and published in 2000 (*Le Retour au Contrat Naturel*, Paris: BNF, 2000); 2) "Retour au Contrat naturel," a conference given at Simon Fraser University in 2006 and available online at *C-theory*; and 3) "Retour au contrat naturel," a conference given at UNESCO in 2006 and published in 2007 (Bindé 169–80). He also includes reflections on the natural contract in many of his recent texts such as *Hominescence*, *L'Incandescent*, *Rameau*, *Petites Chroniques 1*, *La Guerre mondiale*, *Le Mal propre*, and *Écrivains, savants et philosophes font le tour du monde*. It is also possible to find traces of the concept of the natural contract in much earlier books.
32 Serres, *Le Contrat naturel* 4.
33 Serres, *La Naissance de la physique dans le texte de Lucrèce* 116.
34 Harris 43.
35 In direct contrast to Ferry, Daniel Cohen asserts that "philosophical discourse is thoroughly and essentially metaphorical and needs to be interpreted accordingly" (Cohen 3). He then adds: "the very best philosophy is the most profoundly metaphorical" (3).
36 Clark 119.
37 Roger associates Serres's natural contract with the "worst kind of personification of nature" (Roger 153), while Bramoullé cites it as another antihumanist assault on human rights and freedom.

38 Serres, "Peut-on dire encore le pouvoir spirituel ?"
39 Serres, *Hominescence* 15.
40 Serres, *Hominescence* 91–3.
41 Serres, *Hominescence* 144–53.
42 Trans.: "Linguistic pluralism and multiculturalism coexist with biological diversity, as stunning in the variations of individual bodies as in the DNA strands that reproduce the diversity of languages, like a reflection, in and through an alphabet of simple elements" (Serres, *Hominescence* 160).
43 Trans.: "I fluctuate, percolate and am not" (Serres, *Hominescence* 198).
44 Serres, *Hominescence* 258.
45 These writers are part of the regionalist literary movements analysed by Anne-Marie Thiesse in *Écrire la France*. See also the more recent collection of essays edited by Alain Romestaing, *Mondes ruraux, mondes animaux*.
46 See Coyault's "Avant-propos" to a special issue on "The Province in the Contemporary Novel" of *L'Esprit créateur*. Coyault makes a clear distinction between authors of *l'école de Brive* that do celebrate a return to the land, but whose novels are written for solely commercial purposes, and writers of *la province* who write about specific rural regions in France and who are aware of the dangers of representation highlighted by the *Nouveaux Romanciers* (3).
47 It is worth noting an important characteristic of the Cantal region. While Serres cites the low percentage of farmers in the Western world today (he speaks of 3 to 4 per cent), the Cantal region has a relatively important farming population, around 25 per cent compared to 6 to 7 per cent in the rest of France. Most agriculture is related to raising animals, and Cantal is well known for specialized cheeses such as the St Nectaire (mentioned in some of Lafon's novels). Agriculture and tourism are the largest economic drivers in the region.
48 I'm taking this description from Lafon's promotional video for *Les Pays* and *Album*, posted online by her publisher Buchet/Chastel.
49 Lafon's most recent novel, *Joseph* (2014), is also about a rural way of life, and continues to develop many of the themes in the three novels I will be analysing in this chapter.
50 As Lafon explains during an interview, Bergounioux, Millet, and Michon were all "founding figures" for her, as they gave her the courage to write about the rural despite the globalizing turn of the literary world ("Marie-Hélène Lafon: l'heureuse surprise de la rentrée littéraire.")
51 These are some of the verbs that Lafon uses to describe *le pays* in her non-fiction text, *Album*.

52 Trans.: "It must all be embodied." Lafon's promotional video for *Les Pays* and *Album*.
53 In this sense, Lafon's writing fits with Blanc, Chartier, and Pughe's description of *écopoétique* as "un travail sur la perception à travers la langue et la forme esthétique, lequel permet au lecteur de voir différemment" [Trans.: "an exploration of perception through language and aesthetic form, that allows the reader to see differently"] (6).
54 Depardon.
55 Trans.: "A tie of filiation." Lafon's promotional video for *Les Pays* and *Album*.
56 Trans.: "The Santoire family was living on an island, they were the last Indians, the mother said each time the car passed by the tourist information sign for the regional park of the Auvergne volcanoes, we are the last Indians" (Lafon, *Les Derniers Indiens* 58). The comparison to Indigenous groups draws attention to the ways of living with the land that have been lost because of industrialization and globalization. At the same time, it glosses over the fact of European settlers wiping out Indigenous ways of living in the New World.
57 Viart describes Lafon's representation of rural life in the novel as "une mémoire plus âpre que nostalgique" [Trans.: "a memory that is more bitter than nostalgic"] (Viart 256). I prefer Simon's description of the novel *L'Annonce* that I will discuss in the next section of this chapter. According to Simon, *L'Annonce* creates "un monde verbal apte à rivaliser avec la pesanteur terrienne et la désirable âpreté du Cantal" [Trans.: "a verbal world capable of matching Cantal's earthly weight and desirable bitterness"] ("Au 'pays' des bêtes" 219).
58 Trans.: "It is useless to change" (Lafon, *Les Derniers Indiens* 15).
59 Lafon, *Les Derniers Indiens* 56–7.
60 Lafon, *Les Derniers Indiens* 144–6.
61 Trans.: "They were different and the same, the world was inconceivable without them, the other side of the road inconceivable without them, breathing in their air, absorbing their sounds, we invented them, we were attentive to them" (Lafon, *Les Derniers Indiens* 57).
62 Trans.: "At the Santoires', we were not busy, not relevant, soon we would be no more" (Lafon, *Les Derniers Indiens* 155).
63 Trans.: "Alice was a limit, an impossible line, a stretched, vibrating cord beyond which there could be nothing, nothing could occur, nothing could happen, we would no longer matter, it would no longer matter" (Lafon, *Les Derniers Indiens* 149).
64 Sjef Houppermans critiques the rise of regionalist literature in France as purely commercial, asserting that it either celebrates the "little green joys"

of "la France profonde" or revels in its "small miseries" (Houppermans 151–68). He contrasts this with a literature that seeks to understand the profound transformation of the rural in light of other important changes in the history of human civilization (151–2).

65 Trans.: "There, next to the small road, on a patch between the two houses, feet in the thick grass, in the November rain, in the August heat or April hoarfrost, in the snow, in the raw wind, they would give off smells. They would create around them wakes of crumpled fragrances; it was sweet, it was male, it was green, it was warm, fickle, spicy, pungent, acrid, animal, sometimes sour, always radical and overwhelming" (Lafon, *Les Derniers Indiens* 124).

66 Lafon, *Les Derniers Indiens* 167.

67 Girard.

68 Trans.: "A world that has not finished coming to an end and reinventing itself" (Lafon, qtd. in "'Je ne fais pas les romans que je veux, mais les romans que je peux'").

69 Lafon, qtd. in "'Je ne fais pas les romans que je veux, mais les romans que je peux'."

70 In her article "Transformation, recomposition des espaces ruraux et émergence de nouvelles demandes sociales," Jacinthe Bessière identifies the social, emotional, recreational, environmental, and residential as some of the new functions of the rural (Bessière 19–34).

71 Trans.: "Why not the countryside. Elsewhere. To rip away" (Lafon, *L'Annonce* 62).

72 Trans.: "She was learning the light that would wake things, first one thing, then another, visited, taken, haloed; the fields, the trees, the blue-ribonned route, the nestled lanes, the slow cows, the morning tractors, bumping along, willingly red" (Lafon, *L'Annonce* 53).

73 Trans.: "Bodies too, especially bodies. Not relearn, not restart; invent" (Lafon, *L'Annonce* 96).

74 Serres, *The Five Senses* 167.

75 Trans.: "Composing meant everything, day night, the wash the intermingling, food and embraces" (Lafon, *L'Annonce* 79).

76 Lafon, *L'Annonce* 46.

77 Trans.: "Nothing would be passed on, continued, perpetuated" (Lafon, *L'Annonce* 77).

78 Lafon, *L'Annonce* 48.

79 Trans.: "The unfailing alliance that had formed, in plain sight of everyone, as soon as the unknown, unrelated child had arrived on the scene" (Lafon, *L'Annonce* 130).

80 Lafon, *L'Annonce* 15.
81 Éric has a similar relationship to the milking cows, who accept his presence among them while rejecting Annette (she is covered in cow dung the first time she tries to participate in the milking process). The novel describes Éric as having "la bonne façon" as he learns each of the cow's names and individual personalities. The fact that he grew up with no knowledge of animals and yet develops a close relationship with them points once again to the possibilities of new practices in rural places. For a more complete analysis of the role of animals in Lafon's novel, see Simon, "Au 'pays' des bêtes."
82 The novel does challenge this dichotomy between "cruel" farming practices and a humane understanding of animals as feeling and thinking beings in its representation of the milking cows. Nicole, too, calls them by name and treats them as individuals.
83 Serres, "Peut-on dire encore le pouvoir spirituel?"
84 Trans.: "The partnership between humans, living beings and objects, that is now required by and for the Natural Contract, revisits the Latin *familia* and the country farm as a generalized form of peasant dwelling, a global subspecies" (Serres, "Peut-on dire encore le pouvoir spiritual ?" 826).
85 According to the *Trésor de la langue française*, the expressions "faire sa maison," "faire maison nette," and "faire maison propre" were used in the nineteenth and early twentieth centuries to refer to hiring house servants (*Centre National de Ressources Textuelles et Lexicales*, web).
86 Trans.: "That perilous acrobatics of the bit-by-bit, pieced-together couple" (Lafon, *L'Annonce* 35).
87 Trans.: "He anticipated, desired, and gave of himself entirely so that at Fridières, bits and pieces would assemble themselves and make a home. He liked those words, make a home, and used them regularly to refer to the families who continued to stand more-or-less proudly in the squat buildings around Fridières, Jaladis, and Fougerie" (Lafon, *L'Annonce* 105–6).
88 Trans.: "The woman and the child, taken in, were now part of the landscape, had dug the earth around them, taken shape and root" (Lafon, *L'Annonce* 70).
89 The resistance to "strange bodies" also points to the problem of integration in France. Annette and Éric are from the north of France and not from a different country, and yet they still have difficulty being accepted in the small community. How can the practices of ecological dwelling be articulated so as to acknowledge difference and policies of immigration (especially in light of the current political climate in Europe)? The novel's

organic metaphor does not translate into such policies, but does suggest that intimate relationships that include the non-human world are one place to start.

90 Trans.: "In front of the stable door, rooted like sentinels in the granular, rough-looking, grey rock, forged into it, emanating from the building, spit out by it, and destined to stand guard for centuries and centuries" (Lafon, *L'Annonce* 151).

91 Trans.: "The intellectual world, the only one that allowed access to self-awareness" (Coyault 5).

92 Trans.: "By the throw of her body, her voice, her step, her hands, Suzanne belonged to that bit of worn country, the Santoire valley left far behind her" (Lafon, *Les Pays* 27–8).

93 Trans.: "The inevitable agony," "adaptation, innovation, invention" (Lafon, *Les Pays* 20).

94 Trans.: "She had a sharp memory of smells and knew by heart the naked woods in February, the empty barns at the end of spring, the Santoire river swollen with melted snow" (Lafon, *Les Pays* 62).

95 Trans.: "Something too volatile escaped her; during the first months, she had thought that it stank, unquestionably, Paris stank terribly, except in the Chinese laundry quarter where sacks of food, herbs, and unnamed fruits piled up on the sidewalk" (Lafon, *Les Pays* 63).

96 Lafon, *Les Pays* 86.

97 Trans.: "So much splendour and vertical munificence clashed with the organic complicity she shared with beeches and ashes from the first country" (Lafon, *Les Pays* 103).

98 Trans.: "Agricultural roots," "incongruous rural saga" (Lafon, *Les Pays* 124).

99 Trans.: "For the first time, something had been embodied that tightened its grip on her throat, her centre, and demanded from her the mute labour of fitting, of linking together … she would tame and learn to love and seek out that singular emotion roused in her by the appearance of a body, a voice, words dug up from the first world, the ancient, antediluvian one" (Lafon, *Les Pays* 81).

100 Trans.: "Within her, in her blood and under her skin, strong impressions were instilled that *made landscape, composed the world*, there was that in her and she had to broaden her life, earn it and broaden it" (Lafon, *Les Pays* 84, my emphasis).

101 Trans.: "She smells the beloved city, her second skin, she inhales the familiar scent that she is not capable of completely disentangling; it's all mixed together, machine and flesh, gearwheels and sweat, soured breath

and tired smells on greasy dust, it's both animal and mineral; it's on the dirty side and she slips into that stickiness, she finds her place, fits into the flow ... The city is learnt and found by the body" (Lafon, *Les Pays* 154).

102 Trans.: "A city burrow," and "a country burrow" (Lafon, *Les Pays* 156).

103 Lafon, *Les Pays* 156.

104 Trans.: "Perplexed, slightly lost between the large and small screen, the film and documentary ... he nodded and repeated in his throat ... it's us it's us we are like that it's us" (Lafon, *Les Pays* 196).

105 In *Joseph* (2014), she tells the story of a sixty-year old farmhand in Cantal and so comes back to a rural setting after *Les Pays*'s narrative about learning to live in an urban environment.

106 Her collection of short stories, *Histoires* (2015), was awarded the most prestigious French literary prize, the *Prix Goncourt*.

107 Serres, *The Five Senses* 247.

108 Bruno Latour, whom I will discuss in the next chapter, has proposed revisiting James Lovelock's Gaia theory as a way of writing just such a geostory (Latour, "Agency at the time of the Anthropocene").

109 Trans.: "Language: bed, kitchen, workroom, my place, my garden, my country, I mean my home. *Ibi patria* [this is my home/homeland/country]" (Serres, *Habiter* 53).

110 In *Album* (2012), a collection of short non-fiction prose essays, Lafon writes about the non-human world, from trees to tractors, from boots to cows. The chapters are organized alphabetically, but the repetition of some letters and the absence of others, and the mix of natural phenomena, built structures, domestic animals, and manufactured products undo the sense of categories and classification. The title of the book again raises the question of representation – how does a collection of textual photographs portray the continual transformation of rural communities? How does it bring these spaces alive rather than reduce them to *tableaux morts*?

3 Ecological Politics: Latour and Rufin

1 Trans.: "Parties that claim to adhere to political ecology have to commit not to a single platform, but to the creation of a State where legitimate and illegitimate associations can discuss and negotiate the multiple interests of humans and non-humans. They do not *know*. They are not 'for' or 'against.' They commit to guaranteeing that representation will be sought and explored together, and that decisions will be considered rightful by involved stakeholders" (Latour, "Cosmopolitiques, quels chantiers?!" 18).

2 For Simon Estok, to be an ecocritic means extending politics beyond the environment to include animals so that vegetarianism also becomes a defining characteristic of ecocriticism (Estok).

3 See Timothy Morton's critique in *Ecology without Nature*, which traces symptoms of Romanticism in environmentalism's calls to save nature.

4 In "Situated Knowledges: The Science Question in Feminism and the Privilege of Partial Perspective," Haraway critiques, on the one hand, the notion of a purely objective science that removes all traces of subjective practice, and, on the other, the idea of a purely socially constructed reality that leaves no room for nature's agency. The concept of "situated knowledges" allows Haraway to affirm the different positions from which science interacts with the world and the different lenses used to understand reality.

5 Latour, *Politics of Nature* 247.

6 In *L'Éco-pouvoir*, a book from which Latour draws much inspiration, Pierre Lascoumes analyses this possibility even within democratic societies when environmental movements join up with industry, business, and/or government. This book will be discussed in more detail later in the chapter.

7 Rufin was one of the pioneers of *Médecins Sans Frontières*, and spent quite a bit of time in Africa and Latin America in the seventies and eighties. He was president of the organization from 1991 to 1993, and French ambassador to Senegal from 2007 to 2010. He has written quite a few essays dealing with the many issues of humanitarian aid in addition to the novels he has published over the years. Later in the chapter, I will discuss the humanitarian/humanist connection in his novels.

8 Latour, "Arrachement ou attachement à la nature?"

9 This summary of ecocriticism's waves follows, more or less, Buell's version, first articulated in *The Future of Environmental Criticism* and then again in his article "Ecocriticism: Some Emerging Trends."

10 Working in the field of science and literature studies, Bruce Clarke argues that ecocriticism needs to engage more deeply with Latour's thinking. Louisa Mackenzie and I also discuss the importance of Latour's ideas for developing a less dualist ecocriticism (763–8).

11 Many of these articles are available in PDF format on Bruno Latour's website.

12 Whiteside 13.

13 Latour, "L'Alternative compositionniste. Pour en finir aver l'indiscutable." In a 2012 issue of *Écologie & Politique*, Jean Jacob dismisses Latour as another one of those "Americanized thinkers" who have done very little for the Green cause in France. His comment clearly reveals the ways in which

a thinker who does not follow the well-trodden paths of Green politics in France is marginalized; it suffices to associate such a thinker with "American" ideas (Jacob).

14 See, for example, Jean-Paul Deléage's critique of Latour's "mauvaise foi" in "Lutter pour la connaissance et la justice," an editorial piece that appeared in *Écologie & Politique*.

15 Latour, *Politics* 28.

16 Latour draws on Philippe Descola's anthropology, which outlines four different world views or ontologies. According to Descola, the West is the only world view that is founded on nature/culture dualism; the other world views do not have a concept of nature as separate from humans.

17 Latour, *Politics* 38.

18 Latour, *Politics* 39–40.

19 Latour is just as critical of Cultural Studies, which too quickly claims that all is discourse, text, or power relations (*Politics* 48–9). Moreover, he admits to being somewhat shocked by the reaction to his sociological analysis of work being done in scientific laboratories; rather than denying the existence of scientific fact, he saw his analysis as offering a wider range of tools to the sciences for discussing, sharing, and highlighting their work as spokespeople for the non-human world (Latour, "L'Universel, il faut le faire" 952).

20 Latour, *Politics* 114.

21 Latour, *Politics* 124.

22 Latour is critiquing a more American form of environmentalism here. For most French political ecologists, preserving "untouched" nature has not been the main issue. As Alain Lipietz explains, French green parties have always considered social and environmental concerns together.

23 Lipietz 197.

24 As he explains during the 2010 interview cited earlier with Chartier: "Pour moi, l'écologique peut être de tous les sujets possibles, c'est une certaine façon de les aborder, et en particulier d'aborder ces questions d'incertitudes sur les associations. Donc, qu'il s'agisse du chômage, de la drogue, du thon rouge, il y a une façon écologique d'aborder ces questions qui ne se résume pas à dire: 'je suis vert donc je m'intéresse à tel ou tel aspect de cette affaire, par exemple aux questions d'environnement' … Alors que je comprends l'écologie politique comme étant une redistribution du discutable et de l'indiscutable beaucoup plus originale, beaucoup plus démocratique" [Trans.: "For me, the ecological can pertain to all kinds of subjects, it is a certain way of approaching them, and in particular, approaching questions of uncertainty regarding forms of association.

For example, unemployment, drugs, red tuna, are all questions that can be approached in an ecological way, which does not amount to saying: 'I vote green, therefore I am interested in this or that aspect of the matter, for example, environmental issues' … Contrarily, I understand political ecology as a much more original and democratic redistribution of the discussable and the undiscussable" (Latour, "L'Alternative compositionniste" 91–2).

25 Latour, "L'Alternative compositionniste" 81.

26 Latour, "Moderniser ou écologiser: à la recherche de la septième cité" 5–27.

27 Trans.: "To accept ecology as the totality of all relations would be to lose sight of humanity twice, first, in favour of a unity superior to humans, and second in favour of a technocracy of minds superior to that of mere humans" (Latour, "L'Alternative compositionniste" 7).

28 Latour does not address the psychological factors of environmental issues. He asks in *Politics of Nature* why we remain so bound to the modern Constitution and responds by citing Plato's allegory of the cave, which "really weighs heavily" (129). But this response does not get to the heart of the problem (see, for example, Weber). Of course, it is worth noting that Latour is a sociologist and not a psychologist.

29 Latour, *Politics* 57.

30 Latour, *Politics* 94.

31 The terms "experiment," "experimentation," and "experimental" appear repeatedly in Latour's descriptions of everything from metaphysics to anthropology. This illustrates once again the provisionality at the heart of his ecological politics, which refuses deterministic explanations of human history and culture.

32 Latour's political ecology seems much more hopeful about the future than many of environmentalism's gloom-and-doom scenarios. He explains: "What makes the times we are living in so interesting … is that we are progressively discovering that, just at the time when people are despairing at realizing that they might, in the end, have 'no future,' we suddenly have many prospects" ("An Attempt" 486).

33 "It is necessary to *compose* in all possible senses of the term, defining a political program as well as a scientific or aesthetic program" (Latour, "L'Alternative compositionniste" 93, emphasis in original).

34 Latour, "L'Alternative compositionniste" 474.

35 Latour, "An Attempt" 474.

36 Latour, "An Attempt" 487.

37 This parallels the way in which Serres describes the natural contract. On the one hand, it is a reality that we are already living and that we have

been living for quite a while without noticing it (in our relationships with farmed land, in our scientific experiments, and now in our international climate-change talks, etc.). On the other hand, it is something that we must begin to put into practice more conscientiously if we hope to have a symbiotic relationship with the Earth as a whole.

38 Latour, *Politics* 224–5.

39 Latour, *Politics* 94.

40 His emphasis on plurality does not however lead to an everything goes relativism even if this is how his political ecology has been interpreted at times. See, for example, Alain Caillé's critique of Latour's political ecology in "Une politique de la nature sans politique."

41 Latour, "An Attempt" 474.

42 Latour, "L'Universel" 956.

43 Latour, "La Mondialisation fait-elle un monde habitable?"

44 Humphrey.

45 Latour, *Politics* 87.

46 Latour, *Politics* 109–80.

47 Latour, *Politics* 199.

48 Latour, *We Have Never Been Modern* 138.

49 In a recent co-authored article with Émilie Hache, Latour develops the difference between moralism and morality in order to rethink our relationship to animals but also to the environment.

50 I will discuss Animal Studies in further depth in a later section of the book. But it is worth noting here that Latour avoids the debates between environmental ethics and animal ethics regarding whether the ecosystem as a whole or individual animal beings should have more rights.

51 Blok and Jensen 142–3.

52 Whiteside 48.

53 Latour, *We Have Never Been Modern* 136–8.

54 Even if Latour does not use the term "humanism" often, it is telling that he continues to engage with a deeply ingrained French philosophical tradition, or what he calls "the republican heritage of our ancestors" (*Politics* 165). At the end of *Politics of Nature*, he admits, "As I am well aware, I have expressed only one particular viewpoint, one that is not simply European but French, perhaps even social democratic, or worse still, logocentric" (221). Without reducing Latour's political ecology to a single socio-historical context, it is important to acknowledge this intellectual debt.

55 Latour, *Politics* 213.

56 Latour, *Politics* 216.

57 Latour, "Biographie d'une enquête" 549–66.

58 Latour, "Biographie d'une enquête" 553–4.
59 Latour, "Biographie d'une enquête" 558–60.
60 Latour, *Enquête sur les modes d'existence.*
61 Latour, "Biographie" 564–5.
62 Latour, "L'Universel" 960–2.
63 Trans.: "As for me, I see diplomatic undertaking as a heightening of conflicts, at least at first" (Latour, "L'Universel" 955).
64 Trans.: "What interests me in the figure of the diplomat is precisely that no other arbitrator affords the opportunity to define peace" (Latour, "L'Universel" 955–6).
65 Latour is also aware of the necessity of critiquing his own ideas from the perspective of comparative anthropology. In *Enquête,* he categorizes actor-network theory as just one mode of existence among many others, and so contextualizes a theory that he had earlier presented as the one needed to move beyond the modern Constitution. For Kim Fortun, Latour's attempts at creating a common world in *Enquête* remains highly problematic because of its conceptual underpinnings and the design of the digital platform that remain rooted in the logic of late industrial capitalism.
66 Latour, "Agency at the Time of the Anthropocene"; and Latour, Conference Paper, "Anthropology at the Time of the Anthropocene."
67 Latour, "Agency at the Time of the Anthropocene" 13.
68 Latour, "Agency at the Time of the Anthropocene" 15.
69 He is, however, included in Jérôme Garcin's *Dictionnaire des écrivains contemporains de langue française*. And he was elected as a member of the *Académie française* in 2008, a forty-seat ruling body that oversees the official use of the French language and whose members are largely writers in the general sense and include philosophers, lawyers, and even some scientists.
70 Trans.: "This book is born from a desire for unity. Until now, I kept my two kinds of literary production separate: on the one hand, essays about the Third World, North-South relations, humanitarian issues; on the other, novels in which the story took place in the distant past. For me, the two were related, and what I depicted in the past was just a specific example of a general issue that is still current: the encounter of civilizations and the resulting misunderstandings, hopes, and violence" (Rufin, *Globalia* 494).
71 This theme is also taken up by Rufin in his non-fiction books, *Le Piège humanitaire – Quand l'aide humanitaire remplace la guerre*, *L'Empire et les nouveaux barbares*, *La Dictature libérale*, *L'Aventure humanitaire*, and *Géopolitique de la faim – Faim et responsabilité.*

72 For other (at times exagerated) critiques of environmentalism in the French context, see Bramoullé's *La Peste verte*, Larcher's *La Face cachée de l'écologie: Un antihumanisme contemporain*, Paraire's *L'Utopie verte. Écologie des riches, écologie des pauvres*, and more recently, Bruckner's *Le Fanatisme de l'Apocalypse*.

73 The reader has little difficulty identifying Globalia as a fictionalized version of the USA: its flag is made up of stripes and stars, its official motto is "In Globe We Trust," the Head Office of Social Protection is in Washington, DC, and the people speak anglobal (*anglobal* = English + global). But before concluding that the novel is another example of French anti-Americanism, it is worth pointing out that Rufin also caricatures the French motto "Liberté, Égalité, Fraternité." Globalia adopts the words "Sécurité, Prosperité, Liberté" as its official slogan to help brainwash the people into thinking they live in the best of all worlds.

74 The chapters of *Le Parfum d'Adam* are organized in terms of geographical place names, emphasizing its cosmopolitan scope.

75 The fuel used in Globalia has zero emissions, but its fabrication process is extremely harmful to the environment; the factories that produce this fuel are all located in the non-zones (388).

76 According to Ramanchandra Guha and Juan Martinez-Alier, the West has developed a "full-stomach environmentalism" that has at times been at the expense of developing countries. They argue that the love of nature in the West is in part a response to the alienating effects of modernization and industrialization. In countries that have not followed this same historical and economic trajectory, environmentalism has taken on a different form, one that is married to social justice, issues of poverty, and small scale farming. While Rufin does not take up this "hungry-belly environmentalism" in his novel, he does offer a strong critique of "full-stomach environmentalism" (Guha and Martinez-Alier xxi).

77 Trans.: "The muddy ground looked like unending reddish carpet. Here and there, bunches of dry trees formed something like grey filler … As for the rocks, they had cracked in two because of the frost that spread its cruel balm at night on the day's burns" (Rufin, *Globalia* 127).

78 Trans.: "Any differences between the ruins and nature had disappeared, the ruins appeared to be a part of nature" (Rufin, *Globalia* 142).

79 French landscape architect Gilles Clément argues for the virtues of what he calls *le tiers paysage* where nature is left on its own to create landscapes out of what may previously have been an industrial site, an abandoned railyard, etc.

80 As Kawthar Ayed explains in one of the few scholarly articles about Rufin's *Globalia*, it is in the non-zones that Baïkal learns to critique the self/other dualism at the heart of Globalia's politics.

81 Moraru, Rev. of *Globalia*, Jean-Christophe Rufin 51.

82 Trans.: "The reality beneath Globalia's dreams," and "a truth of a different order" (Rufin, *Globalia* 183–4).

83 Trans.: "A tale bordering on the absurd, full of originality and poetry" (Rufin, *Globalia* 182).

84 The novel also deconstructs the country/city opposition in its description of the non-zones. As Baïkal gets closer and closer to a large city, there is more and more agricultural land. Boulevards have been transformed into fields and pastures so that "l'agriculture était une activité urbaine" [Trans.: "agricultural was an urban activity"] and "les paysans étaient en fait des citadins" [Trans.: "farmers were in fact city dwellers"] (254).

85 Baïkal's first name merits further reflection in terms of the novel's critique of nature as pristine or wild. Located in Southern Siberia, Lake Baïkal is celebrated as the world's clearest, deepest, largest (by volume), and oldest freshwater lake. On the one hand, the main character's name references a geological history that dates further back than historical human history. On the other, however, Baïkal's name is given to him as part of his constructed cultural heritage. All Globalians belong to Globalia, but they can apply for a cultural registration. These normalized cultural references act as floating symbolic identifiers, erasing any real attachment to place or history. In other words, one can read the choice of first name as underlining the ways in which nature and landscape are used to construct national or cultural identities (in this case, purely superficial ones).

86 Rufin explicitly contrasts an Anglo-Saxon radical ecology with a shallow French ecologism. In the book's preface, he explains, "Chez nous [en France], l'écologie 'courante' prend le visage débonnaire de mouvement politique ayant pignon sur rue, traversés de querelles bon enfant et préoccupés, lorsqu'ils ont une once de pouvoir, d'améliorer la circulation des vélos ou le recyclage des déchets. Même les actions spectaculaires de Greenpeace ou des faucheurs d'OGM sont vues comme des mises en scène inoffensives. Du coup, on en oublie le visage que peut prendre l'écologie dans d'autres pays, aux États-Unis ou en Angleterre par exemple" [Trans.: "Here in France, 'everyday' ecology takes the form of a good-natured, well-established political movement, involved in friendly quarrels, and, when it has an ounce of power, preoccupied with improving bicycle paths and waste recycling. Even the media-covered actions of Greenpeace or GMO crop destroyers are seen as harmless productions. As a result, the

other forms that ecology can take for example in the USA and England are forgotten" (*Le Parfum d'Adam* 757).

87 Trans.: "This overwhelming nature seemed to her … to leave only a trivial, insignificant spot for the human spectator. Overcome by this beauty, Juliette noted that nature had its own existence and owed man nothing if not destruction" (Rufin, *Le Parfum d'Adam* 304).

88 Juliette assimilates the North American notion of pristine nature to the point of asserting that no nature exists in France and in Europe: "La nature n'existe plus vraiment dans les pays du Vieux Continent. Il n'y a pas un mètre carré qui ne soit cadastré, possédé, travaillé et transformé. Les paysages américains conservent au contraire une force native, indomptée" [Trans.: "Nature does not really exist in Old World countries. Every square metre has been surveyed, registered, owned, cultivated, and transformed. American landscapes, on the other hand, conserve a native, untamed force"] (Rufin, *Le Parfum d'Adam* 305).

89 In the postface, Rufin makes the following claim: "Le terrorisme écologique est pourtant pris très au sérieux par les services de sécurité de ces États. Le FBI a été jusqu'à considérer que l'écoterrorisme constituait la deuxième menace aux E-U, derrière le fondamentalisme islamiste" [Trans.: "Ecoterrorism is however taken very seriously by security services in the USA. The FBI went so far as to rank ecoterrorism the second highest threat in the USA, after Islamic fundamentalism"] (*Le Parfum d'Adam* 757).

90 Trans.: "An action novel," and not "a course lecture" (Rufin, *Le Parfum d'Adam* 759).

91 The novel does capture some of the more nuanced debates within environmentalism – for example, the debate between animal rights activists and environmental philosophers (Harrow argues that hunting animals is part of nature's cycle), and the figure of the "ecological Indian" (Harrow describes the inherently ecological way of life of his Indigenous ancestors, but later the novel reveals that his cultural heritage is largely a construction). For Méryl Pinque, this does nothing, however, to redeem the novel, whose author she castigates for "semer la confusion dans l'esprit du grand public, mentir, salir et déshonorer sous le falicieux prétexte de l'information" [Trans.: "sowing confusion in the general public's mind, corrupting and discrediting, under the pretext of informing"].

92 Trans.: "By strengthening their human side" (Rufin, *Le Parfum d'Adam* 529).

93 Ferry, *The New Ecological Order* 15–16.

94 Ferry, *The New Ecological Order* 133, emphasis in original.

95 Trans.: "The encounter of civilizations and the resulting misunderstandings, hopes, and violence" (Rufin, *Globalia* 493).

96 Trans.: "From the fight against poverty, we are moving towards a war on the poor" (Rufin, *Le Parfum d'Adam* 533).
97 Rufin's novel *Check-point* (2015) takes humanitarian aid as its main theme. Rufin describes it as a "homage" to the world of humanitarian workers, ordinary people who are often placed in extraordinary situations (see his interview with Rudy Le Cours for *La Presse*).
98 Trans.: "Most striking was the wide variety of physical types: all kinds of skin colourings, from the darkest dark to the palest pale, different degrees of pilosity and all kinds of body shapes" (Rufin, *Globalia* 220).
99 As the narrator explains, "Il n'était pas rare de trouver dans un même groupe, dix, vingt, trente origines et langues différentes" [Trans.: "It was not uncommon to have ten, twenty, thirty different languages and ethnic origins in the same group"] (Rufin, *Globalia* 349).
100 Trans.: "The tremendous historical mixing of people in the non-zones" (Rufin, *Globalia* 413).
101 Trans.: "The most powerful arm humans possess" (Rufin, *Globalia* 489).
102 Trans.: "The altermondialist's bible" (Nahapétian).
103 For an overview of the *mouvement altermondialiste* in France, see Agrikoliansky, Fillieule, and Mayer.
104 Trans.: "In keeping with my other novels' themes, it was less a question of me explaining ecological thought in detail than thinking about the gaze we direct towards the Third World and poverty" (Rufin, *Le Parfum d'Adam*, 759).
105 Trans.: "A gigantic machine producing poverty, unhappiness, destruction" (Rufin, *Le Parfum d'Adam* 751).
106 Rufin, *Globalia* 498.
107 Trans.: "A system of unambiguous and dualist values," "a rule of action given to the reader," and "an intertextual doctrine/philosophy" (Suleiman 72–3).
108 Rufin, *Globalia* 253.
109 The novel uses the term "creature" to describe these things, as if to recognize their "liveliness" after their use in the capitalist mode of production (Rufin, *Globalia* 253).
110 Trans.: "A mix of complicated instruments and human intimacies" (Rufin, *Le Parfum d'Adam* 17).
111 Trans.: "Cholera's memory" (Rufin, *Le Parfum d'Adam* 134).
112 Serres gives the example of smallpox, a virus that has been largely eradicated in the world today, but that is nevertheless kept alive in stored samples because of the value of its genetic information (*Hominescence* 31–4).

113 Trans.: "The hidden side of humanity's story" (Rufin, *Le Parfum d'Adam* 227).
114 Trans.: "Cholera is the awareness of our failures, the evidence of our weaknesses, the symbol of the earth to which we still belong, even when our spirit thinks it can fly to the sky of ideas, progress, immortality" (Rufin, *Le Parfum d'Adam* 227).
115 Rufin draws attention to the harsh realities of social inequalities that Latour has been accused of glossing over in his attempts to theorize a common world for all. See, for example, Carolina Miranda's interview with Latour, "A dialog about a new meaning of symmetric anthropology." Unapologetically critical of Latour's belief in the diplomat's capacity to negotiate dispassionately between collectives, Miranda asks, "Where have you seen a negotiation going on? What chance did the Fuegans, for instance, have to negotiate? In 50 years they have been wiped out. All of them. To the last canoe. Who is sent as a diplomat? Guns, microbes, greed, an abominable landgrab. Diplomacy? It's a sickening idea really" (8).
116 Trans.: "Ecological views are defensible on the condition that they are offset by humanism. No, man is not comparable to animals. The human species has something that the others do not. They must therefore be the object of special consideration. If humans are not regarded as sacred, anything is possible and permissible" (Le Fol).
117 Rufin, *Globalia* 480–1.
118 See also Moraru's critique of the novel's use of the literary trope of evasion. A more interesting possibility emerges from the portrait of the *Déchus* in the novel. The tribe's heterogeneity contrasts with the Globalians' conformity to set character and body types, and its name – the Deprived or the Fallen – suggests an alternate narrative trajectory to that of Baïkal. The *Déchus* were a group that chose to leave Globalia when it was first forming and so their freedom predates the totalitarian state (Rufin, *Globalia* 315).
119 Trans.: "Freer than free" (Rufin, *Globalia* 493).
120 Trans.: "Survival instinct," "any memory, any humanity" (Rufin, *Globalia* 508).
121 Trans.: "An excess of body over mind" (Rufin, *Globalia* 508).
122 Ferry, *The New Ecological Order* 15–16.
123 Adopting an even more dramatic tone, Ferry speaks of the opposition between barbarism and humanism, warning that "by considering culture … a simple prolongation of nature, the entire world of the mind is endangered" (*New Ecological Order* 151). Ferry does not reflect on the possibility

that there will be no "world of the [human] mind" at all if the planet becomes uninhabitable for human beings.

124 In addition, Latour explains that we need to move away from a given universalism and towards a future making of the universal. Rather than get rid of universality completely, Latour asks us to examine how today's globalizing forces and ecological condition do (or do not) include the processes of negotiation, discussion, and diplomacy that are key to making a common world (Latour, "L'Universel" 955–6).

125 Trans.: "In the shack's foul-smelling humidity … Juliette felt like she belonged to a family, this one here, and the larger human family beyond that" (Rufin, *Le Parfum d'Adam,* 664).

126 Latour, "On Some of the Affects of Capitalism."

127 Trans.: "At most, a novel can help the reader maintain a well-founded distrust of the future" (Rufin, *Globalia* 495).

128 Latour, "Agency at the Time of the Anthropocene."

4 Ecological Ends: Schaeffer and Houellebecq

1 The poem's title has two slightly different meanings: "Possible Ending to a Path" or "Ending to a Possible Path." In the first case, doubt is raised in terms of the actual end to a direction followed, so that the possibility of continuing on this path remains. In the second case, the ending is not in doubt; rather, it is the path itself that could have been otherwise. Given Houellebecq's general pessimism about the state of contemporary society, the title may in fact refer to the impossibility of choosing a path and then of that path ever actually ending.

Trans.: "Why bother getting restless? I will have lived anyways, / And I will have observed clouds and people / I participated only a little, I nevertheless experienced it all / There were times, especially in the afternoons.

The configuration of furniture in the garden / I knew it well, for want of innocence; / Mass marketing and urban commutes, / And the unmoving boredom of holiday trips.

Here I will have lived, at this century's end / And my journey was not always painful / (The sun on skin and the burn of existence); / I want to rest in the indifferent grass.

Similarly, I am old and very contemporary / The spring fills me with insects and illusions / I will have lived like them, tormented and serene, / The final years of civilisation" (Houellebecq, *Non réconcilié* 53).

2 Rachel Carson's "Fable for Tomorrow" in *Silent Spring* is an oft-cited example of such a success. See also Leeson-Schatz.

3 Buell, *The Environmental Imagination* 285; Garrard, *Ecocriticism* 104–7.
4 Bruckner, Kindle edition, loc. 102.
5 Bruckner, Kindle edition, loc. 3417. Here again, Bruckner sounds a lot like Ferry in his emphasis on technological solutions to environmental problems and his vision of humanity as rising above material constraints (see Ferry's more recent book, *L'Innovation destructrice*).
6 "The meaning of imaginaries whose spread shapes mentalities" (Chelebourg 11).
7 For a more nuanced, historical analysis of environmental apocalypticism, see Afeissa.
8 In her doctoral thesis, Anaïs Boulard takes up the question of reading apocalyptic genres politically and moving French ecocriticism towards a more political engagement with literary texts.
9 According to Marie-Hélène Parizeau, long, heated debates between animal rights philosophers and environmental philosophers mark the anglophone world while being almost completely absent from recent French thinking about the animal question.
10 For an overview of recent work in Animal Studies in France, see my co-edited collection with Louisa Mackenzie, *French Thinking about Animals*.
11 The work of Cary Wolfe exemplifies this shift as it moves from animal rights to posthumanist theory.
12 Buell, "Ecocriticism: Some Emerging Trends" 106.
13 In addition to these two posthumanist branches, one can cite the work of Donna Haraway (even if she rejects the term). Critiquing both animal/human and human/machine binaries, Haraway creates a triangular human-animal-machine figure to counter the long legacy of humanist thought (see in particular her well-known piece "A Cyborg Manifesto: Science, Technology, and Socialist-Feminism in the Late Twentieth Century").
14 Easterlin 20.
15 See her chapter "Minding Ecocriticism" in *A Biocultural Approach* 90–151.
16 Ecocriticism's use of the sciences has drawn some opposition. As Ursula Heise and Dana Phillips explain, ecocriticism tends to become quite reductive when it uses science as a litmus test to determine whether a literary text correctly "records" or not aspects of the natural world (see Heise, "Science and Ecocriticism" 4–6, and Phillips).
17 Schaeffer, *Why Fiction?*
18 Schaeffer, *Why Fiction?* xiii.
19 Schaeffer, *Why Fiction?* 35–40.
20 Schaeffer, *Why Fiction?* 97.

21 Schaeffer, *Why Fiction?* 103.
22 Schaeffer, *Why Fiction?* 108.
23 The case of the "fake" biography in *Marbot* (1981) has an interesting counter-example in the work of nature writer Annie Dillard. When the author revealed that she had added some fictional elements to her factual account of Tinker Creek, many readers, including ecocritics, were very upset. This illustrates once again the strength of the pact that determines the reception of a text as either fact or fiction.
24 Schaeffer, *Why Fiction?* 121–39.
25 Schaeffer, *Why Fiction?* 139–52.
26 Schaeffer, *Why Fiction?* 157.
27 Schaeffer, *Why Fiction?* 160.
28 Schaeffer, *Why Fiction?* 186, emphasis in original.
29 Schaeffer, *Why Fiction?* 205.
30 Schaeffer, *Why Fiction?* 218.
31 Schaeffer, *Why Fiction?* 293.
32 Carroll, Kindle edition, loc. 96.
33 In *On the Origin of Stories: Evolution, Cognition, and Fiction*, literary Darwinist Brian Boyd recognizes the importance of play in highly evolved animals, yet nevertheless concludes that: "Whereas play comes naturally to chimpanzees, the kind of elaborate scenario-building … seems no *normal* part of a *natural* species wide behavior, unlike childhood pretend play. And unlike human art, it seems never to be carried out with others. Human children, by contrast, construct imaginary scenarios perfectly '*naturally*,' without training, alone or in company" (Kindle edition, loc. 619). I italicize Boyd's use of the terms "normal," "natural," and "naturally" to highlight the tension between the human/animal binary in this passage.
34 Schaeffer, *La Fin de l'exception humaine*.
35 Schaeffer, *La Fin de l'exception humaine* 17.
36 Schaeffer, *La Fin de l'exception humaine* 115–29.
37 See, for example, Élisabeth de Fontenay's article "La Bête est sans raison." For a more in-depth discussion, see her book *Le Silence des bêtes: la philosophie à l'épreuve de l'animalité*.
38 Burgat.
39 Lestel.
40 Lestel, back cover.
41 Finding an English equivalent for the term *vivant* has been difficult. I have chosen the expression "the living world," but it can also be understood as "the whole of living beings." For an explanation of the possible ecological resonances and connotations of the expression *le vivant*, see Delannoy.

She argues that ecological awareness starts with an understanding of ourselves as living beings in the living world. This means replacing a past paradigm associated with words like "nature" and "natural" that still separate humans from their environment and embracing a new paradigm of *le vivant* built on connectedness, existence, and life.

42 Delannoy 271.
43 Delannoy 286.
44 Delannoy 383.
45 On the back cover blurb of this book, Schaeffer uses scare quotes around the word *"environnement"* in order to highlight the difference between this term and a general notion of the living world. This positioning echoes a point that I have made earlier about ecological thinking in France. A truly ecological view is seen as going beyond environment (Serres) and/or nature (Latour) and taking up a much larger set of concerns about human and non-human interactions, roles, and responsibilities.
46 Schaeffer, *Petite écologie des études littéraires*, Kindle edition, loc. 41 of 1955. Schaeffer's book participates more generally in a growing movement that seeks to promote the value of humanistic inquiry and critical thought in the face of consumer capitalism and neoliberal politics.
47 His outline does not differ much from the debate about the "two cultures" first outlined by Charles Percy Snow in a 1959 Rede lecture on this very subject.
48 An early defender of comparative ecocriticism, Heise has argued for paying careful attention to the ways in which nature and environment are imagined, discussed, and represented in different national literatures (see her book *Sense of Place, Sense of Planet*: *The Environmental Imagination of the Global*, and, more recently, her article "Globality, Difference, and the International Turn in Ecocriticism").
49 Trans.: "A program, which is open in terms of methodology and accepts 'evidentiary procedures' recognized by all researchers working in the same field" (Schaeffer, *Petite écologie*, Kindle edition, loc. 260 of 1955).
50 Heise, "Globality" 637.
51 Haraway, "Situated Knowledges."
52 Haraway, "Situated Knowledges" 589.
53 Haraway, "Situated Knowledges" 590.
54 This is also true of Schaeffer's more recent book, which aims to understand aesthetic experience not in terms of specific works of art, but instead "dans son caractère générique, c'est-à-dire indépendamment de son object" [Trans.: "generically, independently of its object"] (*L'Expérience esthétique*, Kindle edition, loc. 71 of 6779).

55 The first scandal was related to Houellebecq's ideologically charged comments about his best-selling novel *Les Particules élémentaires*. The second came in the wake of the publication of *Platforme*, when Houellebecq was charged and then acquitted of defamatory remarks about Islam (Sweeney).
56 Sweeney uses this expression in the title of her book about Houellebecq. She concludes her book by hammering home this idea: "Despair is not only inevitable in Houellebecq's work, it is without anticipation of either hope or redemption" (190).
57 In some respects, Houellebecq's pessimism echoes the gloom-and-doom tone of environmentalists enumerating the destructive effects of humans on life on planet Earth. But Houellebecq is not interested in discussing the sixth greatest extinction or global warming or rising sea levels; in fact, his novels openly critique the idea of saving the planet.
58 Even if Houellebecq's novels do not offer hopeful alternatives to our present world, they do reaffirm the power and place of literature and narrative more generally. In this sense, they illustrate another ecological end, the one that aims to use storytelling in all its complexities, reductions, romanticizing, and trivializing.
59 There are actually two English translations, one published in Britain under the title *Atomised* (Random House) and the other in in North America under the title *The Elementary Particles* (Vintage Books). I will cite from this second version, *The Elementary Particles*, hereafter referred to as *EP*.
60 Houellebecq, *The Possibility of an Island* (hereafter referred to as *PI*).
61 Douglas Morrey is one of the few critics to have written about the close resemblance between these two novels.
62 Morton.
63 See Houellebecq's "unofficial" biography, Denis Demonpion's *Houellebecq, non autorisé, Enquête sur un phénomène*.
64 As Laurence Dahan-Gaida notes, Houellebecq represents nature "sous un jour négatif, sous le signe de la domination brutale et de la raison du plus fort, une force aveugle, mauvaise en son principe" [Trans.: "in a negative light, as brutal domination and might as right, as a blind force, as a rule, evil"] (Dahan-Gaida 113).
65 Adopting an ecocritical perspective, Walter Wagner attempts to trace out the "tentation pastorale" in Houellebecq's fiction. He does not quite succeed, however, in explaining the discrepancy between the appreciation for beautiful, natural landscapes and the portrayal of nature as cruel, violent, and savage in the novels.
66 Houellebecq, *EP* 29.

67 Dahan-Gaida 114.
68 Houellebecq, *EP* 4–5.
69 In her book *What is Nature? Culture, Politics, and the Non-Human*, Kate Soper distinguishes three main uses of the word nature: 1) as a metaphysical concept that humanity adopts to think through its difference and specificity; 2) as a realist concept of structures and processes, studied by the sciences; and 3) as a "lay" concept to describe the ordinary, observable features of the natural environment (155–6).
70 Houellebecq, interview with Susannah Hunnewell, "Michel Houellebecq. The Art of Fiction."
71 Houellebecq, *PI* 311.
72 Houellebecq, *PI* 315.
73 Houellebecq, *PI* 334.
74 Houellebecq, *PI* 337.
75 Trans.: "Entanglement thus constructs a closed world with no way out. And *The Possibility of an Island* was precisely that impossibility. When participating in the world becomes impossible, does humanity not also become impossible?" (Granger Remy 11).
76 These opening pages are part of the book's paratextual material. They precede the cover page that indicates the official start of Daniel24's commentary and so pose a problem of authorial voice. They end this way: "No one will be present at the birth of the Spirit, except for the Future Ones; but the Future Ones are not beings, in our sense of the word. Fear what I say." Houellebecq could be warning the reader about his vision of the future; or Daniel24 could be warning future neohumans about the effect that his commentary might have on them. As I noted earlier, Houellebecq's formal experiments in this novel work to blur the boundaries between imagined and real worlds.
77 Houellebecq, *EP* 71.
78 According to Bruno Viard, a "double narrative voice" characterizes Houellebecq's novels: "Sous-jacente à la voix dominante, cynique et pornographique, une autre voix, plus fluette se fait entendre que ne percevront que les lecteurs à l'ouïe fine. La voix du bon Houellebecq qui dit que seul compte l'amour, l'amour maternel et l'amour conjugal, inséparables l'un de l'autre, et que la souffrance est terrible quand l'amour est perdu" [Trans.: "Underneath the dominant, cynical, pornographic voice, another quieter voice makes itself heard that only readers with sharp hearing will perceive. The voice of the good Houellebecq says that only love counts, maternal and marital love, inseparable one from the other, and that suffering is terrible when love is lost"] (B. Viard 71). It is true that at times

the reader must listen very carefully to make out this second voice in Houellebecq's novels.

79 Trans.: "Personally, it seems to me that the only route is to continue to express, uncompromisingly, the contradictions that tear me apart; all the while knowing that these contradictions will prove, in all likelihood, to be representative of my time" (Houellebecq, *Interventions* 118).

80 In his article "Faire la bête," Robert Dion analyses the use of animal fables in Houellebecq's novel *Whatever*. In "Houellebecq, Genetics and Evolutionary Psychology," Douglas Morrey examines Houellebecq's narrative adaptation of evolutionary theory in *Les Particules élémentaires* et *La Possibilité d'une île*. In "Domesticating Hierarchies, Eugenic Hygiene and Exclusion Zones: The Dogs and Clones of Houellebecq's *La Possibilité d'une île*'," Delphine Grass explores Houellebecq's portrayal of cloning. See also my article "Les Enjeux des animaux (humains) chez Michel Houellebecq, du darwinisme au post-humanisme."

81 Dion 59.

82 Houellebecq, *EP* 36.

83 Houellebecq, *EP* 136–7.

84 Houellebecq, *EP* 185.

85 Morrey 231.

86 Trans.: "It is a question of cutting humans off from the traits that dualism uses to establish the thesis of ontological rupture. But this means in reality that the concept of the human remains shackled to the dualist concept of animality, and so, instead of getting rid of the Thesis [of human exceptionalism], they end up collapsing one side of the binary onto the other" (Schaeffer, *La Fin de l'exception humaine* 163).

87 It is worth noting that in *The Possibility of an Island,* Daniel1 acknowledges the problems of such an outdated and reductive version of evolutionary theory. During a conversation with the scientist working on cloning, he is "warned against too blind a belief in the Darwinian vulgate, which was being abandoned more and more by serious researchers; the evolution of species in reality owed far less to natural selection than to genetic drift, that is to say pure chance, and to the appearance of geographical isolates and separate biotopes" (Houellebecq, *PI* 91).

88 Houellebecq, *PI* 331.

89 Houellebecq, *PI* 330.

90 Houellebecq, *PI* 18.

91 Braidotti 1.

92 In her article "Communautés (im)mortelles? La politique posthumaine à l'oeuvre dans les textes de Michel Houellebecq," Susannah Ellis seems

to confuse posthumanism and transhumanism, characterizing the embrace of science and technology in *The Elementary Particles* as "posthumanist" and the critique of this view in *The Possibility of an Island* as "post-post-human."

93 See, for example, Vincent Lloyd's article "Michel Houellebecq and the Theological Virtues," which analyses the recurring themes of faith, hope, and love in *The Possibility of an Island*.

94 See, for example, Jourde and Todorov.

95 Gottschall, Kindle edition, loc. 2054 of 3695.

96 See also Boyd.

97 Houellebecq, *EP* 571.

98 Houellebecq, *EP* 540.

99 Houellebecq, *EP* 12.

100 Trans.: "Poetry is the most natural way to translate pure intuition of a moment. There really is a kernel of pure intuition that can be directly translated in images or words" (Houellebecq, *Interventions* 45).

101 Gottschall, Kindle edition, loc. 1880 of 3695.

102 It is striking that Houellebecq uses this exact expression "*récit de vie*" in the novel rather than a more common literary term like "autobiography." Besides its use in literary Darwinism, the expression "life story" is most often used in psychology. This underlines the fact that the novel is associating life stories with a certain condition of being human rather than with the literary tradition of autobiography.

103 Grass 138.

104 Houellebecq, *PI* 125.

105 Houellebecq, *PI* 290.

106 Houellebecq, *PI* 259.

107 Sweeney 101.

108 Moraru, "The Genomic Imperative" 271.

109 Literary Darwinists attribute very little importance to cultural evolution (see Kramnick).

110 Moraru, "The Genomic Imperative" 282.

111 Romeo 82.

112 This raises the question of why Daniel25 reacts this way when none of the other Daniel clones did. One reason may be that Daniel25 did not stop his reading at the end of Daniel1's life story and asked another neohuman to email him Daniel1's final poem (the poem was part of one of Daniel1's former girlfriend's life story because the poem had been written for her and sent to her). This would support the notion that poetry has more power to move the reader than stories do. Another reason

may be that Houellebecq is once again illustrating the problems with his own reductionist determinism. Despite the clones all being identical, a "swerve" takes place in the ordered flow of atoms, and difference is born (to borrow an image from Lucretius's *The Nature of Things*).

113 Cruikshank 122.

114 Schober 511.

115 Trans.: "Fiction thus represents in Houellebecq's world an essentially testamentary activity, one that must give an account of what is leftover, the human 'residue.' After the end of time, we will still have literature" (Granger Remy 231).

Conclusion

1 I am borrowing the term "render" from Natasha Myers's book in which she examines "how particular enactments *rend the world as molecular*, changing meanings and material realities for practitioners, their students, and wider publics" (Myers 18; emphasis in the original).

2 Braidotti 49.

3 Soper 14.

4 Even Ferry goes so far as to describe a "democratic ecology" that rejects radicalism in favour of reform within the secular Western world: "As a political movement, ecology will not be democratic; as a democratic movement, it must renounce the mirage of grand political visions" (*The New Ecological Order* 148). His reform environmentalism falls far short, however, of the paradigm shift required by the concepts I propose in this book: ecological subjectivity, ecological dwelling, ecological politics, and ecological ends.

5 Whiteside 4.

6 Whiteside 3.

7 Morris.

8 See Biehl.

9 Iovino, "The Human Alien" and "Ecocriticism and a Non-Anthropocentric Humanism."

10 Iovino, "The Human Alien" 54.

11 Iovino, "The Human Alien" 58.

12 Iovino, "The Human Alien" 57.

13 See, for example, her co-edited collection, *Material Ecocriticism*.

14 Trans.: "A decentred humanism, authentically universal for the first time" (Serres, *Hominescence* 185).

15 Whiteside 207.

16 Guattari comes under fire from Ferry for exactly this reason: ecosophy threatens the humanist belief in a free subject who chooses to be part (or not) of the social and political fabric (Ferry, *The New Ecological Order* 112–14).
17 Guattari, "Pratiques écosophiques," in *Qu'est-ce que l'écosophie?* 31–57.
18 Guattari, *Chaosmosis* 6.
19 Guattari, *Chaosmosis* 24.
20 Guattari, *Chaosmosis* 72.
21 See, for example, Montalbetti.
22 As Denis Chartier and Estienne Rodary bluntly put it, Ferry's book aims "more to rehabilitate a certain pride in *French* ideas than to provide any rigorous and in-depth investigation of environmental issues" and it should thus be read largely as a "defence of French identity" (Chartier and Rodary 553–4; emphasis in the original).
23 And yet Ferry himself is full of French nationalist sentiment, a contradiction to which he seems blind in *The New Ecological Order*. Looking back at his 1992 text now, it is possible to identify the strong desire to defend French humanist thought against what was perceived as an American cultural "invasion." With the rise of globalization, Ferry is shoring up the cultural and philosophical walls of a long tradition of rational and liberal humanism dating back to the French Revolution.
24 Ferry, *The New Ecological Order* 138.
25 Ferry, *The New Ecological Order* 151.
26 See, for example, one of the "future issues" identified by Buell, Thornber, and Heise: "Ecocriticism remains disproportionately nation focused … In the future, more emphasis must be placed on analysis of affinities across cultures and planetary-scale tendencies as well as against cultural specificity or uniqueness" (434).
27 Ferry, *A Brief History of Thought* 251.
28 Ferry, *A Brief History of Thought* 249–54.
29 It is useful to remind the reader that some comparatists object to World literature when it too quickly glosses over cultural and linguistic differences. See, for example, Gayatri Spivak's call for a "responsible comparativism" that cultivates "a care for language and idiom" (cited in this book's introduction).
30 Ferry, *A Brief History of Thought* 255.
31 Interestingly, Ferry spends quite a bit of time theorizing the notion of singularity as "a distinctive quality which is not merely that of the particular case, but graduates towards a broader horizon, to attain greater universality" (255). He goes on to link the notion of singularity to our capacity to love another person's individuality, explaining that we are not born with

such an individuality, but that we develop it by withdrawing from the particular and exposing ourselves to the universal (260). Ferry seems to be trying to move beyond the particular/universal binary to construct a kind of synthesis: singularity as a particular universal in the sense of every text, every person having a unique quality.

32 Braidotti 167.

33 Braidotti 166.

34 For example, Juliette is described as an impressionable young woman who falls under the spell of an American outdoorsman, Ted Abbey. At the end of *Le Parfum d'Adam*, Juliette sheds further light on her impressionable nature: "Les médecins m'ont été aimables et, je crois, efficaces. Ils m'ont aidé à prendre conscience de ce qu'ils appellent des troubles cycliques d'humeur … Je n'éprouve plus les profondes crises d'angoisse et de tristesse … En somme, je suis devenue quelqu'un de raisonnable. Cela m'étonne et tantôt me rassure, tantôt fait monter en moi une légère nostalgie" [Trans.: "The doctors have been nice and, I think, efficient. They made me aware of what they call cyclical psychological disorders … I no longer have anxiety attacks and spells of sadness … In short, I have become a reasonable person. It's surprising and sometimes I'm reassured and other times I feel a slight nostalgia welling up in me"] (524).

35 In "Notes Toward a Politics of Location," Adrienne Rich calls attention to the slippery universalist slope of the abstracted body even as she carefully advocates for a return to the material. Situatedness means always asking: "when, where, and under what conditions has the statement been true?" (Rich 10).

36 For example, animal activists may align with ecofeminists to denounce farming practices that keep dairy cows in an almost constant state of lactation. But this does not mean they will do the same for fashion industry practices of wearing fur and leather.

37 Chartier and Rodary.

38 Chartier and Rodary 549–51.

39 Chartier and Rodary 551–2.

40 Chartier and Rodary 552–4.

41 Chartier and Rodary 554–6.

42 Chartier and Rodary 556–8.

43 Chartier and Rodary 557.

44 I have been invited on multiple occasions to speak about ecocriticism in francophone academic settings, but each time I do, I underscore the fact that French literary studies has developed other ways of reading literary representations of nature, space, and place (notably literary landscape studies, *géocritique*, *écopoétique*, and *géopoétique*).

45 Chartier and Rodary 554.

46 In response to the rise of a distinctly East Asian ecocriticism, Hannes Bergthaller critiques the ways in which cultural differences are constructed. Adopting the perspective of systems theory (in particular in the work of Niklas Luhmann), Bergthaller argues the following: "as useful as the study of cultural differences may be, the latter's actual relevance can only properly be gauged if they are set within the larger context of a singular modernity – of world society and the singular environmental crisis that is its correlative, or, as systems theory would have it, of functional differentiation." I appreciate Bergthaller's reminder to pay more attention to the global economic and political systems within which cultures circulate. But I do think he loses sight of the role of literature (and language) as it resists recuperation into such larger systems.

47 Lassi.

48 See, for example, my co-authored article with Élise Salaün.

49 Françoise Lionnet's article "Critical Conventions, Literary Landscapes, and Postcolonial Ecocriticism," is an excellent starting point for thinking about French *écocritique* as a heterogeneous Francophone *écocritique*.

50 Despret, *Bêtes et hommes*.

51 There are many other novels that could be chosen to articulate this particular concept, such as Marie Darrieussecq's *Truismes* and Olivia Rosenthal's *Que font les rennes après Noël?*, to name just a few examples of contemporary French texts that raise the question of the ethical treatment of animals. Sorman's novels bring to light two different angles for examining the animal question, one more contemporary (the tradition of butchering and modern day butchers in France in *Comme une bête*) and one more historical (the treatment of bears since before *Homo sapiens sapiens* to the modern day zoo in *La Peau de l'ours*).

52 Pelluchon, *Éléments pour une éthique de la vulnérabilité*.

53 Pelluchon, *Les Nourritures*.

54 Hache, *Ce à quoi nous tenons*.

55 Another text that should be part of the response to this question is *Les Faiseuses d'histoire, Que font les femmes à la pensée?* in which Vinciane Despret and Isabelle Stengers ask a group of female academics to reflect on how and when they have been able to intervene in and transform their respective disciplines. Some of the responses address the issue of being a woman, and others not at all.

56 For a lucid discussion of the relationship between thought and language, see Deutscher.

Bibliography

Abu-Lughod, Lila. "Writing Against Culture." *Recapturing Anthropology*. Ed. Richard Fox. Santa Fe, NM: School of American Research Press, 1991. 137–62.

Afeissa, Hicham-Stéphane. *La Fin du monde et de l'humanité. Essai de généalogie du discours écologique*. Paris: PUF, 2014.

Agrikoliansky, Éric, Olivier Fillieule, and Nonna Mayer, eds. *L'Altermondialisme en France. La longue histoire d'une nouvelle cause*. Paris: Flammarion, 2005.

Alaimo, Stacy, and Susan Hekman, "Introduction: Emerging Models of Materiality in Feminist Theory." *Material Feminisms*. Eds. Alaimo and Hekman. Bloomington: Indiana UP, 2008. 1–22.

Albrecht, Glenn, et al. "Solastalgia: The Distress caused by environmental change." *Australasian Psychiatry* 15.1 (2007): S95–S98.

Andermatt Conley, Verena. *Ecopolitics. The Environment in Poststructuralist Thought*. London/New York: Routledge, 1997.

Asp, Chantal, and Marie Jacqué. *Environnement et société*. Paris: Éditions Quae, 2012.

Assouline, Pierre. "Marie-Hélène Lafon, d'un pays à l'autre." *La République des livres* 12 Oct. 2012.

Ayed, Kawthar. "L'Anticipation dystopique et le désenchantement modern." *Cycnos* 22.1 (2006).

Badiou, Alain. "French." *Dictionary of Untranslatables, A Philosophical Lexicon*. Ed. Barbara Cassin. Trans. Michael Wood. Princeton: Princeton UP, 2014. 349–54.

Bate, Jonathan. *The Song of the Earth*. Cambridge: Harvard UP, 2000.

Bateson, Gregory. *Steps to an Ecology of Mind*. Chicago: UP Chicago, 1999 [1972].

Bergé, Aline. "Le Tournant paysager de la littérature contemporaine, une traversée des modernités." *Paysage & Modernité(s)*. Eds. Michel Collot and Aline Bergé. Brussels: Vrin, 2007. 87–101.

Bergthaller, Hannes. "The Canon of East Asian Ecocriticism and the Duplicity of Culture." *CLCWeb: Comparative Literature and Culture* 16.6 (2014).

Bess, Michael. *The Light-Green Society: Ecology and Technological Modernity in France, 1960–2000*. Chicago: Chicago UP, 2003.

Bessière, Jacinthe. "Transformation, recomposition des espaces ruraux et émergence de nouvelles demandes sociales." *Innovation et patrimoine alimentaire en espace rural*. Ed. Jacinthe Bessière. Versailles: Editions Quae, 2012. 19–34.

Biehl, Janet. Rev. of *Pioneers of Ecological Humanism*, by Brian Morris. *New Compass* 5 Dec. 2013.

Blanc, Guillaume. *Une histoire environnementale de la nation. Regards croisés sur les parcs nationaux du Canada, d'Éthiopie et de France*. Paris: Publications de la Sorbonne, 2015.

Blanc, Nathalie, Denis Chartier, and Tom Pughe. "Littérature et écologie: Vers une écopoétique." *Écologie & Politique* 36 (2008): 17–28.

Blanc, Nathalie, and Jacques Lolive. "Les Subjectivités cosmopolitiques et la question esthétique." *L'Émergence des cosmopolitiques*. Eds. Jacques Lolive and Olivier Soubeyran. Paris: La Découverte, 2007. 352–82.

Blok, Anders, and Torben Elgaard Jensen. *Bruno Latour: Hybrid Thoughts in a Hybrid World*. London/New York: Routledge, 2012.

Boulard, Anaïs. *Un monde à habiter: Imaginaire de la crise environnementale dans les fictions de l'Anthropocene*. Diss. University of Angers, 2016.

Bouloumié, Arlette, and Isabelle Trivisani-Moreau, eds. *Le Génie du lieu: Des paysages en littérature*. Paris: Imago, 2005.

Bouvet, Rachel, and Stephanie Posthumus, "Eco- and Geo- Approaches in French and Francophone Literary Studies." *The Handbook to Ecocriticism and Cultural Ecology*. Ed. Hubert Zapf. Berlin/Boston: De Gruyter, 2016. 385–412.

Boyd, Brian. *On the Origin of Stories: Evolution, Cognition, and Fiction*. Cambridge: Belknap Press of Harvard UP, 2009. Kindle edition.

Boyle, Clare. "Post-Queer (Un)Made in France?" *Paragraph* 35.2 (2012): 265–80.

Braidotti, Rosi. *The Posthuman*. Cambridge: Polity, 2013.

Bramoullé, Gérard. *La Peste verte*. Paris: Belles Lettres, 1991.

Bramwell, Anna. *Ecology in the 20th Century. A History*. New Haven/London: Yale UP, 1989.

Breidenbach, Joana, and Pál Nyíri, *Seeing Culture Everywhere, from Genocide to Consumer Habits*. Seattle: University of Washington Press, 2009.

Bruckner, Pascal. *Le Fanatisme de l'Apocalypse*. Paris: Grasset & Fasquelle, 2011. Kindle edition.

Buell, Lawrence. "Ecocriticism: Some Emerging Trends." *Qui parle* 19.2 (2011): 87–115.

– *The Environmental Imagination: Thoreau, Nature Writing, and the Formation of American Culture.* Cambridge: Harvard UP, 1995.

– *The Future of Environmental Criticism.* Chicago: Blackwell-Wiley, 2005.

Buell, Lawrence, Karen Thornber, and Ursula Heise. "Literature and Environment." *Annual Review of Environment and Resources* 36 (2011): 417–40.

Burgat, Florence. "Animalité." *Encyclopedia Universalis.* 2013.

Caillé, Alain. "Une politique de la nature sans politique." *Revue du MAUSS* 17 (2001): 94–116.

Campbell, SueEllen. "The Land and Language of Desire: Where Deep Ecology and Poststructuralism Meet." *The Ecocriticism Reader.* Eds. Cheryl Glotfelty and Harold Fromm. Athens, Georgia: UP Georgia, 1996. 124–36.

Carroll, Joseph. *Reading Human Nature: Literary Darwinism in Theory and Practice.* Albany: UP New York State, 2011. Kindle edition.

Cassin, Barbara. "Introduction." *Vocabulaire européen des philosophies.* Ed. Barbara Cassin. Paris: Seuil, 2004. xvii–xx.

– "Introduction." *Dictionary of Untranslatables. A Philosophical Lexicon.* Trans. Michael Wood. Princeton: Princeton UP, 2014. xvii–xx.

Célestin, Roger, Eliane DalMolin, Marc Dambre, and Richard J. Golsan. "Introduction: The French Exception?" *Sites: Contemporary French & Francophone Studies* 12.3 (2008): 317–19.

Chadderton, Helena. *Marie Darrieussecq's Textual Worlds: Self, Society, Language.* Berlin: Peter Lang, 2012.

– "Rendering Memory in the Work of Marie Darrieussecq: The Case of *Bref séjour chez les vivants.*" The 2001 Group Postgraduate Study Day, May 9, 2008.

Chartier, Denis, and Estienne Rodary. "Globalising French *écologie politique*: A Political Necessity." *The International Handbook of Political Ecology.* Ed. Raymond Bryant. Cambridge, Massachusetts: Edward Elgar Publishing, 2015. 547–60.

Chelebourg, Christian. *Les Écofictions. Mythologies de la fin du monde.* Paris: Les Impressions Nouvelles, 2012.

Clark, John. "Aujourd'hui l'écologie?" *Terra Nova: Nature & Culture* 1 (1996): 112–19.

Clarke, Bruce. "Science, Theory, and Systems: A Response to Glen A. Love and Jonathan Levin." *Interdisciplinary Studies in Literature and Environment* 8.1 (2001): 149–65.

Clément, Gilles. *Le Jardin en mouvement.* Paris: Pandora, 1990.

– *Manifeste du tiers paysage.* Montreuil: Sujet-Objet, 2004.

Code, Lorraine. *Ecological Thinking: The Politics of Epistemic Location.* Cambridge: Harvard UP, 2006.

Cohen, Daniel. *Arguments and Metaphors in Philosophy.* Lanham, Maryland: University Press of America, 2003.

Collot, Michel. *Les Enjeux du paysage.* Brussels: Ousia, 1997.

– *Pour une géographie littéraire.* Paris: Corti, 2014.

Collot, Michel, and Aline Bergé. "Avant-propos." *Paysage & Modernité(s).* Eds. Collot and Bergé. Brussels: Vrin, 2007.

Coyault, Sylviane. "Avant-propos." Special Issue: The Province in the Contemporary Novel. *L'Esprit créateur* 42.2 (2002), 3–11.

Coyault-Dublanchet, Sylviane. *La Province en héritage. Pierre Michon, Pierre Bergounioux, Richard Millet.* Genève: Droz, 2002.

Cruikshank, Ruth. *Fin de millénaire French Fiction: The Aesthetics of Crisis.* Oxford: Oxford UP, 2009.

Cusset, François. *French Theory. Foucault, Derrida, Deleuze & Cie et les mutations de la vie intellectuelle aux États-Unis.* Paris: La Découverte/Poche, 2003.

Dahan-Gaida, Laurence. "La Fin de l'histoire (naturelle): *Les Particules élémentaires* de Michel Houellebecq." *Tangence* 73 (2003): 93–114.

Darrieussecq, Marie. *A Brief Stay with the Living.* Trans. Ian Monk. New York: Faber & Faber, 2004.

– "Comment j'écris." Interview by Jean-Marc Terrasse. *La Création en acte.* Eds. Paul Gifford and Marion Schmid. Amsterdam: Rodopi, 2007. 253–68.

– "'Des livres sur la liberté': conversation avec Marie Darrieussecq." Interview by Jeanne Gaudet. *Dalhousie French Studies* 59 (2002): 108–18.

– "Entretien. Je suis devenue psychanalyste." *L'Express* 11 Jan. 2006.

– "Entretien réalisé par Becky Miller et Martha Holmes." *Arizona University* December 2001.

– "Je est unE autre ou pour qui elle se prend." *Écrire l'histoire d'une vie.* Ed. Annie Olivier. Rome: Edizioni Spartaco, 2007. 105–21.

– "Marie Darrieussecq: 'européenne, féministe et athée.'" Interview by Jean-Pierre Bourcier. *La Tribune* 13 Nov. 1996.

– "Marie Darrieussecq parle d'Ovide et du latin." *YouTube.* 6 Jan. 2010.

– *Moments critiques dans l'autobiographie contemporaine. Ironie tragique et autofiction chez George Perec, Michel Leiris, Serge Doubrovsky et Hervé Guibert.* Diss. Université Lille, 1997.

– "Les mots du vide – Propos recueillis par Thomas Flamerion pour Evene. fr." *Even.fr.* October 2007.

– *Le Pays.* Paris: Gallimard/Poche, 2005.

– "*Le Pays* est un livre très utopiste qui imagine une planète faite de petits pays." Interview by Thomas Pierre. *Euskonews.* 8–15 Oct. 2010.

Deitering, Cynthia. "The Postnatural Novel: Toxic Consciousness in Fiction of the 1980s." *The Ecocriticism Reader: Landmarks in Literary Ecology*. Eds. Cheryl Glotfelty and Harold Fromm. Athens, Georgia: UP Georgia, 1996. 196–203.

Deléage, Jean-Paul. "Lutter pour la connaissance et la justice." *Écologie & Politique* 38.1 (2009): 5–13.

Delannoy, Isabelle. "On Being Living Beings: Renewing Perceptions of Our World, Our Society, and Ourselves." *French Thinking about Animals*. Eds. Louisa Mackenzie and Stephanie Posthumus. East Lansing, MI: Michigan State UP, 2015. 135–48.

Demonpion, Denis. *Houellebecq, non autorisé, Enquête sur un phénomène*. Paris: Libella Maren Sell, 2005.

Depardon, Raymond. *La Terre des paysans*. Paris: Seuil, 2008.

Desblache, Lucile. "Profil d'une éco-littérature." *L'Esprit créateur* 46.3 (2006): 1–4.

Descola, Philippe. *Par-delà nature et culture*. Paris: Gallimard, 2005.

Despret, Vinciane. *Bêtes et hommes*. Paris: Gallimard, 2007.

Despret, Vinciane, and Isabelle Stengers, eds. *Les faiseuses d'histoire, Que font les femmes à la pensée?* Paris: La Découverte, 2011.

Deutscher, Guy. *Through the Looking Glass: Why the World Looks Different in Other Languages*. New York: Metropolitan Books, 2010.

Dion, Robert. "Faire la bête." *Michel Houellebecq*. Ed. Sabine van Wesemael. Amsterdam/New York: Rodopi, 2004. 54–66.

Dodds, Joseph. *Psychoanalysis and Ecology at the Edge of Chaos*. London/New York: Routledge, 2011.

Droz, Yvan, and Valérie Miéville-Ott. "Le Paysage de l'anthropologue." *La Polyphonie du paysage*. Eds. Yvan Droz and Valérie Miéville-Ott. Lausanne: Presses polytechniques et universitaires romandes, 2005. 1–20.

Easterlin, Nancy. *A Biocultural Approach to Literary Theory and Interpretation*. Baltimore: John Hopkins UP, 2012.

Ellis, Susannah. "Communautés (im)mortelles? La politique posthumaine à l'œuvre dans les textes de Michel Houellebecq." *Post Humains. Frontières, évolutions, hybridités*. Eds. Élaine Desprès and Hélène Machinal. Rennes: Presses universitaires de Rennes, 2014. 137–52.

Estok, Simon. "Theorizing in a Space of Ambivalent Openness: Ecocriticism and Ecophobia." *Interdisciplinary Studies in Literature and Environment* 16.2 (2009): 203–25.

Evernden, Neil. *The Social Creation of Nature*. Baltimore/London: John Hopkins UP, 1992.

Ferry, Luc. *A Brief History of Thought*. Trans. Theo Cuffe. New York/London: Harper, 2011. Kindle edition.

– *L'Innovation destructrice.* Paris: Plon, 2014.
– *The New Ecological Order*. Trans. Carol Volk. Chicago: Chicago UP, 1995.
de Fontenay, Élisabeth. "La Bête est sans raison." *Critique* 375–6 (1978): 707–29.
– *Le Silence des bêtes: la philosophie à l'épreuve de l'animalité.* Paris: Fayard, 1997.
Ford, Caroline. "Nature, Culture and Conservation in France and Her Colonies 1840-1940." *Past & Present* 183 (2004): 173–98.
Fortun, Kim. "From Latour to Late Industrialism." *Hau: Journal of Ethnographic Theory* 4.1 (2014): 309–29.
Garcin, Jérôme. *Dictionnaire des écrivains contemporains de langue française.* Paris: Éditions Mille et Une Nuits, 2004.
Garrard, Greg. *Ecocriticism*. 2nd edition. London/New York: Routledge, 2012.
– "Heidegger Nazism Ecocriticism." *Interdisciplinary Studies in Literature and the Environment* 17.2 (2010): 251–71.
Genosko, Gary. "Subjectivity and Art in Guattari's *The Three Ecologies*." *Deleuze | Guattari & Ecology*. Ed. Bernd Herzogenrath. New York: Palgrave Macmillan, 2009. 102–15.
Girard, René. *Les Origines de la culture*. Paris: Fayard, 2011 [2004].
Goodbody, Axel. *Nature, Technology, and Cultural Change in Twentieth-Century German Literature: The Challenge of Ecocriticism*. New York: Palgrave-Macmillan, 2007.
Gottschall, Jonathan. *The Storytelling Animal: How Stories Make Us Human*. Boston/New York: Mariner Books, 2013. Kindle edition.
Granger Remy, Maud. "Houellebecq et le monde, contre ou au milieu?" *Le Monde de Houellebecq*. Ed. Gavin Bowd. Glasgow: Glasgow UP, 2006. 1–11.
– "*La Possibilité d'une île* ou "Le Livre des Daniel.'" *Michel Houellebecq à la une*. Eds. Murielle Lucie Clément and Sabine van Wesemael. Amsterdam/New York: Rodopi, 2011. 221–32.
Grass, Delphine. "Domesticating Hierarchies, Eugenic Hygiene and Exclusion Zones: The Dogs and Clones of Houellebecq's *La Possibilité d'une île*." *L'Esprit créateur* 52.2 (2012): 127–40.
Guattari, Félix. *Chaosmosis: An Ethico-Aesthetic Paradigm*. Trans. Paul Bains and Julian Pefanis. Bloomington: Indiana UP, 1995 [1992].
– "Félix Guattari: qu'est ce que l'écosophie?" Interview by Jean-Yves Sparel and Emmanuel Videcoq (1991). *Revue critique d'écosophie* 21 (2006).
– *Qu'est-ce que l'écosophie?* Ed. Stéphane Nadaud. Ardennes: Lignes/IMEC, 2013.
– *The Three Ecologies*. Trans. Ian Pindar and Paul Sutton. London: The Athlone Press, 2000 [1989].
– "Vers une nouvelle démocratie écologique." *Revue Chimères* (1992).
Guha, Ramanchandra, and Juan Martinez-Alier. *Varieties of Environmentalism*. London: Routledge, 1997.

Gunther, Scott. "*Alors*, Are We Queer Yet?" *The Gay & Lesbian Review Worldwide* 12.3 (2005): 23–5.

Hache, Émilie. *Ce à quoi nous tenons. Propositions pour une écologie pragmatique.* Paris: Les Empêcheurs de penser en rond, 2011.

Hache, Émilie, and Bruno Latour. "Morality and Moralism? An Exercise in Sensitization." Trans. Patrick Camillier. *Common Knowledge* 16.2 (2010): 311–30.

Haraway, Donna. "A Cyborg Manifesto: Science, Technology, and Socialist-Feminism in the Late Twentieth Century." *Simians, Cyborgs, and Women: The Reinvention of Nature*. New York/London: Routledge, 2011.

– "Situated Knowledges: The Science Question in Feminism and the Privilege of Partial Perspective." *Feminist Studies* 14.3 (1988): 575–99.

Harris, Paul. "The Itinerant Theorist: Nature and Knowledge/Ecology and Topology in Michel Serres." *SubStance* 83 (1997): 37–58.

Head, Dominique. "The (Im)possibility of Ecocriticism." *Writing the Environment. Ecocriticism and Literature*. Eds. Richard Kerridge and Neil Sammells. London/N.Y.: Zed Books Ltd., 1998. 27–39.

Heise, Ursula. "Globality, Difference, and the International Turn in Ecocriticism." *PMLA* 128.3 (2013): 636–43.

– "The Hitchhiker's Guide to Ecocriticism." *PMLA* 121.2 (2006): 503–16.

– "Science and Ecocriticism." *American Book Review* 18.5 (1997): 4–6.

– *Sense of Place and Sense of Planet: The Environmental Imagination of the Global.* New York: Oxford UP, 2008.

Herzogenrath, Bernd, ed. *Deleuze|Guattari & Ecology*. London: Palgrave Macmillan, 2009.

Houellebecq, Michel. *The Elementary Particles.* Trans. Frank Wynne. New York: Vintage Books, 2000 [1998].

– *Interventions.* Paris: Flammarion, 1998.

– "Michel Houellebecq. The Art of Fiction." Interview by Susannah Hunnewell. *The Paris Review* 194 (2010).

– *Non réconcilié. Anthologie personnelle 1991–2013.* Paris: Gallimard, 2014.

– *The Possibility of an Island.* Trans. Gavin Bowd. New York: Alfred A. Knopf, 2006 [2005].

Houppermans, Sjef. "Le Plateau des mille mystères: Réel et fantastique chez Richard Millet." *European Studies* 18 (2002): 151–68.

Hume, Angela. "Imagining Ecopoetics: An Interview with Robert Hass, Brenda Hillman, Evelyn Reilly, and Jonathan Skinner." *Interdisciplinary Studies in Literature and Environment* 19.4 (2012): 751–66.

Humphrey, Matthew. *Ecological Politics and Democratic Theory: The Challenge to the Deliberative Ideal*. New York/London: Routledge, 2007.

Iovino, Serenella. *Ecocriticism and Italy: Ecology, Resistance, and Liberation*. London: Bloomsbury Academic, 2016.
– "Ecocriticism and a Non-Anthropocentric Humanism." *Local Natures, Global Responsibilities*. Ed. Laurenz Volkmann et al. Amsterdam/New York: Rodopi, 2010. 29–53. Print.
– *Ecologia Litteraria*. Milan: Edizione Ambiente, 2006.
– "The Human Alien. Otherness, Humanism, and the Future of Ecocriticism." *Ecozon@* 1.1 (2010): 53–61.
Iovino, Serenella and Serpil Opperman, eds. *Material Ecocriticism*. Bloomington/Indianapolis: Indiana UP, 2014.
Jaccomard, Hélène. "Écologie, écocritique et littérature (Éditorial)." *Mots Pluriels* 11 (1999).
Jacob, Jean. "Les natures changeantes de l'écologie politique française, une vieille controverse philosophique." *Écologie & Politique* 44.1 (2012): 29–42.
Jourde, Pierre. *La Littérature sans estomac*. Paris: Esprit des péninsules, 2002.
Kalaora, Bernard. *Au-delà de la nature. L'environnement*. Paris: Harmattan, 1998.
Kemp, Simon. "Darrieussecq's Mind." *French Studies* LXII.4 (2008): 429–41.
– "Homeland: Voyageurs et patrie dans les romans de Marie Darrieussecq." *Nomadismes des romancières contemporaines de langue française*. Eds. Audrey Lasserre and Anne Simon. Paris: Presses Sorbonne Nouvelle, 2008. 159–66.
Kramnick, Jonathan. "Against Literary Darwinism." *Critical Inquiry* 37.2 (2011): 315–47.
Lafon, Marie-Hélène. *Album*. Paris: Buchet/Chastel, 2012.
– *L'Annonce*. Paris: Gallimard/Folio, 2011 [2009].
– *Les Derniers Indiens*. Paris: Gallimard/Folio, 2009 [2008].
– *Histoires*. Paris: Buchet/Chastel, 2015.
– "'Je ne fais pas les romans que je veux, mais les romans que je peux' – Marie-Hélène Lafon à Saint Julien en Born." *Medialandes.org*.
– *Joseph*. Paris: Buchet/Chastel, 2014.
– "Marie-Hélène Lafon: l'heureuse surprise de la rentrée littéraire." Interview by Matthieu Falcone. *Culturemag* 9 Sept. 2009.
– *Les Pays*. Paris: Buchet/Chastel, 2012.
Larcher, Laurent. *La Face cachée de l'écologie: Un antihumanisme contemporain*. Paris: Cerf, 2004.
Larrère, Catherine. "Éthiques de l'environnement." *Multitudes* 24.1 (2006): 75–84.
– *Les Philosophies de l'environnement*. Paris: PUF, 1997.
Larrère, Catherine, and Raphaël Larrère. *Du bon usage de la nature. Pour une philosophie de l'environnement*. Paris: Aubier, 1997.

– *Penser et agir avec la nature.* Paris: La Découverte, 2015.

Lascoumes, Pierre. *L'Éco-pouvoir. Environnements et politiques.* Paris: La Découverte, 1994.

Lasserre, Audrey. "Qu'est-ce qu'une histoire de la littérature *française ?*" *La France des écrivains. Éclats d'un mythe (1945–2005).* Eds. Marie-Odile André, Marc Dambre, Michel P. Schmitt. Paris: Presses Sorbonne Nouvelle, 2011. 207–17.

Lassi, Étienne-Marie. "Introduction: De l'engagement sociopolitique à la conscience écologique: les enjeux environnementaux dans la critique postcoloniale." *Aspects écocritiques de l'imaginaire africain.* Ed. Étienne-Marie Lassi. Bamenda, Cameroon: Langaa RPCIG, 2013. 1–18.

Latour, Bruno. "Agency at the time of the Anthropocene." *New Literary History* 45 (2014): 1–18.

– "L'Alternative compositionniste. Pour en finir aver l'indiscutable." Interview by Denis Chartier. *Écologie & Politique* 40.2 (2010): 81–93.

– "Anthropology at the Time of the Anthropocene – A Personal View of What Is to Be Studied." Conference Paper. 113th American Association of Anthropologists meeting. Washington, DC. 5 Nov. 2014.

– "Arrachement ou attachement à la nature?" *Écologie & Politique* 5 (1993): 15–26.

– "An Attempt at a 'Compositionist Manifesto.'" *New Literary History* 41 (2010): 471–90.

– "Biographie d'une enquête." *Archives de philosophie* 75.4 (2012): 549–66.

– "A Dialog about a New Meaning of Symmetric Anthropology." Interview by Carolina Miranda. Proceedings of the Cerisy meeting. August 2013.

– "The Enlightenment Without the Critique: A Word on Michel Serres' Philosophy." *Contemporary French Philosophy.* Ed. A. Phillips Griffiths. Cambridge: Cambridge UP, 1987. 83–98.

– "Moderniser ou écologiser: à la recherche de la septième cité." *Écologie & Politique* 13 (1995): 5–27.

– "La Mondialisation fait-elle un monde habitable ?" *Revue d'étude et de prospective* 2 (2009): 9–18.

– "On Some of the Affects of Capitalism." Conference paper. Royal Academy, Copenhagen. 26 Feb. 2014.

– *Politics of Nature: How to Bring the Sciences into Democracy.* Trans. Catherine Porter, Cambridge: Harvard UP, 2004 [1999].

– "L'Universel, il faut le faire." Interview by Élie During and Laurent Jeanpierre. *Critique* 786.11 (2012): 949–63.

– *We Have Never Been Modern.* Trans. Catherine Porter. Cambridge: Harvard UP, 1993 [1991].

Leeson-Schatz, Joe. "The Importance of Apocalypse: The Value of End-of-the-World Politics While Advancing Ecocriticism." *Journal of Ecocriticism* 4.2 (2012): 20–33.

Le Fol, Sébastien. "Rufin casse les Verts." *Figaro Magazine* 13 Jan. 2007.

Le Goff, Jean-Pierre. *La Fin du village: Une histoire française.* Paris: Gallimard, 2012.

Lestel, Dominique. *L'Animalité, essai sur le statut de l'humain.* Paris: Hatier, 1996.

Lévi-Strauss, Claude. *Mythologiques 3. L'Origine des manières de table.* Paris: Plon, 1968.

– *Tristes tropiques.* Paris: Plon, 1955.

Lévy, Bernard-Henri. "American Talk of the Death of French Culture Says More about Them than about Us." *The Guardian (UK)* 8 Dec. 2007.

Levy, Sydney. "An Ecology of Knowledge: Michel Serres." *SubStance* 83 (1997): 3–5.

Lionnet, Françoise. "Critical Conventions, Literary Landscapes, and Postcolonial Ecocriticism." *French Global.* Eds. Christie McDonald and Susan Rubin Suleiman. New York: Columbia UP, 2010. 127–44.

Lipietz, Alain. *Qu'est-ce que l'écologie politique?* Paris: La Découverte, 1998.

Lloyd, Vincent. "Michel Houellebecq and the Theological Virtues." *Literature & Theology* 23.1 (2009): 84–98.

Locher, Fabien, and Grégory Quenet, "L'histoire environnementale: origines, enjeux et perspectives d'un nouveau chantier." *Revue d'histoire moderne et contemporaine* 56.4 (2009): 7–37.

Love, Glen. *Practical Ecocriticism, Literature, Biology and the Environment.* Charlottesville: UP Virginia, 2003.

Mackenzie, Louisa. "Guillaume Rondelet's Sea-Monsters and Bruno Latour's Modern Constitution." *Animals and Early Modern Identity.* Ed. Pia Cuneo. Burlington: Ashgate, 2014. 329–49.

– "It's a Queer Thing: Early Modern French Ecocriticism." *French Literature Series* 39 (2012): 15–42.

Mackenzie, Louisa, and Stephanie Posthumus. *French Thinking about Animals.* East Lansing, MI: Michigan State UP, 2015.

– "Reading Latour Outside: A Response to the Estok-Robisch Controversy." *Interdisciplinary Studies in Literature and Environment* 20.4 (2013): 757–77.

Maingueneau, Dominique. *Contre Saint Proust: Ou la fin de la littérature.* Paris: Belin, 2006.

Mathieu, Nicole. "La Notion de rural et les rapports ville-campagne en France: les années quatre-vingt-dix." *Économie rurale* 247 (1998): 11–20.

Matts, Tim. "Violent Signs: Ecocriticism and the Symptom." Diss. Cardiff University, Wales, 2011.

Montalbetti, Christine. "Platon *game over*: Aristote au secours de Lara Croft." Rev. of *Pourquoi la fiction?* by Jean-Marie Schaeffer. *Littérature* 117 (2000): 126–7.

Moraru, Christian. "The Genomic Imperative: Michel Houellebecq's *The Possibility of an Island*." *Utopian Studies* 19.2 (2008): 265–83.

– Rev. of *Globalia*, Jean-Christophe Rufin. *Utopian Studies* 17.1 (2006): 248–54.

Morrey, Douglas. "Houellebecq, Genetics and Evolutionary Psychology." *The Evolution of Literature. Legacies of Darwin in European Cultures*. Eds. Nicholas Saul and Simon J. James. Amsterdam/NY: Rodopi, 2011. 227–38.

Morris, Brian. *Pioneers of Ecological Humanism*. London: Book Guild, 2012.

Morrison, Donald. "The Death of French Culture." *Time Magazine* 27 Nov. 2007.

Morton, Timothy. *Ecology without Nature*. Cambridge: Harvard UP, 2007.

"Motion F – Pour des Verts utiles … à la démocratie écologique conviviale." *Les Verts* 19 Oct. 2006.

Murphy, Patrick. *Farther Afield in the Study of Nature-Oriented Literature*. Charlottesville, UP Virginia, 2000.

– *Transversal Ecocritical Praxis*. Lexington: Lexington Books, 2013.

Myers, Natasha. *Rendering Life Molecular*. Durham/London: Duke UP, 2015.

Nabhan, Gary. "Cultural Parallax in Viewing North American Habitats." *Reinventing Nature. Responses to Postmodern Deconstruction*. Eds. Michael Soulé and Gary Lease. Washington/California: Island Press, 1995. 87–101.

Nadaud, Stéphane. "Félix Guattari l'écosophe." *Qu'est-ce que l'écosophie?* Ed. Stéphane Nadaud. Ardennes: Lignes/IMEC, 2013. 7–25.

Naess, Arne. *Ecology, Community and Lifestyle*. Trans. David Rothenberg. Cambridge: UP Cambridge, 1990 [1976].

– "Self Realization: An Ecological Approach to Being in the World." *The Trumpeter* 4.3 (1987): 35–42.

Nahapétian, Naïri. "Cauchemar climatisé." *Alternatives Economiques* 227 (2004).

Paraire, Philippe. *L'Utopie verte. Écologie des riches, écologie des pauvres*. Paris: Hachette, 1992.

Parizeau, Marie-Hélène. "Wild, Domestic, or Technical: What Status for Animals?" *French Thinking about Animals*. Eds. Louisa Mackenzie and Stephanie Posthumus. East Lansing, MI: Michigan State UP, 2015. 163–77.

Paulson, William. "Michel Serres's Utopia of Language." *Configurations* 8.2 (2002): 215–28.

– "Writing that Matters." *SubStance* 83 (1997): 22–36.

Pelluchon, Corine. *Éléments pour une éthique de la vulnérabilité. Les hommes, les animaux, la nature*. Paris: Le Cerf, 2011.

– *Les Nourritures. Philosophie du corps politique*. Paris: Seuil, 2015.

Phillips, Dana. *The Truth of Ecology. Nature, Culture, and Literature in America*. Oxford: Oxford UP, 2003.

Pinque, Méryl. "*Le Parfum d'Adam* ou l'imposture." *Revue Jibrile* June 2007.

Plumwood, Val. *Feminism and the Mastery of Nature*. New York: Routledge, 1993.

Posthumus, Stephanie. "Les Enjeux des animaux (humains) chez Michel Houellebecq, du darwinisme au post-humanisme." *French Studies* LXVIII.3 (2014): 359–76.

– "État des lieux de la pensée écocritique française." *Ecozon@: European Journal of Literature, Culture, Environment* 1.1 (2010): 148–54.

– *La Nature et l'écologie chez Lévi-Strauss, Serres et Tournier*. Sarrebruck: Éditions européennes, 2010.

– "Penser l'imagination environnementale française sous le signe de la différence." *Raison publique* 17 (2012): 15–31.

– "Translating Ecocriticism: Dialoguing with Michel Serres." *Reconstruction* 7.2 (2007): 1–24.

– "Vers une écocritique française: le contrat naturel de Michel Serres." *Mosaic, a Journal for the Interdisciplinary Study of Literature* 44.2 (2011): 85–100.

Posthumus, Stephanie, and Élise Salaün. "'Mon pays, ce n'est pas un pays, c'est l'hiver': Literary Representations of Nature and Ecocritical Thought in Québec." *Greening the Maple: Canadian Ecocriticism in Context*. Eds. Nicholas Bradley and Ella Soper-Jones. Calgary: UP Calgary, 2013. 297–327.

Prasad, Monica. "Why Is France so French? Culture, Institutions, and Neoliberalism." *American Journal of Sociology* 111.2 (2005): 357–407.

Prieto, Eric. "Geocriticism Meets Ecocriticism: Bertrand Westphal and Environmental Thinking." *Épistémocritique* 9 (2011).

Pughe, Tom, and Michel Granger. "Introduction." *Revue française d'études américaines* 106 (2005): 3–7.

Ricardou, Jean. *Pour une théorie du nouveau roman*. Paris: Seuil, 1971.

Rich, Adrienne. "Notes Towards a Politics of Location." *Women, Feminist Identity and Society in the 1980s: Selected Papers*. Ed. Myriam Diaz-Diocaretz. Amsterdam/Philadelphia: John Benjamins Publishing Company, 1985. 7–22.

Richard, Annie. *L'Autofiction et les femmes. Un chemin vers l'altruisme?* Paris: Harmattan, 2013.

Robisch, S.K. "The Woodshed: A Response to 'Ecocriticism and Ecophobia.'" *Interdisciplinary Studies in Literature and Environment* 16.4 (2009): 697–708.

Rodgers, Catherine. "Aux limites du moi, des mots et du monde: Questions d'identité dans *Le Pays* de Marie Darrieussecq." *Le Roman français de*

l'extrême contemporain. Eds. Barbara Havercroft, Pascal Michelucci, and Pascal Riendeau. Québec: Nota bene, 2010. 403–22.
– "Marie Darrieussecq: écrivaine de l'entre-deux." *Women in French Studies* (2009): 105–17.
Roger, Alain. *Court traité du paysage*. Paris: Gallimard, 1997.
Rojas Pérez, Walter. *La Ecocrítica hoy*. San José, Costa Rica: Aire Moderno, 2004.
Romeo, Luigi. *Ecce Homo! A Lexicon of Man*. Amsterdam: John Benjamins PV, 1979.
Romestaing, Alain, ed. *Mondes ruraux, mondes animaux*. Dijon: PU Dijon, 2014.
Rufin, Jean-Christophe. *Check-point*. Paris: Gallimard, 2015.
– *Globalia*. Paris: Gallimard/Folio, 2005 [2004].
– "Jean-Christophe Rufin: humanitaires au XXIe siècle." Interview by Rudy Le Cours. *La Presse* 14 June 2015.
– *Le Parfum d'Adam*. Paris: Gallimard/Folio, 2008 [2007].
Rye, Gill. "Marie Darrieussecq's *Le Pays*: Threshold Worlds." *Redefining the Real: The Fantastic in Contemporary French and Francophone Women's Writing*. Ed. Margaret-Anne Hutton. Bern: Peter Lang, 2009. 31–44.
Schaeffer, Jean-Marie. *L'Expérience esthétique*. Paris: Gallimard, 2015. Kindle edition.
– *La Fin de l'exception humaine*. Paris: Gallimard, 2007.
– *Petite écologie des études littéraires, Pourquoi et comment étudier la littérature?* Vincennes: Editions Thierry Marchaisse, 2011. Kindle edition.
– *Why Fiction?* Trans. Dorrit Cohn. Lincoln: UP Nebraska, 2010 [1999].
Schober, Rita. "Vision du monde et théorie du roman, concepts opératoires des romans de Michel Houellebecq." *Le Roman français au tournant du XXIe siècle*. Eds. Bruno Blanckeman, Aline Mura-Burnel and Marc Dambre. Paris: Presses Sorbonne Nouvelle, 2004. 505–16.
Schoentjes, Pierre. *Ce qui a lieu, Essai d'une écopoétique*. Paris: Wildproject, 2015.
Serres, Michel. *Le Contrat naturel*. Paris: Flammarion, 1990.
– *Détachement*. Paris: Flammarion, 1986 [1983].
– *Éclaircissements*. Paris: Flammarion, 1994.
– *The Five Senses. A Philosophy of Mingled Bodies*. Trans. Margaret Sankey and Peter Cowley. London: Continuum, 2008 [1985].
– *Genesis*. Trans. Geneviève James and James Nielson. Ann Arbor: UP Michigan, 1995 [1982].
– *Habiter*. Paris: Le Pommier, 2011.
– *Hermès V. Le Passage du Nord-Ouest*. Paris: Minuit, 1980.
– *Hominescence*. Paris: Le Pommier, 2001.
– *L'Incandescent*. Paris: Le Pommier, 2003.
– *La Naissance de la physique dans le texte de Lucrèce*. Paris: Minuit, 1977.

– "Peut-on dire encore le pouvoir spirituel ?" *Critique* 726–7 (2007): 803–920.
– *Le Retour au Contrat Naturel*. Paris: BNF, 2000.
– "Retour au contrat naturel." *Signons la paix avec la Terre*. Ed. Jérôme Bindé. Paris: Albin Michel/Éditions UNESCO, 2007. 169–80.
Simon, Anne. "Animality and Contemporary French Literary Studies: Overview and Perspectives." *French Thinking about Animals*. Eds. Louisa Mackenzie and Stephanie Posthumus. East Lansing, MI: Michigan State UP, 2015. 75–88.
– "Au 'pays' des bêtes: écopoétiques de la ruralité contemporaine." *Mondes ruraux, mondes animaux*. Ed. Alain Romestaing. Dijon: Éditions universitaires de Dijon, 2014. 215–27.
Snow, C.P. *Two Cultures and the Scientific Revolution*. New York: Cambridge UP, 1961.
Soper, Kate. *Humanism and Anti-Humanism*. London: Hutchinson, 1986.
– *What Is Nature? Culture, Politics, and the Non-Human*. London: Wiley-Blackwell, 1995.
Sorman, Joy. *Comme une bête*. Paris: Gallimard, 2012.
– *La Peau de l'ours*. Paris: Gallimard, 2014.
Spivak, Gayatri. *An Aesthetic Education in the Era of Globalization*. Cambridge: Harvard UP, 2012.
– *Death of a Discipline*. New York: Columbia UP, 2003.
Stock, Mathis. "'Faire avec de l'espace': Pour une approche de l'habiter par les pratiques." *Habiter. Vers un nouveau concept?* Eds. Brigitte Frelat-Kahn and Olivier Lazzarotti. Paris: Armand Colin, 2012. 57–75.
Suberchicot, Alain. *Littérature et environnement. Pour une écocritique comparée*. Paris: Honoré Champion, 2012.
Suleiman, Susan. *Le Roman à these ou l'autorité fictive*. Paris: PUF, 1983.
Sweeney, Carole. *Michel Houellebecq and the Literature of Despair*. London: Bloomsbury Press, 2013.
Thiesse, Anne-Marie. *Écrire la France*. Paris: PUF, 1991.
Thornber, Karen. *Ecoambiguity: Environmental Crises and East Asian Literatures*. Ann Arbor, Michigan UP, 2012.
Tinnell, John. "Transversalising the Ecological Turn: Four Components of Felix Guattari's Ecosophical Perspective." *The Fibreculture Journal* 18 (2011): 35–64.
Todorov, Tzvetan. *La Littérature en peril*. Paris: Flammarion, 2006.
Van Wyck, Peter. *Primitives in the Wilderness. Deep Ecology and the Missing Human Subject*. Albany: State University of New York Press, 1997.
Vercier, Bruno, and Dominique Viart. *La Littérature française au present*. Paris: Bordas, 2005.
Viard, Bruno. *Houellebecq au scanner: la faute à mai 68*. Nice: Ovadia, 2008.

Viard, Jean. *Le Tiers espace*. Paris: Méridiens Klincksieck, 1990.
Viart, Dominique. *Anthologie de la littérature contemporaine française*. Paris: Armand Colin, 2013.
Wagner, Walter. "La Tentation pastorale de Houellebecq." *Michel Houellebecq à la une*. Eds. Murielle Lucie Clément and Sabine van Wesemael. Amsterdam/New York: Rodopi, 2011. 259–69.
Wald Lasowski, Aliocha. "De Sartre à Félix Guattari." *Temps Modernes* 674–5 (2013): 223–40.
Weber, Elke, and the Task Force on the Interface between Psychology and Global Climate Change. *Psychology and Global Climate Change: Addressing a Multi-Faceted Phenomenon and a Set of Challenges*. American Psychological Association, Washington, DC, 2009.
Westphal, Bertrand. *La Géocritique: Réel, fiction, espace*. Paris: Minuit, 2007.
– *Le Monde plausible*. Paris: Minuit, 2011.
White, Kenneth. "The Great Field of Geopoetics." *The International Institute of Geopoetics: Founding Texts*. 2015.
Whiteside, Kerry. *Divided Natures: French Contributions to Political Ecology*. Cambridge: MIT, 2002.
Wolfe, Cary. *Animal Rites: American Culture, the Discourse of Species, and the Posthumanist Theory*. Chicago: UP Chicago Press, 2003.
– *What Is Posthumanism?* Minneapolis/London: UP Minnesota, 2010.

Index